John McH... ...
Andrews U... ...y. A board member of the Council for Arab British
Understanding and the British Egyptian Society, he is also chair of the
Liberal Democrat Friends of Palestine. McHugo's writing has featured
in *History Today*, *The World Today*, *Jewish Quarterly* and on the BBC
News website. His debut work, *A Concise History of the Arabs*, was
published to critical acclaim in 2013. McHugo was shortlisted for the
Salon Transmission Prize in 2014.

www.johnmchugo.com

'Remarkably prescient ... At the very start of this enlightening read,
McHugo makes the point that to the English-speaking world, Syria is
a far off country which relatively few people have made a serious effort
to understand. In writing this insightful and timely book, he has gone
some considerable way to rectifying this neglect.' *Sunday Herald*

'[A] very timely modern history of Syria ... provides the reader with a
high level of sound analysis' *Journal of Peace Research*

'Tells us with inspirational force how the Syrians have found the ability
to speak out' *Times Literary Supplement*

'A fascinating and timely study ... McHugo places developments in Syria
and the wider region in a solid and coherent context, clearly explaining
the developments of the past century. It should be a pleasure to read for
both experts and a wider audience.' Nikolaos van Dam, author of *The
Struggle for Power in Syria*

'McHugo uncovers uncanny parallels between the pacification strategies
of the French in the 1920s and the Assad regime today, exposing the
continuous role of violence in the region's (flawed) state formation.'
Raymond Hinnebusch, Centre for Syrian Studies, University of St
Andrews

'A fluent introduction to Syri...
backstory to the country's colla...
Andrew Arsan, St John's Colle...

ALSO BY JOHN MCHUGO

A Concise History of the Arabs

SYRIA

A Recent History

JOHN MCHUGO

SAQI

First published 2014 by Saqi Books

This paperback edition published 2015

Copyright © John McHugo 2014

John McHugo has asserted his right under the Copyright, Designs
and Patents Act, 1988, to be identified as the author of this work.

ISBN 978-0-86356-160-3
eISBN 978-0-86356-763-6

A full CIP record for this book is available from the British Library.

Printed and bound by CPI Group (UK) Ltd, Croydon, CR0 4YY

Saqi Books
26 Westbourne Grove
London W2 5RH
www.saqibooks.co.uk

To Benedict

You know and we know, as practical men, that the question of justice arises only between parties equal in strength and that the strong do what they can, and the weak suffer what they must.

Thucydides, *The History of the Peloponnesian War*

Contents

List of Maps

Chronology

331 BC	Alexander the Great of Macedon conquers Persian Empire, including Greater Syria
323 BC	Death of Alexander the Great – partition of Greater Syria between Ptolemaic and Seleucid dynasties
64–3 BC	Greater Syria comes under the sway of Rome
33 AD	Conversion of St Paul in Damascus
630s–40s	Arab Conquest and the coming of Islam to Greater Syria
661–750	Damascus-based Umayyad Caliphate
750	Establishment of Abbasid Caliphate which is based in Iraq
1098	Arrival of Crusaders in Greater Syria
1258	Sack of Baghdad by Mongols and execution of last Abbasid Caliphate
1260	Defeat of Mongols by Egyptian Mamluks at battle of Ayn Jalut and conquest of Greater Syria
1291	Eradication of last Crusader strongholds in Greater Syria
1400–1	Conquest and sack of Damascus by Tamerlane
1516	Conquest of Greater Syria by the Ottoman Emperor Selim the Grim
1683	Breaking of second Ottoman siege of Vienna and beginning of Ottoman decline as a military power

1798–9	Napoleon conquers Egypt and unsuccessfully invades Greater Syria
1831–41	Temporary Egyptian occupation of Greater Syria
1839 & 1856	Ottoman *tanzimat* decrees which attempt to reform the empire. Among the reforms is the abolition of subordinate status of Christians and Jews
1860	Druze defeat Maronites in war on Mount Lebanon and massacres of Christians in Damascus. Establishment of predominantly Maronite autonomous province of Mount Lebanon
1876	Establishment of first Ottoman parliament
1908	Young Turk Revolution
1914	Outbreak of Great War
1915–16	Execution of Arab nationalists in Damascus and Beirut by Turkish viceroy Jamal Pasha
1916	Sykes-Picot Agreement
Outbreak of Arab Revolt in the Hejaz
1917	Balfour Declaration
British conquest of Palestine
1918	British-led conquest of remainder of Greater Syria. Arab armies take Damascus and are first to reach Homs and Aleppo
Armistice at end of Great War; establishment of Arab administration east of coastal mountains and river Jordan but subject to overall British control
1919	The Emir Faisal addresses Paris Peace Conference and pleads for establishment of Arab State
Syrian National Congress elected as a constituent assembly for Greater Syria

1920   Syrian National Congress proclaims Faisal King of Greater Syria

Allied powers agree to partition Greater Syria into French and British Mandates

Battle of Maysaloun – French take control of Syria

French set out to sub-divide their mandated territory, splitting "Greater Lebanon" from the rest of Syria and planning to divide the remainder of Syria into autonomous units which would be dependent on a French presence

Resistance in Alawi mountains; Ibrahim Hananu's rebellion in countryside around Aleppo

1921   France and Turkey agree Syrian border with Turkey

1925–7   Great Syrian rebellion – initial Druze unrest in the Hawran area spreads across much of the country in response to demand for Syrian independence. French temporarily lose control of Hama and then Damascus. Revolt eventually crushed after arrival of French reinforcements

1928   Elections for constituent assembly; emergence of politicians who would form the National Bloc

1930   French accept Syrian constitution but insist it is subject to overriding authority of France as the Mandatory power

1932   Elections; organisational structure given to the National Bloc

1933   Failure of attempt to negotiate treaty between Syria and France

1936   Agreement of treaty with France giving Syria independence which is endorsed by a general election in Syria but which France fails to ratify following fall of the *Front Populaire* government

1939   Cession of the Sanjak of Alexandretta by France to Turkey (although in breach of terms of the Mandate)

Outbreak of World War II. Syria put under martial law and constitution suspended

1940   Fall of France. French administrators in Syria and Lebanon opt to support Vichy

1941   Free French promise Syria sovereign independence and, relying on British support, take control of Syria from pro-Vichy forces. Britain retains ultimate military responsibility.

1943   Elections return National Bloc to power under leadership of Shukri al-Quwwatli

Syrian government gives notice to French that Syria will amend its constitution to provide for complete independence from France

1944   French begin transferring government departments to Syrian control

1945   Syria declares war on Germany and Japan to become founding member of United Nations

French bombard Damascus and shell Syrian parliament in last-ditch attempt to retain their presence in Syria and Lebanon. British garrisons take control. French begin final dismantling of their presence in Syria.

1946   French and British troops leave

Syria now fully independent under leadership of President Shukri al-Quwwatli and his National Party

1947   Syrian parliamentary elections

King Abdullah of Jordan proposes creation of kingdom of Greater Syria

UN General Assembly resolves to partition Palestine giving date for end of British Mandate and triggering civil war in Palestine

Syria initially supports the establishment of the volunteer Arab Liberation Army to assist Palestinian Arabs

1948   State of Israel proclaimed in the teeth of Palestinian and Arab opposition. Syrian army intervenes.

1949   Coup by Colonel Husni Zaim. Unsuccessful attempt to negotiate peace with Israel but ceasefire agreed.

Coup by Colonel Hinnawi. Akram Hourani and the Ba'thist Michel Aflaq enter the cabinet for the first time. Election of constituent assembly.

Coup by Colonel Adib Shishakli

1952   Formation of Arab Socialist Ba'th Party by Michel Aflaq and Salah al-Din Bitar joining forces with Akram Hourani

Adib Shishakli assumes office of president

Overthrow of Egyptian monarchy by the Free Officers led by Nasser

1954   Fall of Adib Shishakli

Restoration of parliamentary rule

1955   Parliament elects Shukri al-Quwwatli as president

Anti-Communist Baghdad Pact

Israeli raid on Gaza

1956   Nasser nationalises the Suez Canal

Syria establishes diplomatic relations with USSR

Syria finally obtains modern armaments from the USSR

Tripartite invasion of Egypt by Britain, France and Israel

1957   Western-backed plots to destabilise Syria

Nasser sends troops to Lattakia to widespread Syrian acclaim

1958   Union with Egypt and establishment of the United Arab Republic

Dissolution of Ba'th Party and suppression of Communists and other political parties

Overthrow of monarchy in Iraq

1961   Military coup in Damascus takes Syria out of UAR

Election of new Syrian parliament

1963   Coup by Ba'thist, Nasserist and officers of other affiliations ends parliamentary rule

           Syria put under Emergency Law

           Suppression of abortive Nasserist coup consolidates power in the hands of Ba'thist officers

1964   Uprising in Hama

1966   Intra-Ba'thist struggle ends with purge of Michel Aflaq and old guard. Salah Jadid becomes de facto ruler of Syria

1967   Six Day War – following diplomatic crisis Israel attacks and defeats Egypt and Jordan then seizes Golan Heights

1969   The minister of defence, Hafez al-Assad, consolidates his position at the expense of Salah Jadid

1970   Hafez al-Assad seizes power

1971   Referendum (in which he is the only candidate) confirms Hafez al-Assad as president of Syria for his first seven-year term

1973   October 1973 War. Syria and Egypt attack Israel but are ultimately defeated. Syrian forces temporarily retake a large part of the Golan Heights but are pushed back almost to twenty-five miles from Damascus

1974   Disengagement of forces between Syria and Israel on Golan Heights

1975   Beginning of Lebanese civil war

1976   Syria intervenes in Lebanese civil war establishing broad control over most of the country.

           Islamist-led discontent appears in Syria and leads to wave of terrorism, including assassinations of prominent Alawis

1977   Jimmy Carter inaugurated as US president. He begins a determined attempt to achieve peace in the Arab-Israeli dispute but eventually has to settle for a separate peace between Israel and Egypt due to the Israeli position. Syria left out in the cold.

1979   Iranian revolution
        Egyptian-Israeli peace treaty
        Aleppo artillery school massacre

1980   Outbreak of the Iran-Iraq War

1981   Israel illegally annexes Golan Heights and treats the area as its own sovereign territory

1982   Brutal and indiscriminate repression of Islamist uprising in Hama

        Israel invades Lebanon, ratcheting violence in the Lebanese civil war up to new levels; siege of West Beirut; evacuation of PLO fighters from Lebanon; assassination of president-elect of Lebanon Bashir Gemayel; election of Amin Gemayel as president of Lebanon

1983   Hafez al-Assad seriously ill; Rif'at al-Assad rises to prominence

1984   "War between the brothers": Hafez al-Assad removes his brother Rif'at from position of power

1987   Outbreak of Intifada in occupied Palestinian territories

1988   End of Iran-Iraq War

1989   Taif Accords provide framework to end Lebanese civil war

1990   Iraq occupies Kuwait

        Syria temporarily rehabilitates itself with the USA and West by joining anti-Iraq coalition

        Syrian troops crush General Aoun; Syria left with hegemonic position in Lebanon

1991   Iraqi forces driven from Kuwait by US-led coalition acting under UN Charter

Syria participates in US-led Madrid conference aimed at finally ending Arab-Israeli dispute

1992   Intermittent negotiations between Syria and Israel begin and continue until 1996 with US encouragement

1993   Oslo Accords produce framework to end Israeli-Palestinian dispute but ultimately fail

1994   Death of Hafez al-Assad's son Basil in car crash
Israel-Jordan peace treaty

1995   Assassination of Israeli Prime Minister Yitzhak Rabin

1996   Election of hardline Israeli government led by Benyamin Netanyahu which does not recognise Syria's right to the Golan Heights

1997   Israeli parliament votes to reiterate Israel's assertion of sovereignty over the Golan Heights

1998   Hafez al-Assad's health in obvious decline; rise of his son Bashar to prominence

2000   Israel withdraws from South Lebanon

Attempt to negotiate peace between Israeli Prime Minister Ehud Barak and Hafez al-Assad fails

Death of Hafez al-Assad from leukemia

Bashar al-Assad takes power

"Damascus Spring"

Ariel Sharon visits Esplanade of the Mosques in East Jerusalem triggering Second Intifada

2001   9/11

Syria shares intelligence with Western powers and is thanked for helping to save American lives

US-led invasion of Afghanistan

2002   Girls given the freedom to wear the hijab at school

2003	US-led invasion of Iraq; demonisation of Syria because of its opposition to the invasion

2003
: US-led invasion of Iraq; demonisation of Syria because of its opposition to the invasion

Foreign fighters use Syrian territory to enter Iraq and join insurgency

USA passes Syrian Accountability Act

2004
: Private banks return to Syria

2005
: Assassination of Lebanese Prime Minister Rafiq Hariri; Syria widely believed to be responsible

Syrian forces withdraw from Lebanon

2006
: War between Israel and Hizbullah; Lebanon devastated

2007
: Nancy Pelosi and other US parliamentarians visit Damascus; signs of thawing of relations between Syria and the West

2009
: Opening of Damascus stock exchange

2010
: Beginning of Arab Spring in Tunisia

2011
: Arab Spring spreads to Syria; regime confronts protests with violence including lethal force

Opposition forms Syrian National Council

Syria suspended from Arab League

2012
: Syria descends into civil war and the country disintegrates

Severe fighting in Homs, Aleppo and suburbs of Damascus

2013
: Much of eastern Syria passes out of government control

Chemical attack in Damascus suburbs

2014
: Regime's military position appears to stabilise

Breakdown of Geneva II diplomatic initiatives

ISIS bulldozes sections of the boundary between Syria and Iraq and proclaims a caliphate

Siege of Kobane

Glossary

Alawi: a member of a secretive Muslim sect which dates from the eleventh century and predominates in the mountains east of Lattakia. The Alawis are also represented in parts of the countryside of the Orontes valley. There are also Alawis in Turkey.

Ba'th: an Arab nationalist party originally formed in Damascus in the early 1940s by Michel Aflaq and Salah al-Din Bitar. Its ideals are Arab unity, freedom from foreign domination, and socialism.

Druze: another secretive sect which is an offshoot of Islam. The Druze are predominant on the Hawran Plateau around Suwayda, south-east of Damascus, and in parts of Mount Lebanon. There are also Druze communities elsewhere in Syria and in the Galilee.

Hashemite: the name of an Arab dynasty descended directly from the Prophet Muhammad which provided the guardians of the Holy Cities of Mecca and Medina until they were forced out by Ibn Saud (the founder of Saudi Arabia) in 1924–5. The Hashemites led an Arab nationalist revolt against the Ottoman Turks during the Great War and briefly established a kingdom of Greater Syria centred on Damascus. More enduring Hashemite kingdoms closely tied to Great Britain were established in Iraq (overthrown in 1958) and Jordan. The Hashemite brand of Arab nationalism was secular but closely tied to British influence.

ISIS: the self-styled 'Islamic State of Iraq and Shaam', also known as ISIL (Islamic State of Iraq and the Levant), IS (Islamic State) and Da'ish (its Arabic acronym). It gained traction among Sunni Arabs in Iraq as a reaction to the sectarianism of the government of Nouri al-Maliki. It expanded into eastern Syria as the forces of Bashar al-Assad withdrew from many areas and established itself in the provincial capital of Raqqa in the spring of 2013. Following its seizure of Mosul in June 2014, its leader, Abu Bakr al-Baghdadi, proclaimed himself Caliph. It uses extreme violence to instil fear and bolster its control.

Mandate: a novel concept in international law established by Article 22 of the Covenant of the League of Nations in 1919. A Mandate was granted to an "advanced nation" to provide "tutelage" to peoples formerly ruled by Turkey or Germany but who were not deemed to be ready "to stand by themselves under the strenuous conditions of the modern world". The intention was that the Mandatory (that is, the power which was granted the Mandate) would prepare the people under its tutelage for full independence. The principle of "the well-being and development" of a people placed under a Mandate was considered to be "a sacred trust of civilisation". Syria and Lebanon were placed under French Mandate, while Britain was granted Mandates over Palestine and Iraq.

Maronite: a member of a Christian sect predominant in parts of Lebanon but also with followers scattered throughout Greater Syria. This sect has retained its own traditions and autonomous structure while being in communion with the Roman Catholic Church since the time of the Crusades.

Millet: a Christian community granted internal self-government by the Ottoman sultan, often (but not necessarily) through the leaders of the clerical structure of their church. The Ottoman Jews were also given the status of a *millet*.

Mukhabarat: an Arabic word for intelligence services – especially the much feared intelligence agencies of the Syrian government.

Notable: a term used to denote important and influential quasi-aristocratic families which provided the backbone of society in Greater Syria during the Ottoman era and later. Notable families provided many administrators and religious leaders. They were based in the principal cities but were often major landlords in the countryside. They were essentially intermediaries of power between the government and the peasantry.

Salafi: literally "a follower of the forefathers". The term is generally used for a Sunni Muslim who follows a rigid and literalist form of Islam and tries to base his life as closely as possible on that of the Prophet and his Companions in the seventh century. Hence, "Salafism". Rather confusingly, the term is also sometimes used for a follower of the reformist and open-minded school of modernist Islam established by the Egyptian reformer Muhammad Abduh at the dawn of the twentieth century, and which he called the Salafiyah. This is very different indeed from Salafism.

Sanjak: a Turkish word for a province.

Syriac: an ancient Semitic language still spoken by a few small pockets of Christians in Syria, Iraq and south-eastern Turkey who are followers of the Syrian Orthodox Church. Once it was the lingua franca of the Fertile Crescent and it has a rich literary heritage. Aramaic, the language spoken by Christ, is a variant of Syriac.

Takfir: declaring another Muslim to be an apostate and therefore worthy of death. Hence "takfiri" – someone who does this.

Tanzimat: a series of nineteenth-century Ottoman reforms.

Taqiyya: a doctrine followed by Shi'is and Alawis under which it is permitted, when need arises, to dissemble about one's true religious beliefs in order to avoid persecution by the Sunni Muslim majority.

Uniate: a term to denote a Christian who belongs to an autonomous church with its own traditions which is in communion with the Roman Catholic Church.

Wahhabi: a strict, puritanical Muslim sect founded by Muhammad Ibn Abdul Wahhab in Central Arabia in the mid-eighteenth century. It is the prevailing ideology of Saudi Arabia. Today, it overlaps with Salafism which Saudi Arabian Wahhabis seek to export to Muslim communities across the world.

Yishuv: a Hebrew word used to denote the Jewish community in Palestine before the establishment of the state of Israel.

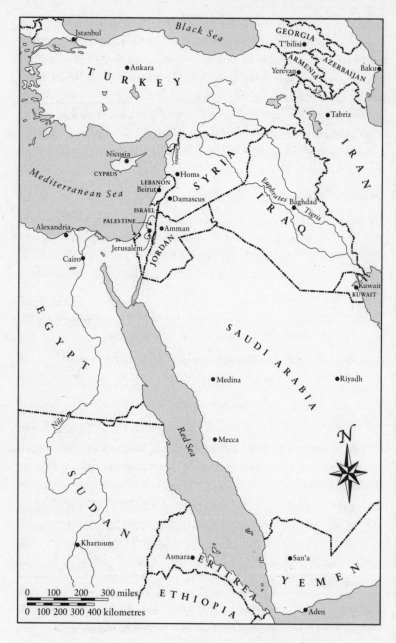

THE MIDDLE EAST SHOWING MODERN POLITICAL BOUNDARIES

Preface

I

The sufferings of the Syrian people since their country descended into civil war in 2011–12 need no recapitulation. The statistics, even if provisional, are terrible. Nobody knows for certain the numbers of dead or injured. Accurate statistics are hard to come by in a war zone, and the numbers are bound to rise. As of December 2014, estimates of those killed have reached 200,000.[1] Out of a population of almost 22.5 million people, over 3.2 million have fled the country,[2] while 6.45 million are internally displaced and 4.6 million 'in need of humanitarian assistance in besieged/hard to access areas'.[3]

To the English-speaking world, Syria is a far-off country which relatively few people have made a serious effort to understand. The "Arab Spring" aroused great interest and excitement, but as the crackdown on protesters in Syria evolved into civil war and a man-made humanitarian crisis began, disaster fatigue seemed all too often to be the general reaction to what was happening. Despite energetic advertising campaigns by relief charities, at first only occasional incidents such as the death of the *Sunday Times* reporter Marie Colvin in Homs in February 2012 brought the unfolding catastrophe home.

For a couple of weeks, the use of chemical weapons in the Damascus suburbs of Ain Tarma and Zamalka which killed hundreds of people on 21 August 2013 shook the world, but it was not enough to persuade British Members of Parliament to give their government the discretion to use force for humanitarian intervention. It was the same with other major world players. As soon as agreement was reached with the Syrian government about the decommissioning and destruction of its chemical weapons, the issue largely faded from the headlines. The killing of Syrians by conventional weaponry and their deaths by starvation, disease and hypothermia did not capture our attention in the same way. Soon enough, public compassion had moved on to fresh humanitarian disasters in other parts of the world.

Following the failure of the talks in Geneva between the Syrian government and opposition politicians on 15 February 2014, the international mediator, Lakhdar Brahimi, stated that he had no alternative but to apologise to the Syrian people.[4] The fighting does not yet seem to have run its course. When the conflict ends – and no one can say when that will be – the world will be presented with yet another traumatised Arab nation. In 1947–9, the majority of the indigenous Arabs of Palestine were forced to flee their homes. Many of them and their descendants are refugees to this day. Among many people in the West, their story remains a taboo topic. But the Palestine problem is just one cause of instability in the region. In the mid-1970s, Lebanon exploded into a civil war which lasted until 1990 and whose embers smoulder still. Then, following the US-led invasion in 2003, Iraq disintegrated along sectarian and ethnic lines. Each of these countries borders Syria, and their tragedies caused severe problems for the Syrian government of the day and Syrian society as a whole. Now it is the turn of Syria itself to look destruction in the face after decades of draconian rule by a government that overreacted to the smallest signs of dissent.

Is the sequential implosion of these closely connected Arab countries just a coincidence? Or is there a deeper, underlying cause that brought conflict to them? In either case, what lessons can be learned? This book provides pointers towards an answer to these questions by reviewing the history of Syria since the Great War of 1914–8, whose one hundredth anniversary the world commemorated in 2014. While the descent into civil war in 2011–2 was certainly the result of failings by the Syrian leadership, there is also an element of culpability and negligence which must be spread much more widely.

The effect of the actions of outside powers on Syria over the last century cannot be overlooked. The country's borders were decided by France and Britain in the immediate aftermath of the Great War. Those two nations thus took upon themselves the momentous responsibility of deciding who was – and who was not – a Syrian. France had a vision of a permanent French presence in Syria, something that conflicted with its "sacred trust of civilisation"[5] to prepare the Syrian people for full, sovereign independence. Furthermore, although this book is not about the Arab-Israeli conflict, its enormous and deleterious effect on Syria cannot be avoided. That conflict was not created by Syrians but they, like their Arab neighbours, had no choice but to assimilate and digest its consequences – something that put both leaders and people under immense strain which has lasted to the present. The Cold War did not help, either. All too easily forgotten today, the global tussle for supremacy between the USA and the USSR turned Syria into a pawn. It was to be moved and, when expedient, sacrificed on the chess board of global politics. In fact, today's Syrian civil war could be said to be the last proxy conflict of the Cold War. The alternative view, which is even more disturbing, is that it is the harbinger of the revival of the Cold War which has now begun in Ukraine. It is not an exaggeration to say that the actions of the great powers in the aftermath of the Great War and over the following decades deprived the people of Syria of any chance of a normal development to nationhood.

But the major international players were not the only ones who have played games in Syria. As will be seen, certain Arab states, particularly Iraq, Jordan, Egypt, Saudi Arabia and latterly even Qatar, have treated Syria as a ball to be prised from their opponents. It has been the same with non-Arab Iran and Turkey. In each period covered by this book, the impact of wars and foreign affairs will be considered before turning to the developments which actually took place inside Syria. This may seem unusual for the history of a country, but in this case it is only logical. Events happening outside Syria circumscribed the freedom of action open to its rulers and foreclosed the options available to them. This does not excuse or justify some of the actions those rulers took, but their actions cannot be examined in isolation from what was going on between Syria and its neighbours.

One of the greatest tragedies in the history of Syrian politics is what happened to Ba'thism. Initially a nationalist movement which seemingly cared deeply about social justice and healing the rifts in society throughout the Arab world, it had the added advantage for Syrians of having been conceived and born in Damascus. The way in which Ba'thism morphed into the dictatorship of the Assads is an object lesson for other Arab countries at the present time. Another salutary example is the chaos of parliamentary life in Syria under the Mandate and the years after independence. The glimpses of that chaos which this book contains are a dire warning. It led to impatience with elected politicians and is part of the story of descent into dictatorship.

Religious politics in Arab countries didn't use to be as important as many people now assume, but they gained in significance as a reaction to the failures of the Ba'thists and other Arab nationalists, and were also linked to the profound sense of alienation from the West which occurred for reasons which this book will make painfully clear. Islamism is not well understood in the West. It is ultimately a quest for authenticity and identity. Values such as honesty, justice and mercy are at the heart of Islam, with the result that the kind of indiscriminate violence practised by some Islamist groups is incompatible with the Muslim ideal of Jihad. Many Syrians may well want a form of democracy that acknowledges in some way the Islamic roots of the majority of the population. Such a democracy could not be more different from the kind of rule offered by militant organisations like al-Qa'ida or ISIS, which are infamous for their brutality and intolerance.

Hafez al-Assad never envisaged the establishment of a democracy in Syria which might threaten his position. If his son ever did so, he left it as a can to be kicked down the road until it was too late. For both father and son, democracy and Islamist militancy were twin threats. To tar the advocates of the former with the brush of the latter was highly expedient. The increasing prominence of militant groups among those fighting the Assad regime today is just part of the price Syrian society has paid for this cynicism.

II

I first went to Syria in November 1974 when I was twenty-three years old and studying Islamic history at postgraduate level at the American University in Cairo. I had planned a week walking in the mountains which run parallel to the coast. Armed with a sleeping bag and ground sheet, I got off the bus at the crossroads below the famous Crusader castle of Krak des Chevaliers. The dark, green hills rising before me had more in common with the Brecon Beacons in Wales than what I had been expecting: the stark rocks of the Arabian desert which I had seen in the film *Lawrence of Arabia*. Rain threatened, and I was only too happy to accept a lift from a taxi driver taking the local vet to visit a sick cow. Ibrahim, the farmer who had summoned the vet, insisted I stay the night as soon as he had greeted us. He was a stocky man in his sixties who wore a white cloth wrapped round his head and the *sherwal*, the traditional black pants of a farmer, tight round the ankles but baggy from the knees upwards.

Western visitors were rare in the mountains then, although that was not so in the years before 2011 – and plenty of hotels have been built since my visit. We communicated that night in a mixture of Arabic, French and English, for Ibrahim had served in the army during the French Mandate and was proud of his French, whilst Karim, his eldest son, was studying English at Aleppo University and was painstakingly ploughing through Thomas Hardy's *The Mayor of Casterbridge* with the same difficulties I was experiencing with classical Arabic works. Towards the end of the evening, when we had got to know each other as well as two people can in such a short time, Ibrahim asked me, "In the West, are there still people who live like us?" I told him there were hill farmers in Wales and in remote parts of England and Scotland, but I wondered how long they could survive in a modern economy. We could detect a sadness in each other's eyes which betrayed our shared regret for the passing of old ways and disquiet at the uncertainties and brutalities of the modern world.

Much earlier, when questioned about myself, I had said I was doing a Master's degree in medieval Islamic studies, which I hoped would lead to a career as a university lecturer. This met with approval, but when I mentioned I was working on a book by the eleventh-century Muslim thinker Abu Hamid al-Ghazali, my hosts did not seem interested and had hardly heard of him. The oval nostrils on Ibrahim's Semitic nose flared ever so slightly and he interjected, "Yes, they have built a mosque here. There has to be one, of course".

A silence followed. Eventually, Ibrahim broke it himself. "It goes back to Nasser. When he ruled Syria as well as Egypt,[6] he thought he would become the great leader of the Arabs. He wanted everyone to think of themselves as the same – as Arabs, not Christians or Muslims. Here you are in the Wadi al-Nasara, which means the Valley of the Christians. He wanted it to be called 'Wadi al-Nadara', 'the valley of the beautiful view'. He could do this by adding just one dot above an Arabic letter in the name on the map. But it did not work. It is still known as Wadi al-Nasara."

Before I met Ibrahim I assumed everyone who wore clothes like his was a Muslim, but I could not have been more wrong. In the morning before I left, two other farmers dressed in the same way called by. They had heard that there was a visitor who lived in Egypt and they wanted to hear about the millions of Egyptian Coptic Christians about whom I knew shamefully little. Ibrahim's family would normally read a story from the Bible together before they went to bed, and I have no doubt his religion, and the identity which flowed from it, were important to him. I had stumbled across a part of the mountains where most people were Christian. Over the following two days as I headed north, I would stop to talk to boys and girls walking home from school who confirmed this, since their first question was about my nationality, but they then immediately asked me my religion and proudly told me theirs. I couldn't help noticing the little Orthodox Church in almost every village.

Ibrahim and his two sons honoured me as a guest in a traditional Arab way. They slept on mattresses on the floor beside me, because they were concerned I might feel lonely so far from home. They even lent me a white nightgown for the occasion. I experienced their hospitality, their generosity and their courtesy – three great Arab virtues. However, I did not meet Ibrahim's wife or daughter, except when they brought in breakfast in the morning and arrived to sweep the floor. Their heads were wrapped in scarves and their arms covered to the wrist: the traditional dress of the mountains for Christian and Muslim women alike. This was a peasant society in which the sexes were segregated to a greater extent than would generally have been the case with peasants in Western Europe. It was a cultural norm that was not a badge of religious identity.

Ibrahim's eyes were moist as I left. Karim accompanied me on the first leg of my journey when I left in the morning. We walked up the green hillside through a mist, spotting the carcass of the cow which the vet had been unable to save lying in a ravine with its stiff legs stretched up to the sky. Quite suddenly, we found ourselves under the walls of the castle where we said goodbye. Karim talked to me about *fasq*, which was a new Arabic word for me and which he did not know how to translate into English. He eventually settled for "moral degeneration". Moral degeneration was the great threat to the modern world, this young Christian Syrian said, then told me it came from the West. I thought guiltily of the trickle of Westerners who came to Egypt as discreet sex tourists: something Muslim friends in Cairo had not hesitated to point out to me. The West, I was beginning to realise, lacked moral authority in the eyes of many Arabs. It might have great power, but it did not necessarily command respect.

My memories of the following days are less clear, and I never achieved again that rare feeling that I had arrived a total stranger and parted a true friend. The next night I was put up by a Christian carpenter who had seven children and was home for a holiday from his work in Saudi Arabia. He was very different from Ibrahim. He talked chiefly about money (a topic Ibrahim did not mention once) and was dazzled by how much he was paid for putting in the wooden fixtures on new buildings in Jeddah. Despite this, he told me he was a *shiyou'i* – a word which, when I was able to look it up in a dictionary, I discovered meant Communist. A day later, I reached Masyaf on the edge of the mountains. This time, I was put up by a young soldier who was obsessed with getting into the Syrian special forces. He said that the secret to beating the Israelis would be to become even tougher than they were.

Masyaf was the point at which I gave up the walk, and shared a taxi down into the plain with an old Ismaili man who told me how wonderful it was to be an Ismaili since there was a tremendous feeling of brotherhood between Ismailis all over the world. The same, of course, goes for the followers of all religious sects. Today the Ismailis (a Shi'i sect who are the spiritual followers of the Aga Khan) are the most peaceable of people, but that was not always so. The Assassins were Ismailis, and it was from their jagged citadel above Masyaf – a puny castle compared with the imposing Krak – that their emissaries set out across Greater Syria to spread terror into the hearts of rulers, Muslim and Christian alike, a thousand years ago.

The taxi dropped me at a village beside an irrigation canal where the people were celebrating the anniversary of the "Corrective Movement" which had brought Hafez al-Assad to power as ruler of Syria exactly four years earlier. At that time, his name meant almost nothing to me. There were bright lights strung between the trees along the canal, while the villagers sat on rows of kitchen chairs and listened to speeches delivered through a megaphone. I continued onwards, by a mixture of hitch-hiking and walking, through the rich agricultural plain of the Ghab before finally taking a bus to Aleppo.

There was generally no mains electricity or water in the mountains or elsewhere in the countryside, and I had been privileged to have the briefest of glimpses of a vanishing way of life. Systematic work was underway to change it for ever. There were trenches being dug beside the roads, and pipes and cables laid in them. I continued to see children in quasi-military school uniforms carrying satchels or clutches of books as they walked along the road on their way back from school in the middle of the day. I was also impressed by the large areas of brown, barren land being planted with trees. Syria seemed to me to be on the move and destined for a better future. Sadly, I could not have been more mistaken.

On that trip I was entertained by Orthodox Christians, Ismaili Muslims and Sunni Muslims (I did not knowingly meet any Alawis or Druze). What struck me most was the great similarity between them all. Whatever differences their religions might have, the likenesses were far greater. Whenever I have returned to Syria (the last time was in

December 2014) I have observed exactly the same thing. At the moment many Syrians are being forced back into their sectarian identities – as is also happening in some other Arab countries. Although conflicts open sectarian wounds, change people permanently for the worse and leave them with hatreds which can endure for generations, I refuse to believe that in Syria the secularism based on mutual respect between members of different faiths has ended. But I also know that many would now call this belief of mine an act of faith. Only time will tell.

III

This book is a narrative history of Syria that broadly follows the chronological sequence of events. In the earlier chapters these coincide more or less with great landmarks in world events. The first chapter deals with the period up to 1919–20, and tells the history of Syria before and during the Great War. It also covers what happened to it in the immediate aftermath of that conflict and ends with the French conquest in 1920. The second chapter covers French rule until the final French soldiers and officials left in 1946. This was the era of the struggle for independence. Chapter Three covers the years after independence. Readers with knowledge of Middle Eastern history might expect it to end with the Six Day War of 1967 in which Israel seized the Golan Heights from Syria. However, the logical turning point in Syrian history occurred three years later when Hafez al-Assad took power in 1970. Chapter Three therefore covers the post-independence era up to that year. Chapters Four and Five cover the rule of Hafez al-Assad. They do not end with the US-led invasion of Iraq in 2003 or another significant event in Middle Eastern history around that time. Instead, they conclude with the transfer of power to Hafez al-Assad's son Bashar in 2000. Chapter Six deals with the era of Bashar al-Assad and includes the descent of Syria into civil war from 2011 onwards.

John McHugo, January 2015

Note on Terminology

The name "Syria" is used exclusively for the modern state of Syria, and the French Mandate which preceded it. The use of the name "Greater Syria" to describe a much larger area is discussed in Chapter One.

In this book, people are frequently described by their religion: as Muslims, Christians, Jews, Alawis, Druze, etc. It is important to stress that references to religion (and sects) are invariably to them as badges of identity which give them an almost tribal quality. Unless indicated otherwise, a reference to someone belonging to a religion or sect is thus not an indication of devoutness (or the lack thereof). Doubts about religion in the Arab Middle East are generally something for the private, rather than the public, sphere. Some of the actors who play a role in this book may have been agnostics or atheists, but that is irrelevant to the identity they possess as members of what Westerners might call their "faith community".

Please note that I refer to Arab Christians of the Greek Orthodox faith as "Orthodox" to avoid the possible confusion that they might be ethnically Greek which, of course, they are not. However, I refer to the "Syrian Orthodox" when I wish to indicate the distinct branch of the Orthodox family of churches which uses the ancient Syriac language in its liturgy. When I use the words "secular" and "secularist" I am referring to the view that religious affiliation should be irrelevant: a view which does not necessarily imply any hostility to religion as such.

For the sake of simplicity, I refer to the state of Jordan throughout, even though during the period of the Palestine Mandate it was "Transjordan".

CHAPTER ONE

The Land that Once was Known as Shaam

I

In Arabic, Bilaad al-Shaam means "the land of Shaam" or possibly "the towns of Shaam", but in its literal sense it means "the land to the left". It acquired this name because an Arab who stands in the middle of Arabia facing north has Shaam to his left. Shaam stretches along the eastern shore of the White Sea, as the Arabs call the Mediterranean, for some 500 miles from the deserts of the Sinai Peninsula until the ground rises to the plateaux of what is now southern Turkey. It is also considered to extend into Anatolia until it meets a natural frontier in the Taurus Mountains. Today, Shaam (or Greater Syria, as it used to be called in the West – and that is the name we will use in this book) is divided between Syria, Lebanon, Israel, Palestine and Jordan, and includes part of southern Turkey. The lines on the map which give these modern states their rather rigid political frontiers were only drawn in the twentieth century.

Rain from the White Sea waters Greater Syria's green coastal plain and the belt of mountains behind. Every winter, the mountains turn white. In spring and summer, they slowly disgorge their snow melt into rivers, some of which flow eastwards into the arid lands beyond. Several millennia ago, one of these gave life to the city of Shaam itself, which is better known as Damascus, and enabled its inhabitants to surround it with orchards and farms. Damascus was a beautiful city, so beautiful in fact that when the Prophet of Islam beheld it at around the end of the sixth century, he is said to have gasped in amazement and turned back. No one, he said, can enter Paradise twice. Slightly over half a millennium earlier still, Paul, the apostle of Christianity to the Gentiles, experienced his conversion "as he neared Damascus":[1] an experience which temporarily blinded him. He was baptised while staying in the city. By then, it was already ancient. It claims to be the oldest known continually inhabited city in the world, but Greater Syria also contains other cities that make this claim: Aleppo in the north and Jericho in the south, near the Dead Sea.

Damascus itself is mentioned by name about thirty-five times in the Old Testament or Hebrew Bible and twenty in the New Testament. It lies at the centre of Greater Syria. More than anywhere else Damascus has been its political and cultural centre, but its pre-eminence has never been guaranteed. Nor has the unity of the land itself, although south of Anatolia most of its people today speak closely related Arabic dialects (save, of course, in Israel where Hebrew is now the majority language). If in the past they described themselves as Shaamis, by and large they were only making a statement about where they happened to come from; and it might indicate either Damascus or the wider land of Greater Syria. This did not mean they had no sense of identity. On the contrary, they identified themselves by their family, their tribe (many, but by no means all, Shaamis had a tribe) and their religion (everyone in Greater Syria without exception had a religion). These identities were very strong. Even today, it is common for ordinary people to be able to trace their ancestry back several hundred years.

Throughout history, Greater Syria has been vulnerable to invasion from all points of the compass, while its geography makes central control extremely difficult. As a cursory glance at a map will show, it contains the land route between Africa and Eurasia. It has constantly been ruled and occupied (and sometimes partitioned) by strong rulers who came from elsewhere. The Pharoahs had a strategic interest in it, and their people depended on its food if the Nile flood failed – as did later rulers of Egypt, who followed the Pharoahs in invading it on many occasions. There were also invaders from the North and East: Hittites, Assyrians, the Achaemenid Persians, and then Alexander the Great of Hellenic Macedonia, who came overland across Anatolia and took over the Achaemenid Empire in the fourth century BC. Following his death in 323 BC, Greater Syria was partitioned between two successor states established by his generals, but fell under the sway of Rome in 64–3 BC. Later Persian empires, the Parthians and the Sasanians, invaded in their turn. Then, in the 630s and 640s, the Arab conquerors came from the south. This ended a thousand years of Greek cultural domination, and led to the overwhelming majority of the population adopting the Arabic language and a sizeable majority of them converting to Islam. These were processes which took hundreds of years.

After the Arab conquest, Greater Syria became the centre of the great Arab empire of the Umayyad Caliphate, which was based in Damascus and lasted from 661 to 750. It left posterity the first two stunning examples of Islamic architecture that endure to this day: the Dome of the Rock in Jerusalem and the Umayyad Mosque in Damascus.

Later, there was a series of invaders from the West. These were the Crusaders who arrived in Greater Syria in 1098 and were only finally driven out in 1291. They were warriors from Western Europe who were inspired by an ideal of Holy War approved by the Pope, and hoped to reconquer lands which had once been part of Christendom from their Muslim rulers. Today, they have left few visible traces save for vast fortifications. But even these are indistinguishable to the non-specialist eye from those built by the Crusaders' opponents, and many were extensions or refurbishments of earlier castles. They have also often been transformed beyond recognition by subsequent rulers. There are even a few localities where people remember today that they have Crusader blood, although they have long since abandoned their Frankish language in favour of Arabic, and sometimes converted to Islam.

The Crusaders were finally crushed by the ruthless Mamluks, a cast of slave warriors which ruled Egypt and perennially replenished itself with recruits purchased as boys in the Caucasus and elsewhere. The Mamluks also fought off another invasion from the East, the Mongols of Hulagu who briefly took Aleppo and Damascus after sacking Baghdad in 1258 and executing the last true caliph.

Another scourge from the East was Tamerlane, whose armies reached Damascus in 1400–1. He massacred the population and kidnapped its craftsmen to decorate his capital in far-off Samarkand. The Mamluks reasserted themselves and won Damascus back, but eventually they, too, had to bow the knee after they were defeated by a fresh invader from the north, the Ottoman Turks. Their sultan, Selim the Grim, conquered Greater Syria and Egypt in 1516. This conquest occurred when the Ottoman Empire was at its height. It had already taken most of the Balkans, including Hungary, and wrestled with the European powers for the control of the Mediterranean. It dreamed of scaling the walls of Vienna (which it besieged in 1529 and 1683) and of planting the flag of Islam in Rome itself. However, in the eighteenth and nineteenth centuries the empire decayed until Greater Syria was one of its last remaining possessions outside its Anatolian heartland. The Ottomans still retained it when the Great War began in 1914.

Although interest in the modern state of Syria has not been widespread in the West, Europeans and Westerners generally have had an intense fascination with Greater Syria. Until quite recent times, memories of the Crusades were generally stronger in Europe than among Arabs. But above all else for Westerners, Greater Syria was the land of the Bible. Christian pilgrims from Europe had been going there since the early centuries of Christianity to visit Palestine where Jesus had lived, died and, his followers believe, risen from the dead. Another major connection with Greater Syria for Europeans was its importance in the history of Classical times. It was a rich part of the empire that was much more significant to the Romans than the lands inhabited by the uncouth Celts who painted themselves with blue woad. As the steamship, telegraph and railway made Greater Syria more accessible in the nineteenth century, visitors from across the Mediterranean came to gape at the splendours of its ruined temples, amphitheatres, colonnades and tombs. These often seemed eerily familiar, particularly when giant Latin inscriptions on granite porticoes or tablets by the side of the road recorded the deeds of gods, emperors and other eminent personages in letters which were still so clear that they might have been carved yesterday.

Europeans also came for trade, particularly to the ports and the great inland entrepôt of Aleppo, a wealthier, more cosmopolitan and, at various periods, larger city than Damascus. Greater Syria had been the western end of the old silk route, and goods from the east were still transported to Europe via the valley of the Euphrates before they were taken by camel and mule to Aleppo and its port of Alexandretta next to Antioch. This route was a rival to the southern one which came up the Red Sea to Egypt. In addition, as the nineteenth century wore on, silk, cotton, tobacco and grain were cultivated for export to Europe. European powers jostled for position, and were helped by the divisions among the peoples of Greater Syria: divisions they were not above fostering for their own ends.

The late nineteenth century and the first years of the twentieth were the age of European imperialism. Europe burned bright with nationalism, and pride and prestige were important for every European nation state that sought to project its influence overseas. Elements of genuine altruism were blended somewhere into this heady brew, giving the European nations a strong self-belief and what would transpire to be a very dangerous sense of their own righteousness. They became envious of each other as they competed to acquire colonies in Africa and Asia. This rivalry could drift into mutual demonisation and was an important part of the run-up to the Great War. The clock was ticking towards a European conflict that would become global.

Ottoman Turkey was a natural focus for European ambition, but its lands in Asia – including Greater Syria – were saved from dismemberment. This was not because of the Ottomans' now faded military might but the constraints of the European balance of power. The Europeans stalked each other, always anxious to prevent their rivals from stealing a march on them. They had also extracted trade privileges which the Ottomans were too weak to resist. These included tax and customs rates which were more favourable than those paid by native merchants. Local Christian and Jewish traders were generally the ones who benefited by establishing links with the foreigners. It was often more advantageous for a merchant in Aleppo, Beirut or Damascus to become the agent of a French or British company than to trade on his own account.

The four powers with the greatest interest in the Ottoman Empire (and therefore in Greater Syria) were Britain, France, Germany and Russia. The last two need only be mentioned briefly. Russia proclaimed itself the protector of the Orthodox Christians in the empire. It also had territorial ambitions in the empire, but not in Greater Syria itself although it established strong links with the sizeable Orthodox communities there. After the Bolsheviks came to power in 1917, it renounced these interests. Russia then becomes largely absent from our story until it re-enters it in the form of the Soviet Union during the Cold War, which lasted from the late 1940s to the end of the 1980s. Germany had no territorial ambitions in the Ottoman Empire, and for that reason was able to pose as the Ottomans' ally and friend with some degree of conviction. It would be this friendship, and the links Germany had established with the Ottoman military, that led to the disastrous Ottoman decision to enter the Great War as Germany's partner in November 1914.

The ambitions and policies of Britain and France require more attention. In the second half of the nineteenth century, Britain took Egypt and Cyprus from Ottoman control and was already the paramount power in the Persian Gulf. Britain's policy now was generally to prop up the Ottoman Empire so as to prevent France, Russia or another rival acquiring its territories and threatening the Suez Canal, which opened in 1869, or Britain's other strategic interests. However, if war eventually came and the Ottoman Empire was dismembered, Britain would have its own objectives to pursue: to control the southern parts of Greater Syria and Iraq as part of a land bridge from Egypt to India, as well as the Iraqi oil wells near Basra. It was vital to British interests that no other power should acquire these areas.

France's interests in Greater Syria were more extensive than those of Britain. It was the main market for the raw materials exported from the area and it had invested more money in Syria's railways, urban utilities and other infrastructure. France saw itself as the protector of the Catholics in the Ottoman Empire, and had done so for much longer than the Russians had deemed themselves the guardians of the Orthodox. The powerful Maronite Christians centred on Mount Lebanon, whose Catholicism can be traced back to the Crusades, were France's most significant Catholic clients, but they were by no means the only ones. In the eighteenth and nineteenth centuries large numbers of other Christians in Greater Syria had converted to Catholicism while maintaining their own self-governing churches. This was what the Maronites had done centuries earlier. These self-governing Catholic communities were known as Uniates. In the Greater Syria of the late nineteenth and early twentieth centuries, many Uniates were prosperous and self-confident.

They were particularly important in Aleppo. In 1849, crosses were carried publicly in processions in the city and traditional Arab celebratory gunfire was heard when the authorities recognised the Melkites, one of the largest Uniate groups, as a separate *millet* or religious community.[2] Uniates frequently engaged in trade between Greater Syria and the West. They represented Western companies and could often speak European languages, especially French. French was also the lingua franca of merchants engaged in international trade throughout the area, and the primary language in which European technical knowledge and the thought of the modern world were disseminated to the elite of Greater Syria and the Ottoman Empire as a whole. Many of that elite could speak and read French, and write well in it too.

These religious, cultural and commercial interests fitted in neatly with the French belief in the uniqueness of the values of France's civilisation, and the desire to spread these values through its self-appointed *mission civilisatrice* or "civilising mission". In Greater Syria, the *mission civilisatrice* was linked in many French minds with the idealised memories of the Crusades which swept France in the nineteenth century. During the French Second Empire (1852–70) *Partant pour la Syrie*, "Setting off for Syria", was used more frequently than the Marseillaise as the national anthem. It was a song about the wish of a Crusader to be the bravest knight and to marry the most beautiful girl in the world, a wish God grants him as a reward for his valour.

It may seem trite to mention this song, but it illustrates an important point. Although there were Western scholars, traders, diplomats, soldiers, clergymen and travellers who had genuine knowledge of Greater Syria, the images Western minds had of the area were also formed by reimagined memories of the past. These were frequently seen through rose-tinted spectacles, and were tinged with both a nostalgic romanticism and the harder edge which the rather intense nationalism of the era added to European perceptions.

II

The mountainous spine which runs parallel to the coast of Greater Syria contains many remote and inaccessible areas. Save for a few gaps, it cuts off the lands behind from the sea. Throughout history, the great inland cities to the east have been natural rivals, especially Damascus and Aleppo but also the smaller Homs and even smaller Hama. Each was surrounded by its own hinterland and had a strong sense of its own identity. The physical geography thus lent itself to divisions among the people or peoples who lived there.

The greatest marker of identity was religion. At the time of the Arab conquest in the seventh century, Greater Syria had been an overwhelmingly Christian country but had been torn apart by heresies, schisms and religious persecutions. When the Ottoman Turks conquered it in 1516–17, Christians may have still made up a third of the population. As the modern era dawned, a lower Christian birth rate and greater Christian emigration, as well as the trickle of conversions to the dominant faith of Islam across the centuries, had led to a further decline in the proportion of Christians. However, they remained numerous and are generally considered to have formed 20 per cent or so of the population in 1914. Although there were still Christians working the land, the cities contained many who were prosperous, well educated and influential. Aleppo at that time was approximately one third Christian.

Christian minorities were usually represented by their bishops or patriarchs, who often fought ferocious turf wars with each other. Ill-feeling between different Christian sects was frequently worse than that between Muslims, Christians and Jews, although the members of the three great monotheistic faiths had tended to live parallel lives for hundreds of years and generally shown disdain for each other's beliefs. Small but ancient Jewish communities which were mostly engaged in commerce were concentrated in a number of cities and major towns, although groups of religious Jews were to be found in Palestine, the land which was the spiritual home of Judaism, where they had settled to lead pious lives.

Most Muslims were Sunnis and followed the form of Islam of their Ottoman sultan. Like earlier Muslim rulers, the sultan had traditionally dealt with his subjects on the basis of their religion, but the Ottoman state did not acknowledge non-Sunni sects, of which the Shi'is were the largest. Greater Syria also contained Alawis and Druze, two small groups which had emerged from Shi'ism but had travelled to the very fringes of Islam. Shi'is, Alawis and Druze sometimes practised *taqiyya*, outwardly appearing as Sunnis so as to avoid drawing attention to themselves and risking persecution.

The coastal mountains provided refuges for minority sects. To the east of Lattakia, Alawis formed the majority overall and their area abutted that of the Ismaili Shi'is around Masyaf and the Orthodox Christians of Wadi al-Nasara to the south. In the massif of Lebanon, substantial areas were predominantly Maronite Christian and Druze. In the mountains, these local sects formed close-knit peasant societies that looked inwards. At times when central government was weak, they could disregard its ordinances and even come down from the mountains in search of pillage and protection money. But they did not all live in compact little enclaves. The Maronite and Druze heartlands might be in the Lebanese mountains, but Maronite and Druze villages were also to be found in many other places. There was also a Druze-dominated area on the Hawran plateau south-east of Damascus. Predominantly Shi'i areas were to be found around Ba'lbek and south of Sidon.

The Ottomans had taken little notice of ethnic, as opposed to religious, divisions. Ethnic markers were therefore administratively invisible. While most Sunni Muslims in Greater Syria were Arabs, some were Kurds and a few were Turks or Circassians (Muslims who had either been ethnically cleansed by the Russians as they conquered lands from the Ottomans, or who had chosen to leave because they wished to continue to live under Muslim rule). Despite the lack of recognition of ethnicity by the authorities, it became increasingly significant as the impact of the modern world came to the region. In the north of Greater Syria, the area that was to remain with Turkey after the Great War, Turks were the largest community, but there were also substantial numbers of Kurds and Armenians, as well as Syriac-speaking Syrian Orthodox Christians and some Arabic speakers. Each of these groups had its own language and a distinct culture.

There were also some rural Kurds further south, as well as substantial Kurdish communities in the big cities – some of which had been there so long that they only spoke Arabic. Meanwhile the migration patterns of Arabic-speaking nomadic tribes known as Bedouin crisscrossed the whole of Greater Syria and dominated the most arid areas. They had their own codes of law, which were administered by tribal elders and were entirely oral. Although they had a symbiotic relationship with settled communities with whom they needed to trade, their arrival in an area could be disquieting to agriculturalists and townsfolk alike. They were unpredictable, and raiding and cattle rustling were an integral part of their life. The Circassians were settled by the sultan in a number of places scattered across Greater Syria, often in the hope that they would provide a counterweight to the lawlessness of the Bedouin. The Circassians also had their own languages and culture.

In the late nineteenth century, Syria's political elite came from wealthy Sunni Muslim families. They were bilingual in Turkish and Arabic, and their blood was a mixture of Arab, Turkish and Kurd. The members of these families were the "notables", those who played a role as intermediaries between the Ottoman state and the people. The names of some Syrian families have a distinctly Turkish ring, such as Qawuqji, Quwwatli or Shishakli. This did not prevent them producing prominent Arab nationalists in the half century or so after the Great War.

This pattern of notable politics was widespread in other regions of the empire and in other Arab countries generally, and was not confined to Sunni Muslims. The same system applied, more or less, to Christians and other minorities, but the Sunni notables of the cities dominated most of Greater Syria. The main source of their wealth was rent and shares of the crops from their vast landholdings in the countryside, although they spent most of their income in the cities where they resided. These families provided the state with administrators and religious leaders, but only rarely military officers. Generally speaking, they looked down on the army as a career choice for their sons. Their patronage networks provided the glue that held the society of Greater Syria together and at the same time bound it into the Ottoman Empire. People depended on the notable families for their livelihoods, both in the countryside and in the cities where they lived in their great houses. Their influence over the population made them useful to the empire, but they depended for their own position on access to state power. They were thus intermediaries of control. They needed a degree of rapport with those who depended on them, so that they could persuade the ordinary people of Greater Syria to acquiesce in Ottoman rule. If they failed to do this, they would cease to be able to carry out the function the empire expected from them.

III

New and unfamiliar ideas like "constitution", "democracy", "liberalism" and "secularism" spread slowly among the educated elite of Greater Syria in the second half of the nineteenth century. These notions came directly from Europe, carried by Syrians returning from their studies as well as by Western intellectuals such as teachers coming to work in missionary and other schools. The ideas also arrived indirectly via Ottoman reformers who hoped to modernise the empire. In 1856, these reformers succeeded – in theory if not always in practice – in abolishing the old distinctions based on religion under which the sultan had governed his non-Muslim subjects through the leaders of their religious communities. They hoped to inspire a sense of Ottoman patriotism among the empire's many ethnic groups. An Ottoman parliament was even established in 1876. The major cities of Greater Syria elected members and gained their first halting acquaintanceship with the democratic process. However, the parliament was suspended within two years and was not reconvened until 1908.

Nationalism enthuses its advocates but creates and reinforces divisions, since by its very nature the idea of a nation to which a particular people belong excludes those who do not. The arrival of nationalism in Greater Syria was slow, but as educated people became conscious of it as an idea hard questions had to be posed. Was Greater Syria a nation? Or was it part of a wider one? Was it merely a geographical expression containing several nations? What were the commonalities of identity which bound its people together? And how could ideas of national identity be reconciled with membership of the Ottoman Empire? The Ottomans might be in obvious decline, but the sultan and his ministers could still turn extremely nasty if they suspected disloyalty. Revolt would not have been an option, even if the nationalist sentiment to begin one had existed – which it did not.

There were some Sunni Muslims who believed national identity should be subsumed into a wider sense of Muslim community. This was known as Pan-Islamism. Latching on to this idea, the Ottoman Sultan Abdul Hamid II, who ruled from 1876 to 1909, tried to advertise himself as the caliph so as to claim the spiritual allegiance of all Sunnis worldwide. He came to be referred to as the "Sultan-Caliph", perhaps on the model of Queen Victoria's title of "Queen-Empress" after she styled herself Empress of India in 1877. Pan-Islamists believed that Greater Syria, being a predominantly Muslim land, should remain part of the Ottoman Empire. They were helped by the fact that the Ottoman reformers had made it easier for non-Turkish subjects to rise in the empire's hierarchy. For the people of Greater Syria, this was perfectly compatible with pride in an Arab identity. After all, was not the word of God revealed in Arabic, and had not the Prophet and his successors been Arab? Arabic was the language of Islam. Such thoughts could be a spur to nationalism. By the first years of the twentieth century some religious reformers in Syria were beginning to question whether it was appropriate for the leaders of Islam to be Turks based in Istanbul, when the birth of the religion had occurred among the Arabs. Because of the large religious minorities in Syria, the reformers were also well aware of the need for pluralism, and tended to favour a constitutional form of government.[3]

Never far from the minds of reformers and everyone else in Greater Syria were the catastrophic "events" of 1860, as they were known. These had shaken Greater Syria and had had reverberations as far away as the chancelleries of Europe. Over the previous decades, relations between the Maronites of Mount Lebanon and their Druze neighbours had deteriorated. In 1860, the area exploded into violence which amounted to full-scale war. Both Maronites and Druze were warlike peoples, but on this occasion the Druze triumphed in a spectacular fashion, probably because of leadership problems and divisions on the Maronite side. That summer, from May to August, Druze warriors rampaged through the Maronite heartland, burning villages and massacring their inhabitants, and even sacking two important towns. Many Maronites fled to Damascus, where tensions mounted.

In Damascus itself, there were causes for resentment against Christians. Many Muslims realised that European political domination was a very real threat, and that some Christians would welcome it. It sometimes seemed as though, in a complete reversal of tradition, Christians (and Jews) were now privileged above Muslims. The reforms of 1856 which had ended the customary superiority of Muslims came at a time when many Muslims were noticing how Christian merchants were benefiting as agents and intermediaries for European trade: something from which Christians were generally better placed to take advantage than Muslims. There was genuine fear that Greater Syria might fall under the sway of France or another European power. After all, thirty years before, France had invaded Algeria and decided to remain there permanently. If Christians were being massacred on Mount Lebanon at that moment, Muslims knew that there had also been massacres of Muslims by Christians in Greece and on Crete.

In July, mobs attacked the Christian quarter of Damascus which was crammed with refugees. The authorities did little or nothing while thousands of Christians were killed. It is important to stress that there were also many Muslims who sheltered Christians, and that Christians in mixed neighbourhoods, such as Maydan,[4] escaped harm. Fearful of intervention by France as the protector of the Maronites, the Ottoman authorities took firm action. They re-established order, ended the disturbances and punished those who had been involved. They executed the governor of Damascus, apparently without due process,[5] as well as many of those who were alleged to have taken part in the disturbances.

The events of 1860 had two long-term consequences. The first was that a feeling of separateness grew among the Maronites of Mount Lebanon. By agreement between the Ottomans and the European powers in 1861, the Maronite heartland on the mountain was declared to be a separate province – the Sanjak or Mutasarrifiyya of Lebanon – with a large degree of autonomy under a Christian governor. It began to be possible to speak of a Maronite nationalism. Idealistic Maronite historians began to claim that they were descendants of the ancient Phoenicians, who had brought the alphabet to Greece and thus introduced it to Europe. Many Maronites increasingly saw themselves as more European than Arab, and wanted their own independent state – although their sanjak was too small to be viable on its own. France was happy to encourage this, and its colonial lobby dreamed what seemed a not unrealistic dream, that one day there would be a Maronite commonwealth voluntarily adding itself to the French Empire.

The second consequence of 1860 flowed from the care taken by the Ottomans to ensure that such disturbances did not recur. They improved security, and invested in infrastructure and education in Greater Syria in a way that was altogether new.[6] The result was that an element of prosperity appeared among Muslims and Christians alike. The events of 1860 thus spawned a paradox: while most Maronites began to feel more apart from other Arabic speakers, Muslims and many other Christians began to feel able to drop their guard against each other a little. They also noticed, perhaps in a self-conscious way that was new, that they all spoke Arabic, which was a major difference between them and their Turkish rulers.

Literacy rates throughout the Arab world had been much lower than in Europe. Reasons included the fact that Turkish was the language of government and the army, and the late arrival of printing in Arabic-speaking countries (almost entirely absent before the nineteenth century). There also existed a strong oral tradition, which included the public recitation of the Qur'an and Arabic poetry. Most Arabic poems had a single rhyme throughout as well as a strong metre, and these were characteristics which made them ideal for declamation to large audiences. Although there were few census returns in Arab countries during the nineteenth century which provide us with relevant data, it has been suggested by one respected scholar that the literacy rate in Egypt may have been as low as 1 per cent in 1800,[7] and there is little to suggest it would have been much higher in Greater Syria as a whole.

Greater Syria played a major role in the revival of the Arabic language during the second half of the nineteenth century – an honour it shared chiefly with Egypt. There were several limbs to this cultural renaissance or the *Nahda*, as it was called. One was the rediscovery of the glories of classical Arabic literature which were printed and disseminated to a growing literate public for the first time. Attempts were even made to revive ancient forms of Arabic literary expression, such as the *maqama*. Based on the picaresque adventures of a well-loved character who quickly became familiar to the listeners, a *maqama* was a short story written in elegant rhymed prose. It combined word-play, humour and eloquence. Dictionaries and grammars were produced to help the reading public, while at the same time men of letters who were also familiar with the thought and culture of contemporary Europe introduced European literary forms and even adapted syntax from European languages to help Arabic modernise. Soon newspapers, magazines and even encyclopaedias were appearing which covered the same topics that were presented to contemporary European readerships, ranging from new scientific discoveries to contemporary liberal ideas. The modern world began to infuse itself into the hearts and minds of many people. Beirut, Istanbul and Cairo became centres of journalism written in Arabic, but as the nineteenth century progressed Cairo came to predominate because it was beyond the reach of the Ottoman censor and many Beirut-based journalists relocated there.[8]

A sense of Arab-ness was now spreading that was distinct from Islamic consciousness, and was shared by many Christians, especially Orthodox, non-Maronite Uniates, and Protestants (many of whom were converted from other Christian sects by American missionaries). Initially, this Arab-ness did not necessarily find its expression in campaigns for political independence: such views were dangerous. But home rule for the Arabic-speaking communities of the empire and the granting of official status to Arabic alongside Turkish as a language for education and government were topics for discussion.

In the last years before the Great War, a final, desperate attempt was made to refashion the Ottoman Empire. In 1908 a group of army officers seized power. They were known in the West as the Young Turks because of the frustration they felt at their country's decline and their determination to sweep away the old order that stood in the way of modernisation. Although in theory they were liberal and secular (they reinstated the Ottoman parliament), they found that the only way they could rule was by turning to authoritarianism. They were also Turkish nationalists before all else. This trumped whatever feelings of pan-Islamism they may have had, and many Arabic speakers sensed their new rulers wanted to turn them into Turks.

The Young Turks tightened the empire's grip on its Arab provinces. Perhaps they feared that Arabs would go the way of Ottoman Balkan subjects who had suddenly "discovered nationalism" and broken free of the empire. If so, their policy backfired. The new rulers insisted on the use of Turkish in administration and education. In reaction, Arab resentment and desire for autonomy, or even independence, began to spread. In 1909, political organisations based on ethnic nationalism were banned. Arab nationalist political societies had to be secret. Two significant such societies were Al-Fatat ("The Youth") and Al-'Ahd ("The Covenant"). Al-Fatat's membership was largely drawn from the notable families of Greater Syria, and its headquarters were moved to Damascus at the outbreak of the Great War. Al-'Ahd was largely a grouping of Arab army officers, chiefly from Iraq but also from Greater Syria and elsewhere.[9]

IV

Turkey joined the Great War on the side of Germany in November 1914, at least in part because the Young Turks were looking for gains at Russia's expense. They hoped to reconquer lost territories in the Caucasus and even dreamed of uniting Turkey with the vast Turkic lands extending all the way to Kazakhstan. As the war progressed these became Turkey's key strategic objectives; by its end the Young Turk leadership looked upon Greater Syria and other Arabic-speaking lands as ultimately expendable.[10]

The war was a calamity for the people of Greater Syria. Food supplies were requisitioned by the Turkish army, all ports were blockaded by the Allied Powers, and peasants were taken from their fields to serve as conscripts, while forests and even orchards were cut down to fuel the railways. Nature supplied a plague of locusts and drought to aggravate the situation. Severe famine affected the mountains of Greater Syria. It is estimated that one fifth of the population of Mount Lebanon died.[11]

In the last twelve months of the war, armies led by Britain's General Sir Edmund Allenby advanced eastwards from the Egyptian border after defeating the Turks at Gaza. Allenby captured Jerusalem in December 1917, then Damascus in October 1918. Aleppo fell just before the armistice the following month, giving him control of virtually the entirety of Greater Syria. Another British army had taken possession of most of the Ottoman territory that would later become Iraq. Legally, these huge areas, which included all the Ottoman Arabic-speaking provinces of the Fertile Crescent, were still Turkish sovereign territory, but under Allied military occupation. Their fate would depend on the small print of the peace treaty which the warring parties would now negotiate. Everyone knew that the reality was that Turkey would be forced to cede this territory. The question was: who would gain it?

The most influential party at the peace conference which decided Turkey's fate would be Britain. It was largely British and imperial troops (especially from India, Australia and New Zealand) that had forced the Turks out of their Arabic-speaking provinces. The strength of Britain's position would ensure that it achieved its main objectives: control of Palestine and Iraq, as well as the deserts that linked them. In the world as it had existed before 1914, Britain would simply have demanded that Turkey cede these territories. Now, however, imperial expansion of that sort was increasingly frowned upon. An idea called "the self-determination of peoples" was beginning to be proclaimed, especially by Woodrow Wilson, the American president, and also by the Communist revolutionaries who were now stamping their grip on the Russian Empire, having taken power in early November 1917. Britain and France felt obliged to make a nod in its direction. On 7 November 1918, a week after the Turkish surrender, they issued a joint declaration:

> The object aimed at by France and Great Britain in prosecuting in the East the War let loose by the ambition of Germany is the complete and definite emancipation of the peoples so long oppressed by the Turks and the establishment of national governments and administrations deriving their authority from the initiative and free choice of the indigenous populations.[12]

These were fine words, but the record of what happened over the following few years suggests that the sentiments they contained always came second to the realpolitik of the powers as they negotiated secretly among themselves. Britain's prime concern remained its own ambitions, but it would have to compromise with the wishes of two other European parties in order to achieve these, and the interests of those parties would have to be satisfied before any thought could be given to the new-fangled and vague concept of self-determination. There was, however, a third party which could rely on self-determination. This party consisted of those Arabs who had begun a rebellion against the Turks in 1916 and, as will shortly be seen, had made a substantial contribution to Britain's victory in Greater Syria.

The first of the European parties was France. It considered that the devastation of eastern France and the other hardships it had suffered during the war entitled it to compensation, including the acquisition of new colonial possessions from the defeated powers. France and Britain watched each other jealously as they rubbed up against each other in the Middle East, often seeking to undermine the other. They would continue to do this until after the Second World War. In 1916, they came to a secret arrangement known to history as the Sykes-Picot agreement[13] on how to carve up Greater Syria and neighbouring parts of the Ottoman Empire. Subject to relatively minor adjustments, the line they drew on a map to delineate their spheres of influence would become the southern frontiers of Syria and Lebanon to this day.

The other European actor was not a sovereign state but a political movement which aimed to implement an ideology. This was Zionism, a form of nationalism which had spread among some European Jews from the late nineteenth century onwards in reaction to the Dreyfus affair and to European anti-Semitism generally. Zionists saw it as their mission to reimagine the Jewish people as a modern nation with a sovereign state in Biblical Palestine, the area they knew from Biblical history as Eretz Israel, or the Land of Israel. Beginning in the 1880s, when the population of Palestine may have been as little as 3 per cent Jewish,[14] Zionists had begun to settle there with the intention of laying the groundwork for this state. By the time of the Great War, their efforts had expanded the Jewish proportion of the population to approximately 10 per cent of the total. The movement increased immeasurably in significance after Arthur Balfour, the British foreign secretary, wrote a letter to a Zionist leader in 1917 promising support. This vague document, whose guarded wording was cast as a single, lawyerly sentence, was soon known as the Balfour Declaration. It committed Britain to do its best to further the Zionist ideal:

His Majesty's Government view with favour the establishment in
Palestine of a national home for the Jewish people, and will use
their best endeavours to facilitate the achievement of this object,
it being clearly understood that nothing may be done which will
prejudice the civil and religious rights of existing non-Jewish
communities in Palestine, or the rights and political status enjoyed
by Jews in any other country.[15]

It added to friction between the Jewish colonists and the indigenous
population of Palestine, on whom the colonists already looked down
disdainfully. Buoyed by the Balfour Declaration, the colonists would
now be all too likely to consider that Palestine was rightfully theirs, and
that the Palestinian Arabs were "natives" who needed to be subdued.[16]
Britain's motives behind issuing the Declaration were a mixture of
pragmatism and emotion. It was hoped to maximise Jewish support
for the struggle against Germany while simultaneously reducing
Jewish immigration into the United Kingdom. These motives were
mixed with a starry-eyed vision held by some Christians, including
the British prime minister, David Lloyd George, of the idea of the
Jews returning to Zion, an apparent fulfilment of Biblical prophecies.

The party which could claim support from the principle of self-
determination was the Arab nationalist movement. Its leader was the
Emir Faisal, a son of the Sharif Hussein of Mecca, who had brought an
Arab uprising to Greater Syria, with support provided by his famous
military adviser, T. E. Lawrence, and other British soldiers. The Sharif
Hussein was the semi-independent ruler of the Hejaz region of Arabia
and the guardian of the Muslim holy places of Mecca and Medina.
He was also a direct descendant of the Prophet Muhammad and a
figure with considerable prestige among Muslims everywhere. At the
start of the war, the Ottomans had feared a nationalist uprising among
their Arab troops. Large numbers were stationed in Greater Syria,
but they were deliberately sent to other fronts. Hangings of dozens of
suspected nationalist activists took place in a reign of terror conducted
by the Turkish viceroy, Jamal Pasha. This embittered ordinary people
against Turkish rule. Faisal had held meetings with members of secret

nationalist societies while on visits to Damascus in 1915. These societies offered support for the revolt which the Sharif Hussein was already contemplating with British encouragement. It would be aimed at establishing an independent Arab state covering the entirety of the Arabic-speaking Ottoman provinces and the whole of the Arabian peninsula, save for the small area around Aden which the nationalists acknowledged was already a British colony.[17] But for the fear which Jamal Pasha's policies had generated and this dispersal of Arab troops, a revolt might well have begun in Greater Syria led by officers and notables who were members of Al-Fatat and Al-'Ahd. In April 1915, while in Damascus, Faisal was sworn in as a member of Al-Fatat. The members of the societies begged him to initiate the revolt.[18]

It was not until June 1916 that the revolt was proclaimed in Mecca. It was on the basis of an agreement with Britain contained in exchanges of letters between the Sharif Hussein and Sir Henry MacMahon, the British High Commissioner in Egypt, in which Britain promised "to recognise and uphold the independence of the Arabs" within the frontiers the Sharif had proposed with the exception of "those portions of Syria lying to the west of the districts of Damascus, Homs, Hama and Aleppo". Their status would be left for subsequent discussion on the grounds that these areas "cannot be said to be purely Arab".[19] The concept of the Arab state claimed by the nationalists in Damascus was thus reflected in Britain's promise, save for the exclusion of the areas along the coast of Greater Syria which run northwards from, approximately, Sidon. Britain inserted these words to give it freedom of manoeuvre in its negotiations with the French. However, the Sharif Hussein had not waived the Arab claim to these areas.

The revolt soon succeeded in taking Mecca from the Sharif Hussein's Ottoman overlords, and besieging Medina, the other Muslim holy city in the Hejaz, where the Turks were resupplied from Damascus by the Hejaz railway. Most of the revolt's followers were local Bedouin tribes. They were joined by others from the eastern desert marches of Greater Syria and in 1917–8 acted as the right flank of the British army as it moved through Palestine into the areas that now make up Syria and Lebanon. Faisal tried hard to raise regular troops, but never succeeded in building a small regular army of more than eight to ten thousand men. He used these men to besiege Ottoman garrisons in what is now Jordan. A battalion or two were recruited from townsmen in Mecca, where the Ottoman garrison surrendered. A few Arabic-speaking Ottoman soldiers deserted to join his cause and a greater number were recruited in prisoner of war camps, where the British authorities encouraged the preaching of the Arab nationalist message by his envoys. In this way, Faisal gained the allegiance of some talented captured officers from both Greater Syria and what would become Iraq.

V

As the guns finally fell silent, Faisal's supporters showed that they were definitely the best organised political force in Greater Syria and had the widest support among the notable class, the section of society that mattered. The Arab flags of the Sharifian revolt, as it was sometimes called, greeted Allenby's soldiers when they arrived in many cities and major towns, including Aleppo, Ba'lbek, Beirut, Damascus, Hama, Homs and Tripoli. Flowers were thrown from balconies, speeches made and banquets held.[20] Although in some places such as the area around Kerak in Jordan the record shows that there were also men who fought for the sultan-caliph against the Arab revolt, this may just have been the instinctive reaction of townsfolk and villagers alike to the approach of a Bedouin army. It cannot be taken as firm evidence for any widespread, lingering support for the Turks. By 1916, if not well before, the Turks had made themselves very unpopular, and their departure in 1918 was generally welcomed. This was acknowledged in the memoirs of Liman von Sanders, the German general who commanded the front, as well as by the Young Turk leadership itself.[21]

When the Allies entered Beirut, they found that a Sharifian administration which contained both Muslims and Christians had already been established there. This was part of a pattern. In the speech he made on the day he entered Damascus to a rapturous welcome, Faisal made a point of reassuring Christians and Jews. He said that he recognised no distinctions between the three monotheistic religions, and that all were equal and entitled to the same rights and subject to the same duties. Furthermore, in his first days in Damascus, he called on the leading clergy of the different Christian denominations. These gestures of goodwill were reciprocated. In the Orthodox cathedral, the patriarch himself offered prayers for King Hussein (as the Sharif now styled himself), his army and the Syrian Arab mayors.[22] In a speech in Aleppo on 11 November Faisal elaborated the secularism that was at the heart of his brand of Arab nationalism, as he had done on a number of other occasions:

> The Arabs were Arabs before Moses, and Jesus and Muhammad. All religions demand that [their adherents] follow what is right and enjoin brotherhood on earth. And anyone who sows discord between Muslim, Christian and Jew is not an Arab. I am an Arab before all else.[23]

Yet there were two weaknesses in Faisal's position. The first was his dependency on British support for military training and advice, arms, money and even grain. The second was that it was ultimately the British, and not the Arab, army that had taken Palestine, and then forced the Turks to abandon the entirety of Greater Syria. Nevertheless, the Arab army had played a major role. It had conquered much of Greater Syria east of the Jordan and the coastal mountains to the north, but it had only been Allenby's right wing. Britain would make sure that this hard reality was reflected in its dealings with Faisal. Indeed, Faisal would find himself repeatedly undercut by British officialdom when this suited its strategic objectives. He was just one of the first of many moderate, reasonable and responsible Arab nationalist leaders who would find their interests betrayed and sacrificed by a Western power with which they had no choice but to cooperate.

There was initially a naive trust in Britain's good intentions on the part of Faisal and many of his followers. Believing their task accomplished when the British officially handed control of Amman over to Faisal's forces, the Palestinian detachment in the Arab army was demobilised. The men returned to their homes west of the Jordan. This would have been unlikely to happen if they had known what the future held.[24]

The British were not frank with Faisal about the Sykes-Picot agreement with France, and he would find himself put under intense pressure to accede to some form of accommodation to reflect Britain's promises to both the French and the Zionists. The question of whether Faisal succumbed to Zionist pressure is still disputed. Initially, he had what his biographer Ali Allawi calls a "partly benign view" of Zionism, believing that Chaim Weizmann and its other leaders were sincere when they said that their movement would work hand in hand with Arabs to help them achieve independence. Although the dangers the Zionist movement posed to Arab self-determination in Palestine were becoming increasingly apparent, and Faisal became aware of this, the weakness of his position made it politically very difficult for him to come out in open opposition to the movement. His British patrons, and in particular his adviser T. E. Lawrence, resorted to ambiguities and possibly outright deceptions to retain his support. One thing is certain. Lawrence, when translating for Faisal, was either incompetent or downright deceitful.[25]

The attitude of Allenby, the British commander, now proved crucial. In Palestine, his policy was to keep the country firmly under British military occupation. This solidified over time, although there were indications of support among the Arabs of Palestine for Faisal and a politically united Greater Syria. In the areas to the north, namely Beirut and along the coast to Alexandretta, Allenby allowed the French to install themselves as envisaged by the Sykes-Picot agreement. The Sharifian governor of Beirut was therefore removed from office. When they could do so, the French advanced inland to take over the spine of the mountain ranges from Mount Lebanon northwards. In the largely Alawi areas east of Lattakia local clans began resisting these foreign troops. Inland, on the other hand, Allenby offered British military assistance to Faisal, who was in control not only of Damascus, but of Aleppo, Homs and the lands east of the Jordan. Allenby was the commander-in-chief and behaved accordingly. He therefore saw both Faisal's administration and that of the French as deriving their authority from himself. This would remain the case until a peace settlement was signed with Turkey, or at least for the foreseeable future.

Whilst nominally observing this framework which Allenby had established, the Sharifian Arab nationalists and French competed with each other to win hearts and minds all over Greater Syria. The memoirs of Faisal's energetic military governor of the province of Aleppo, Jafar al-Askari, give us an insight into this time. A proud Arab and formerly a distinguished Ottoman soldier who had been awarded the Iron Cross by the Germans, he had tried to escape after his capture by the British but joined the Arab cause while in a prisoner of war camp. He was a native of Mosul, the provincial capital of the northernmost of the three provinces which would later make up Iraq. As he went on to play a major role in establishing Iraq as a state and became that country's first minister of defence, he is remembered today as an Iraqi.[26]

But there is a danger in reading history backwards. In 1919–20, when he was in Aleppo, the separation of Iraq from Greater Syria was still only a division between occupation zones. Aleppo had stronger links and greater fellow feeling with Mosul than with Damascus. Both were cosmopolitan, merchant cities which had been trading partners for hundreds of years, if not for millennia, along the Silk Road, and there was no natural frontier between them. The two northern cities, moreover, enjoyed better transport ties than either did with Damascus. They had recently been linked by a modern railway (part of the famous Berlin-Baghdad project) which ran across a flat plain in a fairly straight line. By contrast, the railway south from Aleppo went to a junction near Ba'lbek, where passengers and freight would have to de-train and be moved to a narrow-gauge line to climb over the high Anti-Lebanon mountain range and down through the Barada Gorge before they could reach Damascus.[27]

Jafar al-Askari's first job in Aleppo was to calm the situation in the city where disturbances between Muslims and Armenians had broken out. He was a fair-minded man who possessed strong charisma, and was able to persuade Muslim notables and tribal sheikhs to investigate cases in which Christian Armenian women had been kidnapped and forcibly married after their menfolk had been killed by the Turks. He records how their names were changed by their captors to make it harder for them to be recovered by any survivors of their families. Due to his efforts, some 500 women and their children were rescued. He also helped Armenian refugees who wished to do so to emigrate to Egypt, which had a policy of welcoming them.

But if Jafar al-Askari was implementing Faisal's non-sectarian policies and doing all he could to provide justice across sectarian and ethnic divides, the French seem already to have been following a policy which could have been designed to exacerbate them. His next task was to contend with French attempts to gain the allegiance of local Arabic-speaking notables, especially Christians (and, above all, of Catholics), on whose fears of Muslim domination the French played relentlessly. But he found strong support for the Sharifian cause from many other Christians, including from the Orthodox, Syrian Orthodox and Chaldean bishops of Aleppo. A strong sense of Arab-ness had taken root among many Christians there; their communities had already produced nationalist intellectuals and at least one composer of patriotic songs, Félix Faris.[28] The French also offered gifts in an attempt to gain the loyalty of local Bedouin tribes who were hostile to any form of authority on principle. A sense of Arab patriotism was something quite new to the tribal leaders, but Jafar al-Askari proudly records how he was able to sow its seed on at least one occasion.

Before the end of November 1918, and within weeks of the armistice which ended the fighting, Faisal left for Europe and for the peace conference in Paris where he hoped to put the Arab case. Although he had made Damascus his headquarters, he was refused accreditation as the leader of an Arab delegation and was only acknowledged officially as the "representative of the Hejaz".[29] He addressed the delegates in Arabic, the first time the language was used officially at a major international conference in modern times. Lawrence translated for him. Faisal's tone was conciliatory, and the carefully chosen words of the memorandum he left with the conference betray the problem with which he had to wrestle. How could he placate the powers while not compromising the core Arab demands? The delegates from the "big four" victorious powers – Britain, France, the USA and Italy – were already in the process of deciding the allocation of territory without reference to any Arab leader. Between themselves, they agreed that large inland areas, which included Damascus, would come under French control, as envisaged in the 1916 Sykes-Picot agreement between Britain and France.

Faisal, by contrast, called for an Arab state on all the lands southwards of a line drawn from Alexandretta to the Persian frontier. He was relying on the idea of the self-determination of peoples and on the promises which Britain had made his father, in order to persuade him to rebel against Turkish rule. Faisal said that unity would come to the Arabs, despite the great economic and social differences between their countries, so long as no one tried to force it "by imposing an artificial unity on the whole, or ... by dividing the area as spoils of war among the great Powers." Greater Syria, he said, was "sufficiently advanced politically to manage her own internal affairs".[30] Its independence should not be compromised. He made this point in a perfectly clear, if subtle, way:

> We feel also that foreign technical advice and help [in Greater Syria] will be a most valuable factor in our national growth. We are willing to pay for this help in cash; we cannot sacrifice it for any part of the freedom we have just won for ourselves by force of arms.[31]

However, this was subject to a qualification concerning Palestine. He envisaged that the Palestinian Arabs (who he pointed out were "the enormous majority of the people") and the Jews should coexist and develop the country together. He stated:

> The Jews are very close to the Arabs in blood, and there is no conflict of character between the two races. In principles we are absolutely at one. Nevertheless, the Arabs cannot risk assuming the responsibility of holding level the scales in the clash of races and

religions that have, in this one province, so often involved the world in difficulties. They would wish for the effective super-position of a great trustee, so long as a representative local administration commended itself by actively promoting the material prosperity of the country.[32]

He knew that, in the world of the deliberations of the Western powers, he needed to acknowledge the existence of the Zionist colonies in Palestine, and that some form of supervision of these by a great power was inevitable. But he coupled this with a call for representative government. He felt confident that the Palestinian Arabs wanted to be part of his kingdom. If it had been heeded, his appeal would have led to specific minority rights for Jews in Palestine, but no more than that. Faisal's ambition for an Arab state was not based on a brittle and narrow sense of identity. In his speech in Aleppo on 11 November 1918, in which he set out his political vision, he had clearly envisaged some form of federal structure for the Arab state, or even a confederation of closely tied Arab states. After pledging religious tolerance and stating he would not to forgive anyone trying to sow discord among Arabs on the grounds of religion, he argued passionately that:

> the Arabs are diverse peoples living in different regions The Aleppan is not the same as the Hijazi, nor is the Damascene the same as the Yemeni. That is why my father has made the Arab lands each follow their own special laws that are in accordance with their own circumstances and people ...[33]

But his speech to the peace conference had no impact on the policies that were adopted. For its part, France could show it had support from the Maronites of Lebanon for an independent Lebanese state under a French Mandate, and that this was endorsed by their spiritual leader, the Maronite Patriarch. The wishes of the Zionists were presented to the conference a month later when they submitted their own memorandum which called for recognition of "the historic title of the Jewish people to Palestine and the right of the Jews to reconstitute in Palestine their National Home".[34] They could bring real political pressure to bear on the governments of the "big four" Allies – Britain, France, the USA and

Italy – in a way that Faisal simply could not. They could also play on the links the powers felt they had with Greater Syria for religious and historical reasons, and had native speakers among their number who could confidently address the conference in English and French.

On his return to Damascus in April 1919, Faisal downplayed the fact that in Paris his demands had been ignored. This has made plain the weakness of his position. He therefore attempted to strengthen it by convening an elected assembly. This was hastily elected in accordance with the procedures of the existing Ottoman electoral law, to the extent that this was possible in the difficult circumstances of the moment. The assembly declared itself the National Congress and broadly reflected the opinion of the Arabic speakers of Greater Syria.[35] On 2 July, it called for "absolutely complete political independence" and the establishment of a single state covering the whole of Greater Syria, stretching from the Taurus Mountains in the north to the Sinai Peninsula in the south. This state would be "a democratic civil constitutional monarchy on broad decentralisation principles, safeguarding the rights of minorities".[36] It rejected foreign rule and any attempt to partition Greater Syria. If, however, some form of foreign tutelage was inevitable, then the USA was the preferred power, as it was seen as having no ambitions in the area. Britain was mentioned as very much a second choice, but the National Assembly voiced implacable hostility to France – as it did towards "the pretensions of the Zionists to create a Jewish commonwealth in the southern part of Syria, known as Palestine".[37]

On 28 August 1919, a commission set up by the Allies to ascertain the wishes of the people of Greater Syria presented its report to the peace conference in Paris. It was written by two eminent American figures, Henry C. King and Charles R. Crane, who had been appointed by their government to the commission.[38] It was to this commission that the call of the National Congress of 2 July had been addressed. It had originally been suggested that the report would be authored jointly by representatives of Britain, France and Italy as well, but these states took no part. The findings confirmed that most of the people of Greater Syria (south of the armistice line with Turkey) wished for a single independent state in the form of a decentralised constitutional monarchy under Faisal.

If there *had* to be foreign tutelage, then it should be limited to a fixed period and entrusted to the USA which was not seen as compromised by imperial interests similar to those of Britain and France.

Above all else, a large majority did not want French control. There was support for France among the Maronites and many other Catholics, while other Christian communities were divided. The Alawis in the mountains inland from Lattakia also backed a French Mandate. Only the small Jewish colonies in Palestine supported the Zionist project. By contrast, the Chief Rabbi of Syria had signed a petition in February 1919 backing Faisal as having the right to speak to the Paris peace conference on behalf of all Syrians.[39]

Presciently, the commission observed that the Zionist programme could not be implemented without prejudicing the rights of the Arabs of Palestine and causing conflict:

> No British officer, consulted by the Commissioners, believed that the Zionist programme could be carried out except by force of arms ... That of itself is evidence of the strong sense of the injustice of the Zionist programme, on the part of the non-Jewish populations of Palestine and Syria.[40]

Anyone who cared to read the King-Crane Commission Report would have seen that the partition of Greater Syria by the great powers would be likely to have unwelcome consequences. The fact that it was so successfully sidelined boded ill for the future. Apart from King and Crane, there was another important individual who wrote something which should have led to a pause for reflection. His testimony is all the more impressive because it cuts right against the policies it was his duty to uphold, and which he was, indeed, to proceed loyally to implement. In May 1919, General Sir Edmund Allenby had reported that, in his view, Palestine and Syria should not be separated, since it was "contrary to the wishes and interests of the great majority of the population".[41] He also wrote in the same document that British ideas of the strategic justification for it were misguided, since the Egyptian frontier running to the east of the Sinai Desert, not a border to be drawn in northern

Palestine, provided the best defence for Egypt and the Suez Canal.

By now, however, the wheels set in motion by the decision of the peace conference to partition Greater Syria were beginning to turn. The report by King and Crane was not what the delegates of Britain and France wanted to hear, and it was accordingly kept secret until 1922 when it was published by the US government. Although Faisal was proclaimed king of independent Greater Syria by the Syrian National Congress in March 1920, it was a forlorn gesture. The French would not recognise the complete, sovereign independence that was the demand made by the Congress. They had already offered what seemed to them to be a reasonable settlement. Faisal's kingdom would be allowed to survive, but the French Mandate would have to be accepted, the size of the Syrian army reduced, and control of the country's main railway handed over to French administration. Faisal, whose instincts were diplomacy and compromise, had reluctantly initialled the agreement and recommended its acceptance as the best deal available. Now he complied with Syrian opinion and the wish of the National Congress, and backtracked.

The Allies simply ignored what had taken place in Damascus. At the San Remo conference in April, they formally split Greater Syria into the French Mandate of Syria and Lebanon, and the British Mandate of Palestine (which included Jordan). At the same time, they also allotted the Mandate of Iraq to Britain. The die was cast. France soon ceased to have any dealings with Faisal's government in Damascus

To this day, the history of the pledges made to the Sharif Hussein, the Sykes-Picot agreement, the Balfour Declaration, and the partition into Mandates at San Remo are remembered with bitterness in Syria and many other Arab countries. The Sharif had trusted Britain. His betrayal left him a twisted old man, obsessed with trying to get the world to hear his side of the story until he died in exile in what is now Jordan in 1931, after losing Mecca and Medina to the rival Saudi clan of central Arabia in 1924/5. The Arabic texts of the Sharif's correspondence with Sir Henry MacMahon, the British representative in Cairo, were published in Arabic newspapers. Heedless of this, Britain kept the correspondence secret, and tried for a long while to maintain that the areas it had excluded from its pledges, "those portions of Syria lying to the west of the districts of Damascus, Homs, Hama and Aleppo", included Palestine, when they palpably did not. But it wasn't just over Palestine that the Sharif and the Arabs were betrayed. The same applied to Syria, whose people were subjected to a French tutelage that most of them did not want.

One individual, perhaps above all others, is associated with this treachery in many Arab minds. This is the enigmatic figure of T. E. Lawrence. His part in the story of the Arab revolt was brought to life – albeit with considerable dramatic licence – in David Lean's 1962 film. Even an Arab writer of the 1930s like George Antonius, who admitted Lawrence's military contribution to the Arab cause, was profoundly uneasy about him. Many Arabs were shocked when subsequently released British government papers showed that he tried to persuade Faisal to compromise with the Zionist movement, and had also apparently deceived and misrepresented him.[42] Whatever wishes the Zionists (and the French) might have had for a share of Greater Syria, in Arab eyes there was never any moral or legal justification for their claims.

Both lies and half-lies were told, but voices of conscience also spoke out. Viscount Grey, the British foreign secretary during the first years of the war, had carried ultimate responsibility for the agreement between Britain and the Sharif Hussein. Out of office, he offered his advice from the benches of the House of Lords during a parliamentary debate in March 1923:

It would be very desirable, from the point of view of honour, that all these various pledges should be set side by side, and then, I think, the most honourable thing to do would be to look at them fairly, see what inconsistencies there are between them, and, having regard to the nature of each pledge and the date at which it was given, with all the facts before us, consider what is the fair thing to be done.[43]

But by then the "various pledges" had become a matter of purely academic interest, at least as far as Syria was concerned. Back in the summer of 1920, when King Faisal's final appeals to the Allied powers fell on deaf ears, a French army marched on Damascus. He gave orders that there should be no armed resistance since everyone knew it would be futile.

But these orders were not heeded by the minister of defence, Yusuf al-Azma. On 23 July 1920, the French crushed the Syrian army at the pass of Khan Maysaloun, west of Damascus. The Syrians had stationed some of their small regular forces there, and these were reinforced from Damascus by several hundred men – soldiers and untrained volunteers – who were rushed to the front under the command of al-Azma himself. Some of them were armed only with sticks. There are reports that the contingent included a number of women, although others state that the Syrian feminist Naziq al-Abid, who had given evidence to King and Crane, was the only woman who did so, and rode with the troops as they set off through Damascus with a rifle on her back. She survived the battle.[44]

The total Syrian forces probably numbered fewer than 4,500 men although their exact size is not known. The fallen included Yusuf al-Azma himself. Everyone in his army knew that the Syrians would be slaughtered and the battle lost. They were trying to stop a professional army that was well led, well equipped, and well trained. The French infantry were chiefly colonial troops from Algeria and Senegal. This was probably the first sight Syrians had of the Senegalese who, although they were largely Muslim, would come to be particularly hated during the period of French rule. The French also had tanks and aircraft. The Syrians held the French up for six hours on a hot day on which both sides were equally afflicted by thirst. Their resistance has been described as "spirited, if ill-organised and hopeless".[45] It was fought for the sake of honour, and for that reason it deserves to be remembered.

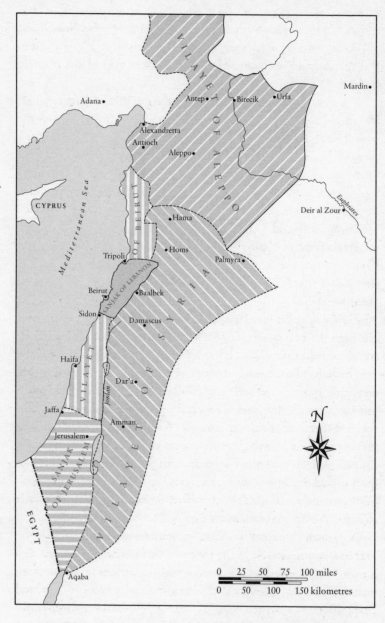

GREATER SYRIA SHOWING THE PROVINCES OF SYRIA AND
ALEPPO AND LATE OTTOMAN ADMINISTRATIVE BOUNDARIES

CHAPTER TWO

French Rule, 1920–1946

I

Initially, France had hoped to control not just the areas covered by Syria and Lebanon today but a substantial portion of territory to the north and west. This extended up to the Taurus Mountains and included the head waters of the Euphrates and Tigris. But no sooner was the Great War over than Turkey began to bounce back. Within two years it was resurgent under the leadership of Mustafa Kemal, who would replace the Ottoman Empire with a republic and take the name "Atatürk", meaning father of the Turkish nation. Although at first technically a rebel against the rule of the Sultan-Caliph, he rallied the still substantial Turkish army behind him. Holding on to the predominantly Turkish areas proved too costly for France, and it withdrew after a number of key garrisons were humiliatingly forced to surrender. This blow only made it consider the retention of Syria all the more important.

A permanent French presence in Syria and Lebanon would give France a lasting interest in the Eastern Mediterranean. Syria was also a useful staging post for France's colonial possessions in the Far East, especially as long-distance air travel might one day become a practical proposition. The French presence was supported by two powerful lobbies in France: the colonial lobby, which saw Syria and Lebanon as markets where French companies could do business on preferential terms, and the Catholic lobby which supported a French presence there in order to protect – and privilege – the local Christians, especially the Maronites and other Uniates.[1] Control of Syria and Lebanon would provide a convenient adjunct to France's domination over much of the Western Mediterranean where it possessed Algeria, Morocco and Tunisia.

But France was not meant to control its portion of Greater Syria for its own benefit. It had been given a "Mandate" to govern Syria and Lebanon in order to prepare them for independence.[2] The source of the Mandate was the League of Nations, the international organisation which had been set up by the victorious powers and was the precursor to the United Nations. Article 22 of its founding covenant provided that the "well-being and development" of the peoples under a Mandate were "a sacred trust of civilisation". The "tutelage" of Syria and Lebanon was expressly "entrusted" to France. Syria and Lebanon were deemed to

> have reached a stage of development where their existence as separate nations can be provisionally recognised subject to the rendering of administrative advice and assistance by a Mandatory until such time as they are able to stand alone.[3]

France would have to account for its rule to the League's Mandates Commission, but the Commission had little power to hold France to account. Article 22 (4) provided that the wishes of the people placed under a Mandate were meant to be a "principal consideration" in the choice of the Mandatory, but this principle had been disregarded. It was a forewarning of the rather cavalier attitude France would show to its sacred trust of civilisation.

The northern boundary of the Mandate was decided in October 1921 in an agreement France executed with Turkey. For much of its length, the Aleppo-Mosul railway was used to separate Syria from the territories that remained Turkish. This railway should have been thought of as a key driver for future economic growth, but its use as a border made it vulnerable to political uncertainty. The border was intended to provide a marker to separate Arabs and Turks, but the neat line along which the railway ran could never be more than an approximation. Many Arabic speakers were left on the Turkish side, while considerable numbers of Turks – especially a substantial minority in the former Ottoman Sanjak of Alexandretta around Antioch – were left on the Syrian side. There were also ethnic communities which were neither Arab nor Turk. Many Kurds, Armenians and Syriac-speaking Christians fled southwards from the new regime in Turkey. This changed the ethnic balance of the north-eastern parts of the Mandate. Kurdish and Arab tribes now competed for the scarce resources of the dry plains east of the Euphrates, while Armenian and Syriac Orthodox refugees made some of the towns of the area predominantly Christian. The city of Diyarbakir, which had provided the main centre for much of this region, was left on the Turkish side of the border. A large part of its rural hinterland was now in the land that was in the process of becoming Syria. That hinterland would be cut off from its main market.

Aleppo was a much greater city than Diyarbakir but was presented with similar problems. It was now in Syria, but only thirty-one miles from the border with Turkey. Much of the economic heartland of its province – and over half of its territory – had been in Anatolia, from which it was now separated. It also had longstanding historic links with Mosul and Baghdad to its east, in an area that was becoming part of the British Mandate of Iraq. It was more populous than Damascus and had a much more sophisticated commercial community. Aleppo's proud notables therefore looked down with disdainful eyes on the city that was now meant to govern them, and saw it as a backwater. It was therefore unsurprising that Turkish agents were able to whisper that Aleppo would do better to remain part of Turkey. If its inhabitants had been given a choice in 1920 between government by France or reincorporation into Turkey, they might well have chosen the latter.[4]

For its part, Damascus had been the capital of an Ottoman province called "Syria" before the war. This province had extended down to Aqaba on the Red Sea, but ended almost immediately north of Hama, which was just over half way between Damascus and Aleppo. Damascus's focus was to the south and west. It had strong links with Beirut and northern Palestine. Throughout the period of French rule, Damascenes would continue to feel more at home in Jerusalem than Aleppo.[5]

Yet another example of the arbitrariness of the Mandate boundaries was the frontier with Iraq. Many tribes lived on both sides of the border. Some localities, such as the provincial capital of Deir al-Zour in the Euphrates valley, could equally well have been placed in Iraq. The border was meaningless for many people, and Iraq had its attractions, especially as its oil revenues increased.

To the south, the Mandate's borders met the British Mandate of Palestine. This included Jordan, although it was made into a separate emirate ruled by another Hashemite, Faisal's brother Abdullah. The Syrian frontier ran along the Jordan and Yarmouk rivers and the eastern shore of the Sea of Galilee. These apparently natural frontiers did not represent ethnic boundaries. They were, in fact, completely arbitrary: as arbitrary as using the Thames and the Severn to partition England. Many communities, some of which were nomadic, lived on both sides of these rivers and were Arabic-speaking. People would cross the border for work. Many of the dockworkers in the Palestinian port of Haifa, for instance, came from the Hawran area which was now inside the French Mandate. New barriers to trade appeared and customs duties were imposed by the governments of the Mandates. The steadily increasing number of people who now had a national sense of themselves as "Arabs" were faced with an invidious choice as to where their true loyalties lay: was it to an indivisible Arab nation, to Greater Syria as a whole, or to the new, foreign-ruled unit which imposed its taxes on them and issued their passports?

At this time, Palestine was still frequently referred to as "southern Syria" and there were no intrinsic marks of difference between its inhabitants and the Arabic speakers in the rest of Greater Syria. Now, instead of being part of the same country, it was by law foreign territory for Damascenes and everybody else who lived north of the new lines drawn by the French and British and approved by the League of Nations. Suddenly, extended families found themselves split. Many owned property in a number of separate jurisdictions and had to cope with different governments which passed their own laws and raised their own taxes.

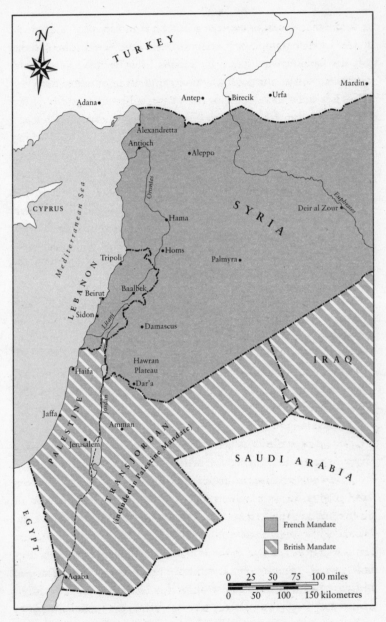

GREATER SYRIA SHOWING THE PARTITION
BY BRITAIN AND FRANCE AFTER THE GREAT WAR

Economic development was a benefit France hoped to bring to Syria. The French public was presented with starry-eyed visions by the colonial lobby which argued, for instance, that French capital could increase cotton production by tapping the water resources of the River Euphrates and thereby bringing prosperity and progress to the Syrian people. Unfortunately, economic conditions were not such in France or the world as a whole at that time for the capital to be raised on anything like the optimistic scale envisaged. The anticipated French investors did not appear, while policies introduced by the French authorities in Syria actually caused an economic decline.

The trade of Syrian merchants was hamstrung by the French decision to peg the Syrian pound to the French franc. France's economy was fragile in the years after the Great War, and its currency fluctuated wildly. In Syria, imported industrial goods could suddenly shoot up in value, making such manufacturing enterprises as existed there uneconomic. Over the nineteenth century, European factory-produced goods had cut into the markets of traditional Syrian handicraft industries, such as weaving and silk production. This process not only continued, but actually accelerated. The new trade barriers set up by the Mandate system had their own deleterious effect. Palestine had been a traditional market for Syrian textiles. This declined because of import tariffs imposed on imports by the British authorities.

One set of statistics speaks more eloquently than any other. The French authorities had to spend very heavily on security and the military. From 1926 onwards, approximately one third of the tax receipts of Syria and Lebanon was spent on the public security budget. Moreover, of the five billion French francs which France invested in Syria during the Mandate, four billion went on defence. It is little wonder, then, that France had little left over to invest in infrastructure and the economy,[6] and France's spending on matters such as education, public works, agriculture and encouragement of local industry was parsimonious.[7] That did not stop it privileging its own citizens who resided in Syria. Under the regime known as the capitulations in the later Ottoman Empire, nationals of many foreign states (including France and the other

European powers) entered into treaties which granted their nationals the right to be tried in special "mixed" courts which had a majority of foreign (that is, European) judges. The Ottomans had abolished these and related privileges in 1914, and the abolition was confirmed in the instrument establishing the Mandate. However, France reintroduced similar provisions and sent judges from France to preside over cases between Syrians and foreigners. To add insult to injury, from 1923 onwards the cost of these courts was born by the Syrian taxpayer. The French authorities also showed blatant favouritism towards French companies in the award of concessions and other contracts – even though this was a clear breach of the terms of the Mandate.

II

France had to fight a battle before its troops could reach Damascus. Official resistance was crushed at Maysaloun in July 1920, and by that time the French authorities were already energetically planning the future of Syria and Lebanon. They now moved to split up the area allocated as their Mandate. They had convinced themselves that they needed to be in Syria for the long term in order to prevent conflict between Syrians, particularly along sectarian fault lines. This presupposed a very negative view of Syrian society generally and of Islam, its dominant religion, in particular. It also created a backlash by some Muslims against Arab Christians who, often unfairly but sometimes fairly, were associated in the minds of many people with support for French policies.

France therefore attempted to turn its Mandate into a patchwork quilt of semi-autonomous but dependant territories, over which it would retain overall control. Already in 1920, the parts of the Ottoman provinces which had been governed from Aleppo and Damascus, but which were now under the Mandate, were reconstituted as separate "states". It was hoped that this would discourage a Syria-wide sense of national feeling, and make it less likely that the elites of both cities would make common cause against French rule. Although they would have local governors who were Syrian, these would be supported by and dependent on French advisers. The district of Alexandretta remained under Aleppo, but was given a semi-autonomous status because of its large Turkish minority.

There were also three areas where a minority sect predominated and which the French now set out to split off from the rest of Syria. The first was the old Sanjak of Mount Lebanon with its Maronite Christians. Within a month of the victory at Maysaloun, the districts around Tripoli, Ba'lbek, Sidon and Tyre were added to it so as to constitute "the State of Greater Lebanon". This gave Lebanon the frontiers it has to this day, although the inhabitants of these four districts were predominantly Muslim and therefore unwilling participants in what was essentially a project to build a Maronite-dominated entity. For a long time, they demanded that their districts be returned to Syria. Although their pleas were disregarded, their presence in Lebanon ultimately ensured that it could never become a wholly Maronite state and would retain a competing Arab identity.

The other two areas were the predominantly Alawi and Druze regions. The Alawi area was centred on Lattakia. Although Alawis were a small minority in the city itself, the mountains to the east were their heartland. The Druze were concentrated in the Hawran around the town of Suwayda. The Hawran was a volcanic plateau south-east of Damascus which had supplied the city with most of its corn since Roman times, if not before. These predominantly Alawi and Druze areas were granted autonomy in 1922 and encouraged to be separate from the rest of Syria to the greatest extent possible. It was not until 1936 that the French officially decreed that they should be treated in the same way as other parts of Syria. In 1939, these districts were separated again and only finally incorporated into Syria in 1942. The steppe and deserts to the east of the Euphrates (known as the Jazirah[8]) were also given their own special regime to reflect the predominance of Bedouin in this area. The French hoped that it would also be insulated from nationalist sentiment which was strongest in the major cities.

Lebanon was to remain separate and would eventually become an independent sovereign state when the Mandate ended. The French

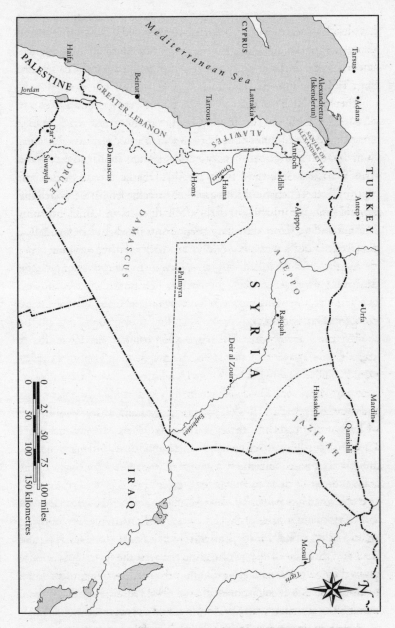

THE MANDATE OF SYRIA SHOWING INTERNAL
BOUNDARIES CREATED BY FRANCE

had at first intended to group the other entities in a Syrian federation. Yet each of them would require its quota of French officials, soldiers and advisers, and this was expensive. Cost led the French to modify these policies in 1924, when Damascus and Aleppo were joined together. Although the Druze and Alawi areas were retained as separate autonomous entities, the Sanjak of Alexandretta, the area around Antioch which contained Aleppo's outlet to the sea, was detached from the rest of Aleppo province to give it a status similar to that of the Alawi and Druze "statelets". In the late 1930s, France would succumb to pressure from Turkey for the return of the Sanjak, which was shamelessly handed over in 1939 and constituted yet another breach of the terms of the Mandate. The transfer was intended to keep Turkey favourably disposed to France in the European war which was then looming.[9]

As the French rolled out their authority across the country, the overwhelming majority of Syrians questioned its legitimacy. Furthermore, the Mandate was often only backed up by slender forces. French military strategy consisted of sending army columns around the country in a show of force. The passing of a column through a district might discourage any uprising from breaking out, but garrisons (which would require much greater numbers of troops) would be needed to control the countryside if a rebellion occurred. Discontent was widespread. People asked what the French were doing in Syria, and by what right they had come there. The success of Atatürk's armies against the French further to the north did not go unnoticed, and many Syrians thought the French might be persuaded to leave quite quickly if life was made sufficiently uncomfortable for them.

France had to subdue the Alawi Mountains before it could extend its authority inland from Lattakia, and it also had to put down an uprising around Aleppo led by Ibrahim Hananu, a local notable who had been an officer in Faisal's army during the Arab Revolt.[10] Turkey gave support to both the Alawis and Ibrahim Hananu until France gave up its claims to parts of Turkey in September 1921. These two insurgencies, although locally based, were portents of future problems which seemed to escape the notice of the French. Alawi tribes had frequently risen up against taxation and other interference by the Ottomans. That had always been a local affair, but this time the Alawis took a further step and cooperated with non-Alawi forces: Faisal's Arab government in Damascus, important Sunni landowners in Lattakia, and Ibrahim Hananu's men.

As for the Hananu rebellion, it recruited in the city of Aleppo as well as rural areas although it operated entirely in the countryside. It had the effect of encouraging the emergence of an Arab nationalist identity among the Muslim elite of the city. Some of the areas in which the rebellion was strongest, such as Jisr al-Shughour, the countryside around Idlib and the mountains of Jebel al-Zawiya where it made its last stand,[11] would become familiar names some ninety years later as rebel areas during the uprising against the rule of Bashar al-Assad.

When his rebellion was finally crushed, Ibrahim Hananu fled into exile. Captured by British intelligence officers while on a visit to Jerusalem, he was extradited and put on trial in March 1922. In court, Fathallah al-Saqqal, a young Christian lawyer from Aleppo who was his counsel, passionately depicted his client as a national hero. Hanunu then spoke from the dock and made his own denunciation of the French presence in Syria as illegal.[12] He was acquitted. At least France knew better than to make him a martyr.

Yet would Syria now be reconciled to the French presence? In order to run the country the French required Syrian administrators, especially in light of the financial constraints on the Mandate government. They therefore needed to co-opt influential notables to their cause. It seemed at first that this would be possible. In rural and tribal areas they could find plenty of figures who seemed to be still untainted by nationalist sentiment. But Damascus, Aleppo, Homs and Hama were the places that really counted. Here, members of the great Sunni Muslim notable families with experience under the Ottomans would be needed to run the administration. By and large, these families detested the French, but they did not form a cohesive group in any of these cities, and there was no cooperation over political matters with the notable families in the other centres. Furthermore, not only did the Sunni notables tend to put the wider interests of their family and city before those of Syria as a whole, but they were not united politically behind any real programme except to end French rule. As that did not seem immediately possible, they often turned their attention to increasing their own individual position under it. It was therefore easy for French officials to play them off against each other. There were also many prominent individuals who relished the chance of regaining the office they had held in Ottoman days, or even a more senior post.

The old politics of the notables therefore resumed, the major landowning families once again acting as intermediaries between rulers and subjects. Below them were the peasant farmers and share croppers who tilled the soil on their country estates, as well as the many who depended on their patronage in the cities where they lived in their palaces and mansions. Above them were the French who, for these purposes, had stepped into the shoes of the Ottomans. Yet the French soon found that the tamer notables who were prepared to work with them lacked the influence in Syrian society which they needed if they were to govern effectively.

At first, the French excluded notables from administrative positions if they had publicly displayed nationalist sentiments. But then a left-wing government took power in Paris in May 1924 and began what might have been a process towards a happier future for the relationship between France and Syria. Like other left-wing governments in France during that era, it was anti-clerical in nature and therefore did not have the same obsession with privileging and protecting Christian minorities.

On 2 January 1925, General Maurice Sarrail, the new High Commissioner for Syria and Lebanon, disembarked at Beirut. His credentials in the eyes of the new government in Paris were impeccable. He had been a hero of the battle of the Marne, which had saved Paris from the Germans in 1914, and he was that comparatively rare creature, a French general of strongly republican, free-thinking and anti-clerical views. He was, however, every bit as authoritarian as any of his right-wing, monarchist and conservative Catholic colleagues among France's top brass. He was also no diplomat. Nevertheless, his first acts included ending martial law, granting permission for the formation of a nationalist political party and stating that there would be elections in October that year.[13]

The political party that was established was called the People's Party which, whether through coincidence or not, had the same name as the successful nationalist party established in Turkey by Kemal Atatürk. It was led by Dr Abdul Rahman Shahbandar, a nationalist from Damascus who had survived the Turkish purges in 1915 and 1916 and who later became Faisal's liaison officer with the British. He had subsequently been imprisoned by the French for nationalist agitation and exiled, but was now allowed to return home by the new French government. The People's Party campaigned for a Syrian constitution which would give the country genuine independence, and demanded an end to religious and class divides and foreign domination of the economy. Its Damascus-based leadership consisted of merchants and members of the professions, and contained some prominent Christians as well as Muslims. It was a grouping of the elite rather than the beginnings of a mass movement, but was nonetheless popular at street level because of the rousing speeches of Shahbandar and his colleagues. Its leaders intended to rally the population behind the nationalist cause, but not in a way that would be recognised today as the conduct of modern, democratic politics. Instead the People's Party adopted the method that occurred naturally to them, and was the traditional one of notables: the dispensing of their patronage to gain support.

Shahbandar's demand for independence included the restoration of the unity of Greater Syria, except for the Maronite enclave on Mount Lebanon. As W. A. Smart, the British consul in Damascus, reported in March 1925, the movement towards reunification was "strong and genuine. It is based on economic and administrative logic. It has behind it a venerable tradition with a powerful sentimental appeal to the Muslim masses."[14] The strength of that appeal was made apparent within weeks. Lord Balfour, a figure of infamy to Syrians because of his promises to the Zionist movement contained in the letter now known as the Balfour Declaration, came to Damascus on 8 April 1925 while touring the region. Ten thousand demonstrators gathered at the Umayyad mosque, the heart of the city, shouting "*yasqut wa'd Balfour!*" – "down with the Balfour Declaration!" The French had to escort him quickly from the city and back to Beirut for his own safety.[15] It was a sharp and poignant contrast to his warm welcome he received from the colonists in Palestine.

III

In July 1925, the Druze of the Hawran exploded in revolt. This lit a fuse for an insurrection that would spread as far north as Hama and the Orontes valley, and as far west as southern Lebanon. For a brief period it even looked as though the French were about to be driven out: a sentiment that was expressed by the famous Arabist Gertrude Bell. She was one of the British officials who had set up the Mandate of Iraq and placed Faisal on its throne, almost as a compensation for his loss of Syria. In a secret report from Baghdad which she wrote that November following a trip to Syria, she expressed the opinion that "it is the Druze who will enable his brother Syrians to evict the French."[16]

This revolt should have been foreseen. The Druze had soon found that the autonomy the French granted them was, in reality, largely a way for the French to interfere in their lives, manipulate disputes between Druze notables to their advantage, and extend their control into the Druze heartland. They were well aware of the French "divide and rule" policies, and observed how they were calculated to insulate the Druze heartland from Damascus, which they resented. They felt much closer to other Syrians than the French were prepared to admit to themselves. Druze leaders such as Sultan al-Atrash had contact with Damascus-based nationalists as well as those in Amman, the capital of Jordan. When their revolt came, it was in the name of Syrian independence – not that of the Druze state-let which the French had carved out for them.

The Hawran had already been restive and seen much discontent, but the straw which broke the camel's back concerned the behaviour of a Captain Carbillet who had been temporarily put in charge of the Druze state-let while the French decided whom to appoint as the next ethnically Druze governor. Appointment of the governor was a delicate question for the authorities, since it meant successfully negotiating their way through the maze of Druze clan politics. Carbillet was a high-minded but arrogant believer in the values of the French republic. He was energetically trying to bring the modern world to the Hawran, and enjoyed High Commissioner Sarrail's full support. But his decision to split common land between peasant families as part of a land reform programme – aimed at ending what he perceived to be "feudalism" – conflicted with customary usages. This made him unpopular, as did his conscription of Druze from all segments of society as forced labour to build roads. Not only did the Druze object to the forced labour on principle, but they considered conscripting their clan leaders an insult to the clan. They also shrewdly observed that the main purpose for the roads would be to bring tax collectors and the French army to their doors.

On 11 July, three Druze leaders arrived in Damascus at Sarrail's invitation to discuss their grievances, while Carbillet had been sent on temporary leave. Sarrail decided to hold them hostage to encourage "good behaviour" among the Druze, and had them taken to Palmyra and imprisoned. This was understandably seen as an appalling breach of the traditions of hospitality and treatment of envoys. A week later, the Hawran rose under the leadership of Sultan al-Atrash, the most important Druze clan leader and an eminent notable whose father had been hanged by the Turks. Although an officer in the Ottoman army, by the end of the Great War he had become a firm partisan of Faisal and the Arab revolt. More recently, he had his own cause for concern as the French had been trying to undermine his pre-eminent position among the Druze.

French columns in the Hawran were ambushed and destroyed, and then a punitive expedition sent from Damascus was forced to retreat. During the first weeks of the rebellion, a thousand French colonial soldiers were killed, and the Druze even captured some artillery. Their revolt soon spread beyond their community, as some local Muslims and Christians joined in. A Druze column marching on Damascus was only stopped outside the city in late August by an air attack and a Moroccan cavalry squadron. Leaflets signed by Sultan al-Atrash appeared in many neighbourhoods. They combined Arabic rhetoric with that of the French Revolution, and clearly demonstrated that intellectuals in Damascus had had a hand in drafting them. They denounced the French attempts to divide Syria – as well as the partition of Greater Syria itself:

> The imperialists have stolen what is yours. They have laid hands on the very sources of your wealth and raised barriers and divided your homeland. They have separated the nation into religious sects and states. They have strangled freedom of religion, thought, conscience, speech and action. We are no longer allowed to move about freely in our own country.[17]

They ended with four demands:

1. The complete independence of Arab Syria, one and indivisible, sea coast and interior;
2. The institution of a Popular Government and the free election of a Constituent Assembly for the framing of an Organic Law;
3. The evacuation of the foreign army of occupation and the creation of a national army for the maintenance of security;
4. The application of the principles of the French Revolution and the Rights of Man.

> To arms! God is with us.
> Long live independent Syria!
> Sultan al-Atrash,
> Commander of the Syrian Revolutionary Armies[18]

Within days, the countryside around Damascus had ceased to be secure territory for the Mandate forces. The French clamped down in Damascus itself, arresting such leading lights of the People's Party as they could find, but many had escaped, including Dr Shahbandar who fled to the Hawran where he attempted to establish a provisional rebel government on 9 September.[19] With the help of reinforcements, the French tried to stamp out the source of the rebellion. At first the army successfully penetrated the Hawran, inflicted a bloody defeat on the Druze and relieved the French garrison at Suwayda which had been besieged in the citadel. But then it had to withdraw because of its supply situation. For the Druze, defeat was turned into victory.

This was the point at which the revolt spread in a major way. On 4 October, the Syrian troops in Hama mutinied under the leadership of Fawzi al-Qawuqji, a survivor of the Syrian forces at the battle of Maysaloun. He had joined the army of the French Mandate and was now a captain in a cavalry unit. The Hama uprising had been carefully timed, and Qawuqji waited until most of the garrison had been transferred to reinforce the French in the Hawran. Rapidly taking control of the city, he besieged the remaining French in their headquarters. The authorities, however, hit back by sending their air force to bomb Hama into submission. Local notables persuaded Qawuqji and his followers to leave so as to avoid further destruction, but the insurgents took refuge in the surrounding countryside and waged guerrilla war against French communications.

The French also lost control of the Ghouta, the countryside around Damascus, and insurgent bands also began to appear in many other parts of Syria. Counter-attacks against the insurgency were frequently ineffectual, so the authorities resorted to reprisals and collective punishments. The French recruited gangs from the Circassian and Armenian minorities to carry out their dirty work. It was a sign of how nervous they were becoming about trusting Arabic-speaking Syrians. Villages, including the Druze settlement of Jaramana just outside Damascus, were systematically destroyed, and prisoners shot. On one occasion, the authorities executed up to 100 inhabitants of villages in the Ghouta, and brought a further sixteen young men back to Damascus to be shot in the central Marja square, where the bodies were left on public display. After this incident, the French had an unpleasant surprise a few days later. The corpses of a dozen captured Circassian militiamen were discovered lying near Bab Sharqi, the eastern gate of the city. The hands of the rebels were far from clean.

Insurgent bands engaged in extortion to finance and supply the revolt. They also attacked villages which refused to cooperate, and cases of naked brigandage occurred.

On 18 October the rebels took control of most of Damascus, burning and looting much of the sprawling Azm Palace, the governor's residence, where they had hoped to capture General Sarrail. They also slaughtered Armenian refugees who had fled from Turkey, and were now encamped to the south of the city at Qadam. These refugees were alleged to have been members of militias which had taken part in massacres in the Ghouta. Police and gendarmes melted away from their posts, and French armoured cars were reduced to firing blindly as they passed through the streets, terrorising but failing to hold neighbourhoods. Many people from the Christian and Jewish quarters had participated in a big nationalist demonstration which had taken place during the Muslim religious celebrations for the Prophet's birthday a few weeks earlier. All districts of the city were now backing the insurgency, but the rebels took special care to reassure and safeguard the Christians and Jews as they moved through Damascus.[20] This prompted an ironic comment by W. A. Smart, the British consul, in a report to his superiors: "These Moslem interventions assured the Christian quarters against pillage. In other words it was Islam and not the *Protectrice des Chrétiens en Orient* which protected the Christians in those critical days."[21] This incident illustrates that, contrary to what the French tended to feel instinctively, the nationalism they were encountering did not fit the label of the "Muslim fanaticism" which they constantly attempted to pin on those who opposed them. Their obsession with seeing Arab nationalism through this particular prism made it very hard for them to understand it, let alone come to terms with it.

Now the French did as they had done in Hama, with equal success but greater violence, even though the protests their actions caused led to the recall of Sarrail. For two days, they shelled Damascus, leaving much of it in ruins and on fire. One area was so thoroughly destroyed that when it was rebuilt the original street pattern was abandoned. It also acquired a new name, "*Hariqah*", meaning "Fire". One thousand

five hundred people are estimated to have been killed in the bombardment (in Hama, the inhabitants had claimed the death total was 344,
mostly civilian – the French admitted to 76, all of them insurgents).
As in Hama, a delegation of notables persuaded the rebels to leave the
city. The delegation also agreed to pay the authorities a hefty fine in
exchange for ending the bombardment.

Once again, the rebels were forced out of the urban areas into the
suburbs such as Maydan and the surrounding belts of farmland, where
they disrupted French communications with, for a time, increasing
success. That winter, the rail link into Damascus was regularly cut by
the activities of co-ordinated bands of insurgents who now dominated
virtually the whole of the southern half of Syria. The French air force
conducted what may well have been the most intensive and systematic aerial bombardments against a civilian population that had taken
place up to that time anywhere in the world, as their planes returned to
bomb villages on a daily basis. The intention of the bombardments was
to punish and deter, but initially it bred hatred and made its victims
flock to join the rebels.[22] Maydan suffered repeated assaults because of
its obstinacy, and was cut in half by a new road and barbed wire as the
French built a security barrier round the city.

The final French assault on Maydan in May 1926 was savage and
brutal. One thousand houses and shops were destroyed by incendiary
bombs dropped by the air force and up to 1000 people were killed –
many of whom were women and children and only about fifty were
fighters. A neighbourhood where 30,000 people had lived was now
a desolate ruin. But the onslaught achieved its objective. On 17 May,
lights shone again from the minarets in the city, something that had
not been seen for months. Refugees from Maydan now thronged into
the Old City to join those from the Ghouta, the Hawran and other
areas. The French did little to help them. It has been suggested that
this was deliberate. The French "relied on the growing state of misery,
which they attributed to the rebellion, to force the rebels and their
supporters into submission".[23]

The Maronites of Mount Lebanon and many other Uniates
generally supported the French, but many Orthodox Christians

backed or joined the rebels. In some Christian communities, such as the small towns of Ma'loula and Saydnaya, the Christians may have split more or less on sectarian lines between Uniates and Orthodox. The ancient Orthodox convent of Saydnaya tended wounded rebels and collected food for the fighters. At least one letter has survived from the leader of a rebel band to an Orthodox notable in Damascus asking him to provide young men from his community to fight in the insurgency.[24] There were also areas, such as Aleppo, where there was nationalist agitation but no explosion of revolt, even though on one occasion Moroccan cavalrymen dispersed a demonstration in the city and killed at least fifteen people with their sabres. The Alawi area was also quiet. This may have reflected its relative isolation compared with the Hawran. The Alawis had no equivalent to the longstanding corn trade links with Damascus which had hampered the French attempt to separate the Druze from the rest of Syria.

Minor rural and provincial notables like Sultan al-Atrash and Fawzi al-Qawuqji, who were often former Ottoman army officers, provided most of the military leadership for the revolt. Many city notables with large rural estates supplied the revolt with arms, money and men, and it was also widely supported by urban merchants, particularly the Damascus grain merchants of Maydan and Shaghur. Much of the rank and file were peasants, those who had left the land and were destitute because they could no longer make a living there, and the urban poor. Economic factors, including drought, also played their part in boosting recruitment. The rebels had more support and sympathy among the young than the old, and there were elements of what might be called class struggle in the demands sometimes made of leading notables to provide funds, men and other support. Among the wealthier sections of society, many people sat uncomfortably on the sidelines, and more than a few were quietly relieved when the revolt was crushed.

Sometimes, but not always, there was a religious tinge to the revolt: the use of traditional Muslim warrior rhetoric and appeals for jihad against the unbelieving French. For the French to rule a predominantly Muslim country was, in the eyes of Syria's Muslim majority, a scandal of monumental proportions. Fawzi al-Qawuqji exploited this fully in Hama where, before the revolt began, he had founded his own political party known as Hizbullah, or "the Party of God",[25] to appeal to the conservative Sunni population of the city. He also grew a beard to mark himself out as a devout Muslim, and spent many evenings in mosques where he encouraged preachers to support him and give sermons on jihad.

For obvious reasons, neither class warfare nor this populist/religious current chimed well with the elite nationalists. When Dr Shahbandar proclaimed a provisional government, he used purely secular language in his communiqué. Yet it would be wrong to see the nationalism of the elite as entirely secular. Because they saw themselves as the leaders of Syria, they considered that they should represent its people. The religious rhetoric of Islam has its place in any sense of Arab pride, and was an obvious rallying cry. Ordinary people felt their customs, their way of life and their religion were under attack from alien forces. The nationalist elite shared this perception, and it was only natural for it to use religious symbolism on appropriate occasions. Nor did this lead to a neat sectarian divide. In 1923, right at the start of the Mandate, Yusuf al-'Issa, a Christian, had suggested in the Damascus newspaper he edited that "the birthday of the Arab prophet" should be made a national holiday. He saw it as a way to unite all the "communities" that speak Arabic – the entire Arabic-speaking nation.[26]

By the summer of 1927, France had succeeded in crushing the revolt. This would have been impossible without large numbers of additional colonial troops who were brought in from Algeria, Senegal and Madagascar. A significant role was also played by the badly disciplined militias. These were particularly important in the earlier stages of the rebellion when they were short of troops. As the French regained territory and maintained their grip on it, the heart went out of the rebellion. In October 1926, Sultan al-Atrash and Dr Shahbandar took refuge in Jordan. Fawzi al-Qawuqji fought on into the following spring, by which time he and his followers could no longer find the welcome and support from the local population which they would once have received. State terror had done its work. By the very end, more than 6,000 rebel fighters had been killed and 100,000 people – a staggering number in the Syria of the mid-1920s – had seen their homes destroyed.[27]

IV

The Druze rebellion started over very specific, local grievances which merged naturally with resentments that were shared by many people all over Syria. These included resentments about the French presence and a general perception that the Mandate had no legitimacy, as well as grievances over French economic policies which had devastated the urban economy. The rebellion also showed that Sunni Muslims and some Christians were prepared to join with the Druze to make common cause against the French. Sectarianism clearly did not divide all Syrians.

Nationalist uprisings are normally perceived as responses to calls from urban political leaders. They occur after a people's sense of national identity has already been articulated by intellectuals. Nationalism is often seen as beginning as a form of self-awareness among the intelligentsia and only percolating into other sections of society, especially the less educated ones, after those same intellectuals have formulated a more focused nationalist message. In the Syria of 1925, it does not seem to have happened quite like this.[28] The revolt was started by peasants and artisans who were more often than not illiterate, and swept along destitute people who had been forced off the land because of drought. The uprising also appealed to the large numbers in the cities who had no secure livelihood. Very few of these people were intellectuals. What seems to have happened is that people became Syrian nationalists as they rose up in arms, and saw that the cause they were fighting for was shared by others with whom they might not previously have sensed that they had much in common. French atrocities, collective punishments and generally high-handed behaviour brought communities together and united them with neighbouring ones. Although they were militarily successful, on the ideological plane the French policies backfired spectacularly. They had the unintended consequence of spreading nationalist sentiment far and wide.

By the time the rebellion was over, there could be no denying that a strong sense of Syrian national identity had taken deep root. It was felt strongest among the Sunni Arab majority and the Druze, but there were also leading nationalists from the Christian communities – to which both Faisal's short-lived kingdom and more recently the People's Party had already addressed appeals. However, anyone who had had a leadership role in the revolt was now dead, in prison, or in exile, while the People's Party had been outlawed. On the other hand the French, too, were exhausted. The campaign to suppress the revolt had cost them dear in terms of casualties and money. France needed, more than ever, the assistance of eminent Syrians to govern. The tamer notables would still be given offices and positions, but it was clear that they would never be enough on their own. The French would have to persuade notables who were nationalists to take part in running the country.

These were the politicians who emerged in the late 1920s and became known as the National Bloc at the beginning of the 1930s. A study of the Bloc's leading lights has revealed that more than 90 per cent of them were Sunni Muslim, and all came from the four cities of Damascus, Aleppo, Homs and Hama. Two thirds of them were from the land-owning class of notables, and a quarter were merchants. Their educational background is also interesting. The overwhelming majority had had a modern secular education and no less than half had been trained in Istanbul to be Ottoman administrators. One in five had received a university education in Europe or at the Syrian Protestant College in Beirut (today the American University of Beirut) which provided a Western tertiary education to the same standard.[29] These were cultured and sophisticated men who wanted complete political independence for their country and the wider Arab nation. But that did not mean they necessarily wanted to transform Syrian society. On the contrary, their main preoccupation was ensuring that they retained their place at its apex: a position that they instinctively felt was threatened by the rule of the alien French. They were prepared to negotiate and compromise with France in order to achieve independence, which they accepted could only come over a period of years. This became known as the policy of "honourable cooperation".[30] They were therefore moderates. Yet the Bloc had its weaknesses: a propensity to factionalism, a reliance on the power of patronage to win votes, and an absence of thought-through policies with which to provide the country with effective government. It also failed to develop a following in rural areas or among the Alawis and Druze.

Elections for a constituent assembly took place in the spring of 1928. These were the first elections for a single body to represent all Syrians since the arrival of the French. The National Bloc won less than a third of the seats. The remainder of the delegates were independents, chiefly elected to represent rural or tribal areas where they were local notables. The French had hoped that this majority of unaffiliated delegates would be putty in their hands and could be used to marginalise the nationalist movement, but there was no rival banner for them to unite behind. The majority had few arguments to counter those of the nationalist deputies, who persuaded the assembly to adopt a draft constitution on European lines which some of the country's leading lawyers had written.

This document aimed to make Syria a parliamentary republic in which deputies would be elected by universal male suffrage in a two-stage process, which had also been adopted in neighbouring Iraq. There would be equality for members of all religions, although the president of the republic had to be a Sunni Muslim. The constitution gave the president power to execute treaties and the other prerogatives usual for the head of an independent state. It also declared that Syria, Lebanon, Palestine and Jordan constituted a single nation. These provisions made it utterly unacceptable to France, even though the High Commissioner feared that rejecting it would be unwise.[31] Instead, he was forced by Paris to resort to legalism and declare that the constitution could not be adopted because it would have breached the terms on which France had been granted the Mandate. After attempts at compromise failed, the assembly was suspended.

In the years leading up to the Second World War, there were further attempts to win French acquiescence to a constitutional settlement which would make Syria independent. In 1930, High Commissioner

Henri Ponsot finally accepted the constitution but only after he had added an article that made it subject to the overriding authority of France on any matter that affected its rights and obligations as the Mandatory power. He also issued separate organic laws governing the Druze and Alawi majority areas, as well as the Sanjak of Alexandretta, all of which would be semi-detached from the rest of Syria. Ponsot had succeeded in safeguarding France's position without any real reduction in its power. Elections followed in 1932. The French indulged in the manipulation which they had used in previous elections, as well as outright gerrymandering and ballot rigging. Even so, seventeen of the sixty-nine elected deputies were committed nationalists.[32] As before, the bulk of the remainder were local figures who were ill-equipped to oppose the nationalist leaders. The nationalists consolidated their position as a political party. A congress held in Homs in 1932 gave the National Bloc an organisational structure. This took the form of a permanent office with seven elected members.[33]

The politicians of the Bloc put honourable cooperation into practice. There now seemed to be a way forward, so long as the French were prepared to make compromises, and the Bloc, for its part, was willing to play the game according to the rules set by the French. But both sides had incompatible goals. The best hope for the Syrians would be to change French attitudes, something that seemed possible since French politicians of the left were hostile to the colonial lobby, and many French people increasingly realised that the Mandate was a drain on French resources. At times, the French seemed to move towards a position in which they would grant a greater degree of political independence. Some officials recognised this as inevitable, since it was the only way to gain Syrian goodwill and the enduring role for themselves in Syria that was the ultimate French objective. Yet high commissioners were political appointments who had to bow to the prevailing wind in Paris. Sometimes the direction of this wind could change abruptly following the fall of a government. The decade before the outbreak of the Second World War was marked by shifts in French policy in Syria, while the National Bloc was forced into inconsistent positions in order to win French concessions.

During the 1930s, French officials sometimes glanced enviously at how well Britain seemed to be doing with its Mandate next door in Iraq. Iraq's boundaries, like those of Syria, had no inherent logic and had also been drawn on maps at international conferences. Iraq had been constituted as an independent kingdom, and until his death in 1933, was ruled by the same Faisal who had led the Arab revolt and who had briefly been king of Syria. The French Mandate for Syria and Lebanon took the form of a resolution of the Council of the League of Nations, as did the British Mandate over Palestine. Yet there was a major difference of form if not substance in the Iraqi Mandate. It consisted of a treaty of alliance between Britain and Iraq, ostensibly as equals. However, the treaty provided that the king of Iraq "agrees to be guided" by British advice "on all important matters affecting the international and financial obligations and interests of His Britannic Majesty".[34] This provision was not included in a fresh treaty of alliance which was concluded in 1930 and gave Iraq a sufficient degree of independence to terminate the Mandate and qualify for membership of the League of Nations. Britain nonetheless retained important powers under the new treaty. These included two airbases, the right to station its forces in Iraq, and a requirement that British training should be preferred for the Iraqi army over that of any other foreign power.

Some French officials thought wistfully about making Syria a monarchy on the Iraqi model: the Mandate would be replaced by a treaty which would give Syria independence of a sort, and in exchange the king would bind it to France in a similar way. But who would be the French-appointed king of Syria? There were several possible candidates who might be suitable from a French perspective, but they would have been men of straw who could not hope to gain the essential support and cooperation of the nationalists. Other candidates, such as a Hashemite prince from the same family as Faisal (or even Faisal himself while he lived), might turn out to support a nationalist agenda once in power, particularly the reunification of Greater Syria. Yet, when all was said and done, the idea of a monarchy did not appeal to most French officials. Some Syrian nationalists supported a monarchy but for diametrically opposed reasons to those advanced by French officials. To place Syria under a member of the Hashemite family might be a step on the road to complete independence and to Arab unity. Nevertheless, discussions on both the French and nationalist sides never moved beyond the purely theoretical.

An attempt to negotiate a treaty in 1933 failed. France refused to back down on the question of separating the Druze and Alawi areas from Syria, and required that these would continue to be administered by France. The proposed treaty also suggested that France intended to retain its grip on Syria, and the vagueness on this major point of principle led to it being withdrawn from consideration by the Syrian Chamber of Deputies.[35]

A younger generation of nationalists was now rising up who had received their education after the end of the Ottoman period in an overtly Arab nationalist environment. They could observe how honourable cooperation was forcing the National Bloc to moderate its sympathy for the struggles of Arabs outside Syria. In 1931, the leading lights in the Bloc were reluctant to speak out or to join demonstrations against Italian atrocities in Libya. They even felt unable to commemorate the hanging of nationalists by the Turks in 1915–6.[36] A new generation put the Bloc under pressure to retreat from this policy, but its leaders remained trapped by the need to work with the French. For this reason, and because of a wish not to alienate Britain (a power which might be able to offer support for an independent Syria if it ever considered this expedient), the Bloc's official leadership found itself tongue-tied in 1936 when much of Palestine finally exploded into revolt in frustration at Britain's continued support for the Zionist project. The leaders of the Bloc were forced to part company with public opinion, since Syrians sympathised deeply with the Palestinian struggle. The Palestinian revolt also had much in common with the great Syrian uprising of 1925. However, speaking out would have been likely to antagonise the French and prejudice the negotiations for Syria's own chance of independence.[37]

In those years the Bloc was headed by the moderate Jamil Mardam, an aristocrat from Damascus who had been educated in Paris and had impeccable nationalist credentials, as he had unambiguously thrown himself behind the 1925 revolt. However, his need to placate the French opened a space for two major figures on the political scene who offered more robust varieties of pan-Arab nationalism. The first was the charismatic Dr Shahbandar, the founder of the People's Party who had once attempted to establish a provisional government based in the Hawran during the 1925 rebellion, and who had therefore been Jamil Mardam's leader at that time. Now he stood for reuniting the whole of Greater Syria in a confederation under the leadership of the Emir Abdullah of Jordan. He picked up support in areas which the National Bloc failed to reach – such as the Druze and Alawi heartlands and the Jazirah east of the Euphrates. He was sometimes dubbed the leader of the opposition, although he worked outside parliament and was frequently exiled by the French. Shahbandar would eventually be assassinated in Damascus in June 1940. Who was behind the murder is not known for certain, although his rivals in the National Bloc and the French were suspected. The motive may have been his support for the Emir Abdullah's pan-Syrian ambitions and rumours that he was a British agent.[38]

The other pan-Arab figure was Shukri al-Quwwatli. He had been a member of the nationalist secret society Al-Fatat who had joined the Arab revolt. He had been imprisoned and possibly tortured in Damascus by the Turks during the Great War. This made him a national hero. He had worked for Faisal's administration but fled into exile after the French conquest. He later became very anti-Hashemite and anti-British, probably because, like many other Syrians, he felt a sense of betrayal. The French considered him one of the most dangerous Syrian figures in exile. Al-Quwwatli worked tirelessly for the reunification of Syria and Palestine, and came from a family which had commercial relations with a rising star in the Arab world. This was Ibn Saud, the tribal strongman from Nejd in central Arabia and advocate of the puritanical brand of Islam known as Wahhabism. Ibn Saud had driven the Hashemites from the Hejaz and its holy cities of Mecca and Medina in 1924–5. He thus displaced the elderly King Hussein, the Sharif who had risen against the Turks in 1916. He united most of the Arabian peninsula in a kingdom named after himself which was formally proclaimed as Saudi Arabia in 1932. The Hashemites of Iraq and Jordan never forgot or forgave this. Ibn Saud therefore became a figure to whom anti-Hashemite factions in

Syrian politics could look for support. Naturally enough, Ibn Saud was sympathetic to Shukri al-Quwwatli who was eventually permitted to return to Syria and became one of the founding fathers of the National Bloc when it held its inaugural congress in Homs in 1932. He opposed the policy of honourable cooperation with the French from inside the party. In 1936, he spoke out forcefully on Palestine and thus established some distance between himself and the party's official leadership.

Public anger mounted throughout the early 1930s. It was intensified by the economic decline brought on by the Great Depression and manifested itself in strikes and civil disturbances, as well as boycotts of French-owned businesses. In January 1936, matters reached a climax when four protesters were killed outside the Umayyad Mosque in Damascus. Twenty thousand people attended their funeral the next day, and a general strike and riots rippled across the country. This was by far the most serious resistance to the French since the revolt of 1925. Yet, even as Syria risked becoming ungovernable, it looked for a moment as though the policy of honourable cooperation might be working. In March, a delegation from the National Bloc left for Paris. At first, negotiations were bogged down in old sticking points, such as the French insistence that there should be French governors for the Druze and Alawi semi-autonomous regions. However, the French government of the day collapsed. The socialist *Front Populaire* came to power under Léon Blum. The *Front* took a very different approach. When negotiations resumed in June, the French delegation was led by Pierre Viénot, the new under-secretary of state for foreign affairs, who accepted that the Mandate was "transitory", and that if France did not acknowledge this it would lose all influence in Syria.[39]

The result was a treaty which France would ratify after a three-year probationary period. It accepted the principle of Syrian unity, although in return the National Bloc waived Syria's claim to the four districts which France had added to Lebanon in 1920 – Tripoli, Ba'lbek, Sidon and Tyre – and recognised Lebanon's existence as a separate state. There would be a degree of autonomy for the Druze and Alawi areas, as well as the Sanjak of Alexandretta. The treaty gave provisions defining the garrisons that France would retain in Syria, some of which would be stationed in the Druze and Alawi areas for a period of five years. France would also have two airbases (the same number as Britain had in Iraq) and communications facilities for its military. The treaty was endorsed by a general election in Syria in which the National Bloc triumphed. Rural delegates who did not belong to the Bloc also declared themselves as nationalists. The agreement was signed in Damascus on behalf of France by Pierre Viénot, and the Syrian prime minister, Jamil Mardam, on 22 December 1936.

This was Mardam's great achievement but, as has so often been the case with moderate Arab nationalists, it was taken away from him. Although the treaty was ratified unanimously by the Syrian parliament five days later, it was never implemented because the *Front Populaire* government in France fell from power in 1937. Opponents of the treaty in Paris were then able to lobby successfully against ratification. Those opposed were not limited to the old colonial lobby. The looming prospect of war with Germany and Italy made the military more cautious about anything that might dilute France's strength – or perceived strength – in the eastern Mediterranean. At the same time, every opportunity was given for Syrian opponents of the treaty, who were chiefly drawn from the Christian minorities, to put their case in Paris.

Jamil Mardam tried to find compromises but public opinion in Syria would not allow this. He came under sustained attack with implications of treachery, as when a newspaper article alleged that he was "a lion in Damascus and a fox in Paris".[40] Further humiliations were forced upon him. France gradually prised the Sanjak of Alexandretta away from Syria in tacit acceptance of Turkish claims to it, although only a minority of its population was ethnically Turkish. Mardam was also seen as compromised because of his failure to speak up in support of the Palestinians. Such were the perils of honourable cooperation with France. As support drained away from his government, he finally resigned on 18 February 1939.

At the start of the Second World War, Syrian independence seemed as distant as it had at the very beginning of the French Mandate. In July 1939, France suspended the constitution, increased the autonomy of the Alawi and Druze areas, and established direct control over the east of the country, the Jazirah. A month earlier, it had formally ceded the Sanjak of Alexandretta to Turkey. Syria seemed quiescent and reconciled to its lot. Nationalists were now reduced to looking abroad for support – but this led to factionalism. While Dr Shahbandar wanted the Hashemite Emir Abdullah of Jordan to be proclaimed king of Syria, the National Bloc politicians sought support from his rival, Ibn Saud. Syria thus became tied up in a contest between Arab dynasties. The French, as might have been expected, played a less than helpful role. The High Commissioner, Gabriel Puaux, toyed with the idea of a Syrian kingdom under a member of the Saudi family. Not only was the official ideology of Saudi Arabia based on Islam rather than the Arab nationalism which was the ideology of the Hashemites of Jordan and Iraq, but Saudi Arabia was the deadly rival of the other two monarchies and much less close to Britain. Islam was seen as less threatening to French interests than Arab nationalism. A Saudi king of Syria would also be the end of hope for the reunification of Greater Syria or a pan-Arab federation with Iraq which encompassed all the Arabic-speaking former Ottoman provinces.[41]

V

The population of Syria and the other Mandates grew steadily during the period between the two world wars. Towns were unable to absorb all new arrivals from the countryside or give them productive occupations. The number of Damascenes doubled during the twenty years following the arrival of the French in 1920. City quarters became more crowded, while the notable class and the better off began to move to new suburbs in the surrounding countryside. These were built on European lines and reflected a more Europeanised way of life, leaving the Old City and the long-established districts outside its walls to people who were, by and large, poorer and more traditional in their attitudes. The old extended family had tried to live in a single house arranged round a complex of courtyards. Now, though, the arrangement became less cohesive, as different sons made their way in different professions. They no longer lived in the same space, even if they frequently built a house next door or were at least close neighbours.

Adding to this changing urban complexity, many of the traditional merchant class remained in the city because they needed to do so in order to be close to their business. New, European-style class divisions began to appear, as did an educational divide. Those who remained in the old quarters were much less exposed to modern education. The number of secondary school pupils in government schools doubled between 1924 and 1934, but education was still largely for the elite – and girls' education lagged far behind that of boys.[42]

The vicissitudes of the Great Depression reached Syria. There were high levels of inflation and many bankruptcies. Nevertheless, there were some positive new economic developments which were financed by Syrian capital and skill. A particular success and source of pride was the introduction for the first time of an efficient supply of running water to Damascus homes from the spring of 'Ayn al-Fija (also well known today as a leading local brand of bottled mineral water). Local cement production was providing 60 per cent of Syrian needs by 1938, and modern factories began producing fruit conserves, leather goods, textiles and soap. Sometimes mechanisation actually rescued old handicraft industries which had been at death's door. New tariff barriers kept out imports, which further helped these local industries; but by the same token these levies hindered exports to traditional market destinations, such as Palestine and Iraq. In fact, the tariff barriers could work directly against Syrian industry. Damascus is renowned for its confectionery, but in Syria sugar was subject to duty. In Palestine it was not, and therefore the sweet makers of Damascus faced unfair competition from Palestinian imports.

The old ways under which people looked to the notables for patronage were slowly breaking down. Although a new middle class was appearing, neither this phenomenon nor the beginnings of economic development were sufficient to meet the needs of the increasing population. For most Syrians, life was not getting better. While the National Bloc continued to dominate parliament, a political space was opening up lower down the social scale. Fresh movements emerged, ranging right across the spectrum from Communists to Muslim revivalists. Each aimed at building a new Syria based on its own, particular vision. A large part of their appeals centred on concern for social justice. If, one day, Syria became free of the French, Syrians would need to consider how to remodel their society, and revolutionary issues would come to the fore. For the moment such impulses could only find a limited expression, since workers, students and the rising bourgeoisie alike shared the National Bloc's focus on ending the French presence.

Sunni Muslims constituted nearly three quarters of the population of the territory of the Mandate. The Sunnism of Syria tended to be tolerant and accepting of the country's diversity, although already in the nineteenth century Sunnis were very conscious that their culture and identity were being put under strain as a result of the pressures of a rapidly changing world. This awareness increased when they suffered the grotesque humiliation of rule by France, some of whose soldiers and officials fantasised about the Crusades as some kind of golden age. Many Sunnis suspected that the French intended to do whatever they could to detach Syrians from Islam and their traditional values. This meant that at a popular level there was often an instinctive resistance to modernisation. In fact, modernisation could all too easily be caricatured as "Christian" or "atheist" – words which, in this context, would have seemed almost interchangeable to Sunni Muslims.

Much thought was given by Sunni thinkers to the dilemmas of the modern world, and it is important today to stress that such thought was not in principle xenophobic, anti-Western or anti-Christian, even if it was, understandably, hostile to European imperialism. The values of Islam were eternal, and corrupt Muslim rulers were seen as having sacrificed them. Muslims could see much to admire in the progress of the West. Muhammad Abduh, the great Egyptian religious reformer of the late nineteenth century, once visited Britain, and is reported to have said that in Egypt he had seen Muslims but no Islam, while in London he had seen Islam but no Muslims. But he was also well aware of how the penetration of Western education and values might threaten Islam in his home country unless it could renew itself from within. He feared that if this did not happen, the religion would be discarded like an old garment.[43]

Ideas similar to those of Abduh were well received in Syria and were developed by local thinkers, but the influence of the traditional religious elite was declining as young men – and women – flocked to obtain a secular education in the increasing number of places where it was available. Religious leaders had been important as the custodians of the values and morals of society, but now their grip on the educated young was steadily weakening. Few religious leaders were prominent in the nationalist movement. In fact, their own sons were often among the most eager to receive a modern education and become members of this new world of doctors, engineers and lawyers. Over a couple of generations, many of the great religious families forsook a career as scholars in favour of the prestigious careers that were now available in these modern professions.[44]

Nevertheless, the ranks of the religious scholars were constantly replenished from below, and they retained an important constituency. The old quarters of the cities were still densely populated by merchants and artisans who had not received a modern education, and remained their spiritual fiefdoms. As people left the land and flocked to the cities, this world of fidelity to old religious norms was the one they naturally gravitated towards. Many merchants and artisans looked to the religious scholars for guidance, while a kind of devout but unlettered proletariat, constantly swelling in numbers, joined these traditional constituencies. Sunni Islam was the focal point of identity for many people. This sentiment blended naturally and easily into a sense of Arab nationalism. In fact, one of the reasons for the popular growth of Arab nationalism under the French was that it was a way for many people to express their allegiance to Islam, the threatened cornerstone of their identity.

There was therefore much pressure on governments to uphold the values and practices of Islam. Muslim benevolent societies were founded to encourage education in Islam and for other charitable purposes, and also to lobby governments to hold fast to Muslim traditions. Many of these societies were founded in Damascus, but others were set up in Aleppo, Homs and Hama. They tended to remain locally based in the city where they originated, and had their own youth movements. Organisations worked at a popular level, and the term "Islamic populists" was coined for them and their members.[45] The perception that Islam was under attack led to a certain brittleness. This deepened a sense of identity politics that was simultaneously tied up with the cultural struggle between modernisers and conservatives. Perhaps the most extraordinary manifestation of this was the opinion by the Mufti of Damascus in 1933 that the yo-yo, a brightly coloured children's toy which rolls itself up and down a piece of string held between forefinger and thumb, should be forbidden because it was the cause of the severe drought the country was suffering. The opinion was sufficiently influential for the minister of the interior to issue a decree banning the innocent plaything.[46]

The Sunni elite from which most nationalist leaders came was not necessarily pious, although some of those leaders were devout individuals. So long as Islamic precepts were upheld in public, a blind eye could be turned to behaviour that did not conform in private. One leading and highly respected figure in the National Bloc, for instance, Fakhri al-Barudi, was well known to have a taste for alcohol and a sexual preference for young men, but he was discreet and does not seem to have caused scandals which might have threatened his position – or that of the Nationalist movement.[47]

But red lines were drawn over public behaviour. Conservative scholars and popular preachers attacked early signs of the emancipation of women, such as the discarding of face veils and headscarves by feminists, the mixing of the sexes in public, and women walking along the street on the arm of their husband. Many saw the adoption of Western dress by women as a betrayal of their culture, nation and identity, and there was horror when women began to attend the theatre and the cinema (both deplorable innovations in the eyes of more inflexible conservatives). A *cause célèbre* occurred in 1944 when a charity ball was organised in Damascus by the wife of the minister of education. The event had to be cancelled after demonstrations turned into riots, in protest at the anticipated participation by Muslim women who would be unveiled.[48] The position of women thus became one of the dividing lines between secularists and Islamists. Although there seems to have been little or no opposition to female education as such among Islamists, there was intense hostility to women moving out of their traditional roles and into a modern work place. Nevertheless, women increasingly took part in political activities, especially demonstrations.

Another red line concerned the position of Islam in the state. Ottoman reformers had removed the ancient legal disabilities on non-Muslims, such as the payment of extra taxes, in the middle of the nineteenth century. This established equality for all, but left each religious community its own law of personal status governing such matters as inheritance, divorce and family law. On several occasions during the Mandate period, but most notably in 1938, the French proposed legislation to institute a unified personal status law which would allow freedom of religious conversion as a basic right – including, for the first time, explicit freedom for Muslims to convert to other religions or for a Muslim woman to marry a non-Muslim. The motives of the French in introducing such legislation were mischievous. They knew it would be seen as an attack on Islam and an attempt to strip Islam of its privileged position as the religion of the majority of Syrians. They also knew that an attack on Muslim identity would be an attack on Syrian identity. Following an outcry, they were forced to back down.

But was the Sunnism of a large majority of the population a threat to Christians and other religious minorities, as the French liked to maintain? The French had their own highly particular view of their mission to provide "tutelage" to Syria. They were also worried that Arab nationalism could spread to their North African possessions of Algeria, Morocco and Tunisia. This undoubtedly affected the way they ruled Syria, where they attempted to adapt policies which had been developed in Morocco to prevent Moroccans uniting against them.[49] The French in general considered that what lay behind Arab nationalism was hostility to the modern world, which it was France's duty to eradicate through its *mission civilisatrice*. Arab nationalism was just a new pigment taken on by the malign chameleon of "Muslim fanaticism". This led the French to favour religious minorities and non-Arab ethnic groups and to try to co-opt them. Minorities in the mountains such as Maronites, Orthodox Christians, Alawis and Druze could even be seen by French administrators as racially superior to the "physically mediocre, less intelligent, fanatic and untrustworthy" peoples of the towns and plains.[50]

There were those who saw the futility and dangers of this approach and the unpleasant mind-set which lay behind it. As the distinguished French scholar Louis Massignon (who is just about the only Orientalist for whom Edward Said shows some genuine respect in his famous *Orientalism*) noted in June 1936, in a comment he wrote as a French government adviser during the negotiations on the abortive 1936 treaty:

> Because we are in Syria for cultural ends and to maintain our promises to the Christians, it is necessary that we reposition the defence of minorities in the framework of a frankly pro-Arab political culture ... this way we will win the Syrian wafd [delegation] to our side and reach an agreement.[51]

But Massignon and similar voices were crying in a French wilderness. A "pro-Arab political culture" was anathema to the prevailing ethos in the ministries of Paris. The French were able to find separatist voices among the Alawis and, to a lesser extent, among the Druze, but in both cases these were balanced by unionists who wanted either full unity with Syria, or unity with some measure of local autonomy. A strong sense of local identity was not incompatible with a sense of Syrian – or pan-Arab – nationalism. Furthermore, as the case of Lebanon shows, a Maronite state was impossible without incorporating large tracts of land inhabited by non-Maronites. Viewed with the hindsight of today, this arguably defeated the purpose of the establishment of the state of "Greater Lebanon" in the first place. Similar problems would have been faced by an independent Alawi or Druze state. To be viable, it would have had to incorporate many people who did not belong to the supposedly dominant sect for which the state was established.

This is particularly obvious in the case of the Alawis. Although Alawis constituted 62 per cent of the population of the Alawi state which the French proposed, they were the third most numerous community – behind Sunni Muslims and Christians – in Lattakia, its capital. According to a report in a Damascus newspaper written in 1923,[52] at a time when the French were actively encouraging Alawi separatism, much of the impulse for separatism came from local Christian bureaucrats who feared the loss of their positions if the area was incorporated into a wider Syria. Although the writer also notes separatist feeling among Alawis, he suggests that to a very large extent it had been planted in the minds of Alawi notables by the French. Many of these notables would probably have been barely literate. Yet further partition of Syria would also have been economically disastrous. Shorn of the Alawi area as well as Palestine, Lebanon and Alexandretta, Syria and its inland cities would have had no access to the sea.

Even the Maronites eventually tired of the French. In 1935, Mgr. Arida, the Maronite Patriarch, showed his displeasure at France's refusal to grant Lebanon "true independence".[53] In consequence, the Patriarch even visited the leaders of the Syrian National Bloc, and thereby "raised hopes for a Muslim-Christian *entente* and for the unification and consolidation of opposition to the French".[54] Within a few years, Muslims and Christians in Lebanon would be cooperating to get rid of the Mandatory power. Left to their own devices, the nationalists of Syria would have created a "pro-Arab political culture" such as that which Massignon had recommended to the French Ministry of Foreign Affairs.

VI

After the fall of France to Hitler in June 1940, the French authorities in Lebanon and Syria declared their allegiance to the Vichy regime which collaborated with the Nazis. A year later Vichy appeared on the brink of allowing the Axis to establish airbases in Syria. The Allies had to respond. On 8 June 1941, planes flying from British-controlled Palestine dropped leaflets across the southern parts of Syria and

Lebanon promising independence. These were signed by General Catroux, the representative of the Free French forces of General de Gaulle who had continued to fight on after France surrendered to the Germans in June 1940. The Free French were now poised to invade, although their military venture was only possible with the support of a very substantial British army and the Jordanian Arab legion. The Free French proclamation written on the leaflets was unequivocal:

> You will become henceforth a free and sovereign people; you will be able to compose for yourselves separate states or unite yourselves into a single state. And in either of these cases, your independence and sovereignty will be guaranteed in a treaty to make clear the relations between us ... A great time in your history is drawing near. With the voices of its sons fighting for its life, and for the sake of the world's freedom, France declares your independence.[55]

Yet problems emerged as soon as the forces loyal to Vichy had surrendered. General de Gaulle was a passionate believer in the greatness of France. He aimed to preserve France's control of its overseas possessions, including its Mandate over Syria and Lebanon. It seems that the wording of the proclamation Catroux signed went further than de Gaulle had intended. The promise of independence was not meant to be unconditional. Rather, it would be based on the well-worn precedent of Britain's termination of the Iraqi Mandate which had enabled Iraq to become a member of the League of Nations in 1932. France would grant Syria and Lebanon independence, but only when they had executed treaties granting back to France rights at least equal to those Britain had retained for itself in Iraq. France intended to preserve its privileged position in Syria and Lebanon, including the right to station forces there.[56]

Once the Free French had established their administrative control, they tried to put independence on the backburner. They feared that any renunciation of French rights in any part of their empire would be seized upon by their Vichy opponents, who would be delivered a propaganda victory in France itself. Once again, it seemed as though the domestic interests of a European power might be about to decide the fate of Syria, and the feelings of Syrians could be safely disregarded. The Free French now made it their policy to extract treaties from Syria and Lebanon along the lines originally intended by de Gaulle. Pending this, they acted on the assumption that the Mandate would continue in perpetuity. However, they were now in a much weaker position than ever before. Their presence in Syria and Lebanon was ultimately dependent on British goodwill. There were now British troops garrisoning Syria alongside the French, and Britain had endorsed the proclamation promising independence.

Some kind of concession therefore had to be made to the nationalists. In September, Catroux issued a declaration of Syrian independence, but it stated that France would retain control of the armed forces and police, all public services, communications and the economy.[57] As the constitution was still suspended, he was able to appoint as president a non-nationalist notable with a reputation for compliance. However, Allied victories in North Africa weakened the argument that Syria had to be kept under tight control because of the war. This fact and British pressure led to elections being held in July 1943. The resultant vote returned the National Bloc to power under the leadership of Shukri al-Quwwatli, whom the new chamber elected as president of the republic. This ended any possibility of France gaining the treaty it so coveted. In Lebanon, which had also held elections, an alliance between the dominant Christians and Sunni Muslim Arab nationalists ensured that the Lebanese, too, stood firm and united against the French. Most Lebanese Sunnis had by now reconciled themselves to remaining part of Lebanon. The transfer of the four districts lost to Syria in order to create "Greater Lebanon" was accepted as permanent, but there were compensations. Sunni merchants were now joining with their Christian counterparts in trade with Europe, while helping to open the Syrian market to foreign goods.

The final chapter of the Mandate was a display of extremely bad grace by the frustrated French. In October 1943, the Syrian and Lebanese governments gave notice to the French representative, Jean Helleu, who had succeeded General Catroux, that they intended to amend their constitutions to provide for complete independence. In Lebanon, the French arrested the president, prime minister and others on 11 November, but were soon forced to release them after strikes and demonstrations showed that Lebanon was united against them. Demonstrations in Syria and other Arab countries also helped to force the French to back down, as did British pressure.

From that point onwards, the French no longer attempted to challenge constitutional changes made by the Syrian and Lebanese parliaments. In December 1943, the Syrian prime minister stated that the Mandate was not recognised, and deputies took their oath of allegiance to a constitution which had been drafted accordingly.[58] Over the course of 1944 and early 1945, France handed over most governmental powers, save for the *Troupes Spéciales*, the army which the French had recruited predominantly from minority communities. The French also strengthened their military forces, reluctant to accept that their role in the two countries was at an end. They had not yet given up on shackling Syria with a treaty which preserved at least some of France's interests, but the two new states of Syria and Lebanon were intent on demonstrating their independence. They declared war on Germany and Japan in February 1945, thereby entitling them to be founder members of the United Nations.

Britain used its influence to try to persuade the Syrians to compromise. This led to a stand-up row between Winston Churchill and Shukri al-Quwwatli when the British prime minister met the Syrian president at a summit of Arab leaders in Egypt in February 1945. As the minister in the British government with responsibility for the Middle East in the immediate aftermath of the Great War, Churchill had been a firm opponent of complete independence for either Iraq or Egypt, as well as a staunch advocate of the Zionist programme in Palestine. In his meeting with Quwwatli, Churchill begged at first, arguing that it was necessary to placate France for the sake of the war effort. When this got him nowhere, he then turned to bullying. Quwwatli responded by pointing at the sea and saying, evidently with some heat, "We will not sign a treaty with France even if the waters of this sea turn red! We are willing to spill enough blood to turn the clear waters red, Mr

Churchill!" Churchill angrily rose to his feet and accused the Syrian leader of threatening him. "Do you know who I am?" he shouted. "I am the commander-in-chief of the Allied forces. I will not let anyone in this world threaten or intimidate me." But it was Quwwatli who was being intimidated, and he refused to give way. Years later he recounted that he was afraid Churchill was going to strangle him, and said that Churchill had "instantly turned from an angry man into a mad man". The encounter ended with Quwwatli gaining the British prime minister's respect. Churchill told Roosevelt that the Syrians were lucky to have such a leader.[59]

Still the French persisted, and continued to build up their forces. In response, there were strikes and demonstrations in Damascus and Beirut on 19 May 1945, followed by disturbances in many areas, including Aleppo, Homs, Hama, Deir al-Zour, and the Druze and Alawi districts. Towards the end of the month, law and order were clearly breaking down. French troops and aircraft shelled and bombed Damascus on 29 and 30 May 1945. They reportedly killed 400 people, although – as so often – no reliable statistics exist.[60] When the guards outside Syria's parliament building refused to salute a French flag, the French responded by attacking it in the hope of arresting the government. It was then almost entirely destroyed by French shelling.[61] This wanton destruction could be said to have been a symbol of France's failure to fulfil the promise to prepare Syria for independence which it had made when it first accepted the Mandate.

Following an appeal from President Shukri al-Quwwatli, Britain now acted. It already had enough reasons to feel nervous about public opinion in Arab countries, and could not risk adding yet further fuel to the fires of Arab hostility. The British garrisons in Syria took control and restored law and order. Thereafter, it was only a matter of time before France's adventure in Greater Syria came to an end. Paris gave permission for control of the *Troupes Speciales* to be handed over. In 1946, the last French troops left Damascus and Beirut. By agreement with France, the British forces did so at the same time.

CHAPTER THREE

From Independence to Hafez al-Assad,
1946–1970

I

The story of how independence came to Syria was told in the final section of the last chapter. Every single concession had to be wrung out of the French in the teeth of their determined opposition. This was far from an ideal way for a new nation to be born. It also left it unprepared for the challenges ahead. It had no allies and has been aptly described as "a political orphan".[1] Syrians now had their own state and a democracy, but that democracy was fragile – as were the state and its sense of nationhood.

During the twenty years of French rule before the outbreak of the Second World War, there had probably been no overall advance in per capita income in Syria.[2] Public expenditure by the French had concentrated on security and administration, with the result that little was left for transport, infrastructure, education or social expenditure. Government neglect of education also had the effect of disadvantaging the Sunnis and other Muslims. These communities had few schools of their own compared with those which the Christian churches built for their flocks, and which were often helped and funded by missionaries.

There were estimated to have been some 3 million people living in Syria in 1932, an increase from 2.14 million, according to the only French census which was conducted in 1921–2. It is reasonable to guess that there were over 3.5 million Syrians in 1945, since the next census which took place in 1960 gave the country's population as 4.5 million. The war years had been characterised by shortages and terrible inflation, which had totalled 830 per cent in Damascus, according to the retail price index for the period 1939–45. The economic achievements of the Mandate period were generally unimpressive. Some successful import substitution industries were set up in the 1930s, and by 1938 local production for cement and cotton thread produced about half the country's needs, as well as a third of its cotton textile requirements. There had also been some extension of the area of cultivated land. Nevertheless, railways and most utilities were owned by French concessions which had been granted monopolies. The transport network was still very limited, and the country relied largely on the Lebanese ports of Beirut and Tripoli as it did not have a port of its own which could take large ocean-going vessels.

Was it possible to speak of a genuine Syrian nation in 1946? Or was the newly independent state no more than a still freshly-minted geographical expression? Syria was almost entirely Arabic-speaking, save for the approximately 8 or 10 per cent of population who belonged to the Kurdish minority that was concentrated in parts of the north and east of the country, and much smaller Armenian and Circassian minorities, which had no geographical base. Yet the arbitrariness of the Mandate boundaries would haunt the new state. Aleppo, still at the time probably Syria's largest city and certainly the country's commercial hub, had retained its links with Mosul and Baghdad throughout the Mandate years. Many politicians from the city favoured Syria joining Iraq in a federation, or even a full union. There was also resentment of the domination of Damascus, particularly in important provincial centres like Homs and Deir al-Zour. In the south, the Druze around Suwayda were passionately Arab, but their tribal leaders were equally firm about their wish to regulate their own affairs in the way they had always done. There was a general consensus that the existing divisions between the Arab states which had once been Ottoman provinces were artificial.

Syria was menaced from almost all points of the compass. Indeed, it seemed surrounded by ravenous wolves. To the north, its relationship with Turkey was uneasy and clouded by fear and distrust, especially after the loss of Alexandretta, now recast as the Turkish province of Hatay. To the east lay Iraq, still ruled by the Hashemite monarchy originally established by Faisal, who had briefly been king in Damascus. Iraq had substantial oil revenues and was a rising power. Britain retained very substantial influence there. Many Syrians feared Iraq would now try to dominate or absorb Syria so as to convert it into a British protectorate, while others wondered if some form of rule by Baghdad which allowed for local autonomy might be preferable to their present situation. To the south lay Jordan which was ruled by King Abdullah, another Hashemite who was a close friend of Britain. His army was by far the most effective in the Arab world, and he dreamed of becoming king of a reconstituted Greater Syria and transferring his capital to Damascus.

Then there was Palestine, which now had a border with Syria along the river Jordan and the eastern shore of the Sea of Galilee.[3] A terrorist campaign by Zionist militias was underway to force Britain to allow more Jewish refugees from Europe into the country, and to establish a Jewish state on Palestinian soil. If Britain withdrew, this could only lead to civil war between the Jewish and Arab populations. The repercussions for Syria if Palestine imploded would be catastrophic. Of Syria's closest neighbours, only Lebanon offered no threat. The two newly independent states were cooperating on many matters but they would grow further apart. In 1950, different economic policies ended their currency union which had survived throughout the Mandate period, and for the first time each state charged customs duty on goods exported from the other. Yet another little split had been created in the Arab world, and this time it had been caused by two Arab governments.

The Arab League, a grouping of the independent Arab states, had been formed in Cairo in March 1945. Syria was a founding member. The League established a club of nations of which Egypt, because of its sheer size, would be the natural leader. Egypt's only serious rival was Iraq. On its own Iraq could not compete with Egypt, but, if the former Ottoman provinces could be reunited, this would challenge Cairo's dominance. Yet this reunification would be difficult to achieve. Although Iraq and Jordan were separate Hashemite kingdoms, they were natural allies against everyone else. If Syria could be enticed into their orbit, they might succeed in establishing a confederation or even a federal state which would be the strongest independent Arab entity. This was obviously anathema to Egypt, as it was to Saudi Arabia which was ruled by the Al Saud family, the dynastic rivals of the Hashemites. Egypt and Saudi Arabia therefore formed their own unspoken alliance. Egypt, Iraq, Jordan and Saudi Arabia would keep a close eye on Syrian politics and do whatever they could to increase their own influence at the expense of the others.

This inevitably meant that these Arab states would exploit whatever divisions they could open up in Syrian society. Nationalism had been the creed that most Syrians could unite behind because they wanted the departure of the French, but that left open the vexed question of national identity: should the unification of Greater Syria or a wider, pan-Arab entity be the goal to which all should strive? Consideration of such issues involved not just identity and ideology but the complexities of practical politics.

The politicians now running Syria as a parliamentary republic were from the old notable families. They had been elected because of their leading positions in Syrian society and the patronage they could exercise. Parliamentary deputies were meant to represent their constituents, but in practice they looked after the special interests of the groups which had backed them during the election campaign. These would invariably be the local notable or clan leaders who had asked them to stand for parliament in the first place; often they were members of their own families. Independent members who had no party affiliation constituted the largest single bloc in parliament, while political parties were weak, undisciplined and poorly organised.

With the French no longer ensconced in their forts and offices up and down the country, there was no agreed programme behind which to unite a majority in parliament. Those elected to parliament included some deputies who were illiterate, while there were others who spoke Kurdish or Armenian as their native language and were less than fluent in Arabic. The National Bloc which had led the country to independence under Shukri al-Quwwatli was divided into factions which were essentially for or against the personality of its leader. These factions also reflected the rivalry between Damascus and Aleppo. The National Bloc duly split, with the president's Damascus-based followers constituting themselves as the National Party, while its Aleppo-based rival became the People's Party which was formally set up in 1948. As Patrick Seale has eloquently put it, after independence Syria was governed through "a western constitutional formula stretched like a new skin over the fissures of a traditional society".[4] That skin was all too likely to crack. This was the reason why Syrian politics in the post-independence years would be so chaotic and bewildering.

II

Syria was changing. Despite the neglect of the Mandate years, education was becoming gradually more widespread. The nationalism of the young was not the same as the nationalism which had been adopted by the notable families twenty, thirty or fifty years earlier. National consciousness – both of the pan-Arab variety and belief in a united Greater Syria – was strong among students in secondary schools and university institutions as well as in the professions. Young intellectuals wanted to see a proud, new Syria that would be part of a modern Arab world. This inevitably meant some kind of social revolution. There was no shortage of ideological currents eager to fill the intellectual vacuum independence had exposed in Syrian politics, or of zealous idealists anxious to turn these currents into political movements to transform Syria.

At one extreme of the ideological spectrum was the Syrian National Party[5] of Antun Sa'ada, originally founded in 1932.[6] He was an Orthodox Christian with powerful charisma who espoused a narrative of an eternal, united Greater Syria, which he saw as extending from the Taurus Mountains across the Sinai Desert to the Suez Canal and the Red Sea, as well as eastwards to the Zagros Mountains, which form the border between Iraq and Iran, then down to the Persian Gulf. His was a territorially based nationalism. The entire Fertile Crescent was the crescent moon of Greater Syria. He subsequently added Cyprus to this notional homeland, as the star within that crescent. For Antun Sa'ada, there was an unbreakable, indivisible link between this land and its people, who were the descendants of all the glorious ancient civilisations which had inhabited its area. This meant that his Syrian National Party rejected notions of Islam or the Arabic language as a source of nationhood, and was not a pan-Arab movement. The party was strongly influenced by European Fascist ideas and, like many other political organisations of the time, established paramilitary youth movements. It also believed in the complete separation of politics from religion and opposed any separatist impulses – including those of the Lebanese Maronites.

At the other extreme of the spectrum was the small Syrian Communist Party. The Syrian industrial proletariat was too small to form a power base for the party, which often made sure to campaign on a moderate platform. It was led by Khaled Baqdash, a very talented Kurdish lawyer from Damascus. Backing came from other Kurds as well as from a significant number of Damascenes amongst whom his family was highly regarded. His social position meant that he could expect a degree of support regardless of ideology. Ironically for a Communist, this made him resemble a notable politician of the old school. On the other hand, the Communists sought alliances with other left-wing groups to extend their influence. Once women with a primary school education received the vote, many of them were minded to cast it for the Communists because of their support for women's rights.

Then there was Islamism. The main concern of Islamists was the struggle for a return to the moral roots of Islam, and the fight against the westernisation of society. Their entry into politics was gradual, and initially they backed individual candidates who were known to be supportive of Muslim values. The Muslim Brotherhood had been founded in Egypt in 1928. A Syrian branch was officially set up in 1945/6, but its roots lay in the Islamic benevolent societies and youth movements which dated from the Mandate, some of which now provided the Brotherhood with an organised base. Under its leader Mustafa al-Siba'i, it believed that Islam endorsed no one form of rule, but only general principles which had to be adapted to different times and places. This meant that Muslims could participate freely in democratic politics under a ruler who was elected but upheld the precepts of Islam.[7]

Its programme was based on "trying to revive Islam from its current putrefaction" by means of social reform and "the liberation of Arab and Islamic people from foreign domination".[8] In some respects it differed from its Egyptian parent. There was friction between factions from different Syrian cities, which made the Cairo-focused centralisation that has characterised the Egyptian Brotherhood to this day difficult to copy. It also showed much greater sensitivity to the position of the religious minorities than the Egyptian Brotherhood did with regard to Egypt's Coptic Christian minority.

In both the 1947 and the 1949 elections, Islamist candidates backed by the Brotherhood won three seats.[9] Islamist ministers also entered the cabinet. During the debates over the constitution in 1950, the Islamists failed to win backing for a provision that would make Islam the state religion. In a compromise which the Brotherhood accepted (to the dismay of some Islamic scholars), it was decreed that Islam should be the religion of the head of state, and that Islamic legal reasoning, or Sharia, should be the "main source" of legislation. At the same time the rights of other religious communities were to be explicitly recognised. The Brotherhood's decision to be flexible showed that a moderate Islamist agenda resonated with a substantial section of the public. This was also evidenced by the popularity of the Brotherhood's newspaper in Damascus. A back-handed compliment to its influence came when the authorities suspended its publication for a period in 1947. The government had noted the Brotherhood's arrival as a political player and feared that its influence would increase.[10]

Neither the eccentric nationalism of Antun Sa'ada nor the Communism of Khaled Baqdash would survive as a major player into our own day, but both movements were very influential in the Syria of the late 1940s and 1950s. Islamism, by contrast, has endured and become a very powerful force. However, the ideology that was to take deepest root in Syria and affect the country and its identity the most during the period covered by this chapter was Ba'thism. For most Westerners, Ba'thism conjures up images of the brutality of the Syrian government's forces in the civil war that began in 2011/12 or reports of torture in Ba'thist prisons, to say nothing of the massive suffering caused by the pointless wars started by the Iraqi Ba'thist dictator Saddam Hussein. When the American-led "Coalition Provisional Authority" took charge of Iraq after invading the country in 2003, one of its first acts was to "de-ba'thify" the bureaucracy. This was modelled on, or at least inspired by, the de-Nazification of Germany by the Allied powers at the end of World War II.[11] Ba'thism, in the minds of many Western people, was an evil ideology. To them, drawing comparisons between it and Nazism seemed entirely natural and appropriate.

It therefore comes as something of a surprise today to learn that Michel Aflaq, the thinker behind Ba'thism, was once described by a not necessarily well-disposed analyst as "having a stature that other Arab nationalist writers do not possess".[12] In 1959 Aflaq's admirers were reported in *The Times* as seeing him as "the Ghandi of Arab nationalism". He was, said *The Times* correspondent, "a pale slight man of painful shyness, deep sincerity and debilitatingly frugal habits," who was "working from a modest home which he shares with his mother in Damascus".[13] The word "*ba'th*" means rebirth or resurrection, and this renewal of Arab-ness was Michel Aflaq's aim. It meant the end of lesser loyalties that contradicted this unity, especially sectarian and regional ones. There was an altruism behind this that was aimed at improving society in Syria and all other Arab countries. In the early decades of the Ba'th Party, the 1940s and 1950s, some Ba'thist doctors in Syria devoted their spare time to travelling the countryside operating impromptu free clinics, while there were cases of prosperous party members financing the education of bright sons of peasants.

The story of Ba'thism begins with the friendship between Michel Aflaq and Salah al-Din Bitar when they were students in Paris between 1929 and 1934. They both came from the Damascus suburb of Maydan, which at that time was the southernmost extension of the city's urban area and had grown up around the main road leading out of the city. In Maydan, Muslims, Christians and Druze lived side by side. It was a place where people settled when they came into the city from the countryside for the first time. During the massacres of Christians in 1860, those living in Maydan were not attacked.[14] It was also, as was seen in Chapter Two, an insurgent stronghold during the great rebellion against the Mandate in 1925–7, and suffered dreadfully when it was besieged and pummelled into submission by the French. The links between its corn merchants and the Hawran, where the initial Druze rebellion began, played an important role in the spread of the revolt. It may have been no coincidence that Michel Aflaq and Salah al-Din Bitar were themselves both sons of corn merchants. Maydani merchants had also lost out because of the partition of Greater Syria, and the restrictions the Mandates imposed on trade for Syrians with Palestine and Jordan.

The two young men were already strong nationalists before they went to France, but in Paris they encountered another European idea, socialism. On their return home their eyes were opened to the social problems of Syria. Michel Aflaq related how the politicians who aspired to lead the nation "could not see beyond their family and social interests". He also stated that the two friends also observed how Syrians "were suffering not only from national wounds inflicted by the foreigner but also from social wounds because our society was sunk in ignorance and falsehood. We then understood that the struggle against the foreigner had to be waged by the people as a whole."[15] On another occasion, he wrote that colonialism was "an effect rather than a cause: an effect of the deficiencies and distortions in our society".[16]

Back in Syria, they both taught at the Tajhiz, the elite government secondary school for boys in Damascus. Salah al-Din Bitar became the movement's organiser, while Michel Aflaq developed its ideology.[17] He formulated three goals for the movement: unity, freedom and socialism, and coloured them with a particular tinge which reflected the lived experience of Arabs. As regards unity, the physical boundaries between the Arab countries were artificial and had frequently been imposed by foreigners. The Arabs must therefore rise up and abolish them so that Arab civilisation could flourish and renew itself. As regards freedom, Ba'thism preached personal freedom:

freedom of speech, assembly and belief, as well as the freedom of artistic expression. But when placed alongside unity and socialism, Aflaq was thinking primarily of freedom from foreign domination. It was therefore closely connected with unity.

His conception of Arab socialism was rather different from the materialist socialism and Marxism of Europe which he had encountered in Paris, the struggle of the dispossessed proletariat which was, by its very nature, hostile to nationalist sentiment. For Michel Aflaq, socialism was like a stream that mingles with nationalism. The Arab people have to join together in a vision of unity. This would be the source of their socialism, while the vision this socialism gave them was essential in order to enable unity to be achieved. Unity, freedom and socialism were so intertwined that they were inseparable from each other. Their attainment was a spiritual quest.[18] The salvation for the Arab people lay in love for each other, for the Arab nation as a whole, and for its land. This led him to proclaim that "nationalism is love before everything else".[19] He envisaged not just a political revolution but a revolution in the Arab soul.

He maintained that it is impossible to be a true Arab without acknowledging and taking pride in Islam as the supreme achievement of the Arabs as a people. He held that nationalism, "like religion ... flows from the heart and issues from the will of God; they walk arm in arm, supporting each other, especially when religion represents the genius of the nationality and is in harmony with its nature."[20] This idea of Aflaq's is particularly interesting, since he was an Orthodox Christian who saw no contradiction in this view of Islam for non-Muslim Arabs like himself.[21] He and Bitar (a Sunni Muslim) were very conscious of the sectarian and other divisions which were running sores in Syrian society and which, as we have seen, the French had used to full advantage in order to divide and rule. They were therefore intensely hostile to interference by religion in politics and to all discrimination based on religion.

There were, however, problems at the very heart of Ba'thist ideology. Article one of its Constitution, which was adopted in 1947, provided that "the Arab homeland is an indivisible political and economic unit. No region of it may complete the conditions for its life in isolation from the other(s)."[22] Each Arab country was thus merely a region of the wider

Arab homeland. It therefore had its "regional committee" which was the body organising the Ba'th within its territory. Above the regional committees was a "national committee" headed by Aflaq himself, the supreme governing organ of Ba'thism in the entire Arab world. It was through coordination of the regional parties by the national party that Arab unification was to be achieved. There was certainly nothing wrong with a political party fighting for such an ideal in democratic elections. However, within a couple of years democracy would begin to be replaced in Syrian politics by periods of military rule, and the Ba'thists would be fighting for their ideals in governments which had not been elected. Aflaq's ideology was a revolutionary one: it envisaged overthrowing the existing order, not merely a gradualist and piecemeal approach.[23] As time passed, the Ba'thists would put means before ends, and would employ coercion in the way they went about trying to achieve their ideals. Ba'thism also raised other questions: what was the position of Arabs who did not wish to take part in the unity for which the Ba'thists strove? And what did it have to offer to Kurds and other groups in Syria which did not consider themselves Arab? The answer to both questions would be a stark choice between allowing themselves to be co-opted and being subjected to repression.

Michel Aflaq and Salah al-Din Bitar were not the only idealists in Syria in the period immediately after independence who cared about the poor, the selfishness of the elite and the backwardness of society. In the parliament elected in 1943, one solitary deputy did not come from a notable family and was not an independent elected to represent vested local interests. At the age of thirty-one, he was also by far the youngest member of parliament and stood out because of his relatively humble background. This was Akram Hourani, the son of a Hama weaver who was a Sufi sheikh. This city and the countryside around it were dominated by a handful of extremely wealthy landowning families.

After taking a law degree in Damascus, he returned home and, to-gether with a cousin, soon set up a movement to fight for the rights of peasants. He was radicalised further in 1942 when the daughter of a member of one of the town's three richest families was murdered by her cousin in what was portrayed as an honour killing, but was in reality a successful attempt to gain her inheritance. Hourani was legal counsel for the victim's father. He was able to show from the autopsy that the girl had been a virgin and therefore had not been engaged in a clandestine affair, but the court still acquitted the cousin.[24] It was a case study of how the judicial process had been corrupted by the reluctance of the judges to convict a member of one of the town's most powerful families.

At election time, every landlord would expect his tenants to vote for his chosen candidate. Akram Hourani challenged this and travelled the villages to tell the peasants that they were free to make their own choice. On the last night of the election campaign, the crowd that applauded him began chanting "Fetch the basket and the shovel to bury the *agha* and the *bey*." *Agha* and *bey* were two titles of honour used by large landowners, who expected their tenants to address them with due deference. Riots and violence followed.[25] Pressure was put on him to withdraw his candidacy, but he refused and won a seat in parliament where he instantly proved an energetic campaigner. One of his first targets for attack was the continuation of the subsidies the French had paid to tribal chiefs as a reward for loyalty. Surely, he argued, this was incompatible with the new, democratic Syria where all should be citizens equal before the law? He also noted, pragmatically, how these same chiefs worked hand in glove with his enemies, the rural landlords, and bolstered the latter's power. His campaign was successful, and the special regime governing the Bedouin tribes was abolished.

When the first election after independence was fought in July 1947, an alliance on the left was formed which included Hourani and the Ba'thists, as well as Communists and others. They won a total of thirty-three seats, and there were an additional twenty opposition deputies. Shukri al-Quwwatli's National Party only won twenty-four but he was able to survive with support from independents. He was able to force through a constitutional amendment which would enable him to stand for a second term as president. The old elite had reasserted itself, and Shukri al-Quwwatli was now its representative. Politics would remain business as usual, and the scramble for monopolies and commissions granted to those with a cosy relationship with government – the normal business of politics in Syria – would continue.

III

In 1947, Britain decided to renounce its Mandate in Palestine and turn the matter over to the United Nations. In November 1947, the United Nations General Assembly resolved to partition Palestine into Jewish and Arab states, although because of their immense religious significance Jerusalem and Bethlehem were to be made a special area over which no one would have sovereignty. All Arab states voted against the resolution. The UN partition resolution itself had no legal effect, save for the fact that it terminated the British Mandate, but it set in train a series of events that would be catastrophic for the Arab people of Palestine. The Palestinian Jewish community, the *Yishuv*, was overwhelmingly composed of immigrants from Europe, many of them refugees from Hitler's Germany and the lands of the Holocaust. Genocide had wiped out communities that dated back centuries, killing a total of six million people. Among the survivors, many Jews who had hitherto had no Zionist sympathies fled to Palestine after other countries – including Britain and the USA – shut their doors. Most of the *Yishuv* had little understanding of or sympathy with Arab culture, and their leadership rejected Arab suggestions of a single state in which the Jewish minority would be granted specific rights. Trust on both sides had broken down, and Palestine descended into chaos as the British prepared to depart and a civil war between Jews and Arabs became inevitable. The Jewish state of Israel was proclaimed on 14 May 1948 but it was not a viable proposition unless it also seized territory allocated for the putative Arab state. No Arab state was proclaimed, and the suggested procedures contained in the partition resolution to establish the two states jointly were quietly forgotten.[26]

It was, in reality, impossible to establish a Jewish state in Palestine without evicting a large part, very probably the majority, of the native Arab Muslim and Christian population. No plebiscite was held on the question of partition, and the passing of the UN resolution led directly to war. Initially, local bands of Arab rebels attempted to cut the roads to Jewish traffic and to rekindle the 1936 rebellion. In the early months of 1948, before the Mandate had even ended, the Zionist militias began seizing control over as much of the country as they could. Unprepared, uncoordinated and badly led, Palestinian society quite simply collapsed.[27] Large numbers of Palestinians fled, encouraged by Zionist militias which often cleansed whole areas. Once Israel declared itself a sovereign state, Syria had no moral alternative to sending its army to intervene – on humanitarian grounds as well as for strategic reasons and for national pride – but it did not have the means to do so effectively.

The Syrian army was in no state to fight a war. President al-Quwwatli saw the military as a potential threat to his own position. In Iraq, the army had entered politics soon after the country became formally independent in 1932. In 1936, General Bakr Sidqi staged a coup in Baghdad in favour of his preferred nominee as prime minister but was executed in a counter-coup a year later. These two coups did not overthrow Iraq's constitutional order, but subverted it. From that point on, elected Iraqi politicians had to look over their shoulders at powerful figures in the army who soon built up their own power bases in the wider country. It was quite understandable for President al-Quwwatli to fear the same might happen one day in Syria.

Under the French, the purpose of the military had not been external defence but internal control of the country. After independence, President al-Quwwatli was mindful of the dangers it posed to his rule. When he realised it was too difficult to reform it in the short term, he began to reduce the size of the army (down to 6,000–7,000 men from 30,000 under the French). He was reluctant to see it acquire new weapons until he had restructured it and assured himself of its loyalty. In the meantime, he preferred it to be weak, corrupt and incompetent.[28] He was also well aware that the notable class was poorly represented in the officer corps and that the French had preferred to recruit, whenever possible, from minority groups and rural populations in which nationalist sentiment was weaker.

Beyond the question of the army's loyalty lay a wider concern: the threat to Syria posed by its Arab neighbours. The result was that, for its president, his main enemy was Jordan, not the Jewish *Yishuv* in Palestine or the shortly to be proclaimed state of Israel. This was despite the shared anger of Syrians and Jordanians at what the Zionist militias were inflicting on the Palestinian Arabs – something that Syria, a parliamentary democracy, could not ignore because of the pressure of public opinion. If the army of King Abdullah of Jordan entered Syria it might be welcomed by sympathisers – not least by many senior officers in the Syrian army who favoured King Abdullah's brand of conservative Arab nationalism.

There was also a degree of support for him in the wider country and some newspapers even supported a monarchist movement. The Druze of the Hawran, including Sultan al-Atrash, the now venerable old warrior who had led the 1925 rebellion and was perhaps Syria's greatest national hero, supported him. They were strategically close to the Jordanian border. What if they marched on Damascus as they had done in 1925, but this time under King Abdullah's banner? In August 1947, following the Syrian elections, King Abdullah even called in a radio broadcast for a constituent assembly to be established to plan the unification of Jordan, Syria and Iraq. He followed it up with a letter to President al-Quwwatli and every newly elected Syrian parliamentarian.

President al-Quwwatli supported the establishment of a volunteer Arab Liberation Army to fight in Palestine, but it soon became clear that it stood no chance against the militias of the *Yishuv*. The truth was that the Arab Liberation Army was created for two ulterior objectives: to stop the Jordanian army occupying the parts of northern Palestine allocated to the Palestinian Arabs in the UN partition plan, and to ward King Abdullah off from Syria. Once Israel declared its independence, President al-Quwwatli was forced to commit the Syrian army, but he still looked nervously over his shoulder at King Abdullah. This meant he opposed peace moves with Israel which would have benefited the king's position. In the fighting in Palestine, the Syrian army never tried to do more than take a few Zionist settlements around the Sea of Galilee and the marshes to the north. By the time of the final ceasefire, it was in occupation of merely 66.5 square kilometres of Palestinian soil.[29]

The consequences were all too predictable. Fiery speeches by politicians had led the public to expect an easy victory over the Zionists.

Now Syrians were enraged by the suffering of their kin in Palestine, and soon learned about it at first hand from the starving refugees who flooded across the border with their stories of Israeli war crimes and dispossession. Martial law had to be imposed in response to riots, strikes and demonstrations. The Syrian Jewish community suffered as a result. The community was one of the longest established in the world and was Arabic-speaking. It was approximately 30,000 strong, and was concentrated in Damascus and Aleppo where synagogues were now attacked by mobs. Following Israeli seizure of the property of Palestinians in December 1948, restrictions were placed on Jews moving within Syria. Jewish bank accounts were frozen and real estate transactions banned. Over the following decades, life became very uncomfortable for Syrian Jews. When they had the chance, they emigrated until the community was reduced to around 5,000 by the early 1970s.[30] It would disappear virtually in its entirety before the year 2000.

The army felt humiliated by the politicians who had sent it off to fight with inadequate equipment and supplies. Army officers were also enraged by being made the scapegoats for the disaster. The situation was aggravated by a trial of strength between President al-Quwwatli and the head of the army, Colonel Husni Zaim, over the president's demand for the arrest of an officer close to Colonel Zaim over a scandal involving the supply of sub-standard cooking fat.[31]

On 30 March 1949, troops occupied key positions in Damascus. The president was arrested and sent into exile. Although no blood was shed, the conspirators went one stage further than their Iraqi counterparts had done in 1936. Colonel Husni Zaim installed himself as head of state.

IV

Husni Zaim was of Kurdish origins. He had been a soldier in the Ottoman army and had subsequently served in the French forces during the Mandate, but was discharged by the Free French who believed he had received funds from Vichy. He may have been more fluent in French than in Arabic. President Quwwatli had been persuaded to reinstate him, and was therefore completely taken aback by his treachery.

A shadowy aspect of the story of the coup is the role of the American Embassy in Damascus and the fledgling US Central Intelligence Agency, which had been established in 1947. The Americans were displeased with the Syria of Shukri al-Quwwatli. At the time of the coup, Syria had still not signed an armistice with Israel, although all other frontline Arab states had done so, and was refusing to permit the construction of a pipeline carrying Saudi Arabian oil to cross its territory. The CIA officer in Damascus at the time, Miles Copeland, claims in his book *Game of Nations* that he reported to his superiors that it was necessary to find an officer who would be prepared to "take unpopular decisions" such as making peace with Israel. He stated baldly, "the only kind of leader who can acquire such power is one who deeply desires power for the mere sake of it. Husni al-Zaim was power crazy."[32]

The Americans certainly knew that Colonel Zaim was plotting his takeover because he told them in advance, but there is debate as to whether they were actually involved. What is certain is that they were surprised and very pleased when he said that he wanted to make peace with Israel, and equally delighted when he handed them a list of Communists in the army. Colonel Zaim told Major Meade, an assistant attaché at the American Embassy, that he envisaged a four-stage plan for taking over Syria and bringing it close to the USA. In the first stage, he would install a figurehead as president but exercise real power himself as minister of defence. The USA would then, in the second stage, provide Syria with aid. This would help to legitimise his coup in the eyes of the people. In the third stage, the USA would supply the Syrians with modern weapons. In the final stage, he would expand the army and reform Syria, taking the Turkish leader Kemal Atatürk as his role model.

Meade reported back to Washington and commented, "although unscrupulous, bombastic and a complete egoist, it must be admitted that he has a strong personality, unlimited ambition and the backing of the Syrian army. If the ever-present element of fate happens to be in his favour, Zaim may realise his desire to be dictator in Syria."[33] On another occasion, Meade described him as "a 'banana republic' dictator type".[34] Husni Zaim certainly had a vainglorious side. He promoted himself to *Maréchal* and wore a magnificent uniform complete with a baton which cost $3,000 – a princely sum in 1949.[35] He was headstrong in pushing through policies which met resistance in the country. A poor politician, he antagonised many of those who had encouraged him to carry out his coup. Unsurprisingly, some wonder if he had no real programme except personal aggrandisement.[36]

That said, many of his actions were positive. He gave civil servants ten days to choose between their government jobs and their business interests. He also secretly made his offer of peace to Israel. This offer included full normalisation of relations and the settlement by Syria of 250,000 or 300,000 dispossessed Palestinians on its soil – many more than the 85,000 who had already fled to Syria. If knowledge of this had become public in Syria, it would have caused outrage and it is doubtful whether he would have had the political strength to push it through. However, he never needed to inform the Syrian public because David Ben Gurion, the Israeli prime minister, rejected it. Israel refused to negotiate peace until an armistice had been signed. In exchange for agreeing to this, it insisted on a Syrian withdrawal from small areas of the former Mandate of Palestine which had been under Syrian occupation at the time of the ceasefire.[37] In other words, Israel – the stronger party militarily – was demanding a concession which would weaken Syria's bargaining position as a condition for entering into peace negotiations.

Husni Zaim's coup marked the beginning of a new era in Syrian politics. As in Iraq, the views of the military top brass now mattered. Some, like the veteran nationalist Faris al-Khury, were plunged into despair by the army's assumption of power. Khury, a constitutional expert and founding member of the National Bloc, was speaker of parliament at the time. Military rule reminded him of the shredding of the equally fragile Ottoman constitutional order in the years leading up to the Great War. Others, however, had been unimpressed by the performance of the elected politicians. This category included such figures as Akram Hourani and Michel Aflaq. These two radicals had become popular among young people who were the first generation in their families to receive a modern education.

The coup was just the first of three that year. On 14 August, less than four and a half months after his seizure of power, Husni Zaim was arrested in his pyjamas at home early in the morning. He was beaten up and subsequently shot. His overthrow seems to have had nothing to do with his attempt to make peace. The group of officers in the army who had deposed him were members of Antun Sa'ada's Syrian National Party, and were acting in revenge for the death of their leader who had been executed by the Lebanese authorities after launching a guerrilla campaign to overthrow the Lebanese state. These officers held Husni Zaim responsible because he had delivered Antun Sa'ada into Lebanese hands. Their leader, Colonel Sami Hinnawi, intended to restore the constitutional order. He organised elections for a constituent assembly but on 19 December, only a week after the assembly had met for the first time, he was overthrown in his turn by another colonel. This was Adib Shishakli who would rule Syria until February 1954, a period of over four years.

For most of that time, Shishakli chose to keep himself in the background and work through a nominee as president. The politicians knew they could not challenge him, and that he would tell them what to do when he considered it necessary. His rule was thus initially indirect, but he set the direction of the country and was its de facto dictator. He gave Syrians their first real taste of extended military rule. Initially he was popular, especially with younger army officers whom he took pains to cultivate. He built up the armed forces. Initially reduced to 7,000 men by President Quwwatli, the size of the army was increased to 18,000 during the Palestine war. Husni Zaim had raised the strength to 31,500 during his brief rule, while Adib Shishakli increased it to 43,000 by the end of 1951.[38] What had happened in Palestine had shown this was necessary, to say nothing of potential threats from Turkey, Jordan or Iraq. He bought new military equipment from France and intended to diversify Syria's sources of supply when this became possible. Officers were sent to be trained in France, Britain, the USA, West Germany and Italy.

But the modern, mechanised army he constructed was not just for external defence. It was also intended to prevent local rebellion in Syria itself. No longer could bands of tribesmen brandishing rifles swoop down on Damascus and try to bend the government to their will. Shishakli set out to unify Syria, trying to flatten any regional or local sentiment. State controls were extended over foreign schools, and he discouraged minority ethnic and religious groups having their own separate scouting associations or sporting clubs. The sale of land to foreigners was prohibited, and he refused to accept American aid as a matter of principle.

Akram Hourani and the Ba'thists saw the coups of 1949 as opening up opportunities to prise the right to rule away from the patrician, notable class. The interim government formed after Hinnawi's coup was dominated by the Aleppo-based People's Party, but it also included Michel Aflaq as minister of education (because of his influence with university students) and Akram Hourani as minister of agriculture (because of his influence with the peasantry). Like Hourani, Shishakli was from Hama and the two had known each other as boys. They had also fought together in Palestine in 1947–9. Hourani denied involvement in the coup which brought Shishakli to power, but they were both opposed to a movement to unite the country with Iraq. This was advocated by the People's Party and was backed by merchants in Aleppo who would have welcomed it, as well as deputies from the landlord class who saw no problem joining with their Iraqi counterparts under a pro-British monarchy which would preserve their positions.

Adib Shishakli seized power to make sure that this did not happen. At first, the two men got on well, almost as comrades. Akram Hourani proceeded to build a peasants' movement in the countryside around Hama which transcended sectarian boundaries. He notched up a number of successes. The old tobacco monopoly, which had been inherited from French days and effectively reduced some peasants to a form of slavery, was abolished. A maximum size was decreed for landholdings, with the balance to be distributed to destitute peasants. But then, as Adib Shishakli became increasingly authoritarian, the two parted company.

This brought Akram Hourani and the Ba'thist leaders close. They united their political parties in 1952 to create the Arab Socialist Ba'th

Party. The urban activism of the Ba'th, which had been particularly successful among intellectuals and students who came from a rural background, was now joined with Akram Hourani's rural base around Hama. They had much in common. Hourani had returned from the Palestine war with the conviction that the antiquated Arab social order was the root cause of the disaster. He linked the struggle to emancipate the peasants with the struggle to unite the Arab people, and encouraged his followers of humble origin to enrol in the military academy at Homs. Like Michel Aflaq and Salah al-Din Bitar, he believed firmly that politics should be secular. He was well aware how some Sunni Muslim preachers were used by landlords to stir up antipathy to reforms. Now, however, instead of fighting for their policies in a parliamentary democracy, the three men found themselves fleeing to Lebanon together after Adib Shishakli made Syria a one party state in August 1952.

Shishakli fell on 25 February 1954. For months, strikes and demonstrations had been organised against his rule. Secretly encouraged by Iraq, these had begun in Aleppo, and spread quickly to Homs, Hama and even Damascus. At first, it seemed he was succeeding in retaining control. However, when there were demonstrations in the Hawran town of Suwayda, he feared the igniting of an uprising among the Druze like that of 1925. He sent in the army, which used artillery to bombard towns into submission. This brutality may have been his undoing. A military revolt began in Aleppo and spread like wild fire through garrisons across the country, but the initial conspiracy to unseat him had begun among Druze officers in Deir al-Zour.[39] He fled to Beirut, and ended his days in Brazil, where he was assassinated by a Druze in 1964, probably in revenge for the many Druze he had killed during the Hawran crackdown.

Parliamentary rule was restored later that year. The Arab Socialist Ba'th Party became a powerful force during the final period of democratic rule in Syria, which lasted until the union with Egypt in 1958. This period saw further reforms, such as the introduction of the secret ballot which the landlords had resolutely opposed. Yet, even so, the militant nationalists found themselves continually frustrated. The Ba'th and forces allied to it never succeeded in winning a parliamentary majority, while foreign powers continued to meddle. Saudi Arabia, for instance, is widely believed to have supported the successful bid by Shukri al-Quwwatli to return to the presidency in 1955 by providing funds to distribute to parliamentary deputies. Saudi Arabia's rivals, the Hashemite monarchists of Iraq, also continued to plot with Syrian politicians until they themselves were overthrown in a bloody coup in 1958.

V

During these years, the titanic struggle of the Cold War loomed over Syria and its rulers like a dark shadow. America, Western Europe and their allies were pitted against the Soviet Union and its satellites. For America and the Soviet Union, this struggle was existential. Communism was feared in the West above all else. Over the first two decades of the Cold War the old colonial empires melted away. As these empires weakened, freedom would appear to be there for the taking by the peoples they had once ruled – subject to a few noteworthy exceptions such as the Palestinians. But all too often the leaders of these peoples would be distracted from the task of building and developing their nations. While there were frequently flaws in their own leadership, the insistent demands of the powers engaged in the Cold War were also a factor. Those powers were not above engaging in the same kinds of pressure and manipulation as their predecessors, the colonial powers of earlier generations.

Visiting statesmen and resident diplomats from Western countries would harangue Syrian leaders about the dangers of Soviet Communism. They would argue that Russian forces might one day smash their way through Turkey and Iran to the Mediterranean and the Indian Ocean, and thereby achieve dominance over the Arab countries. They would also point out the risk of Communist subversion from within. On the whole Syrian leaders were probably bemused as they listened to this hectoring. They had other, much more pressing, concerns. The issues that preoccupied them were building a state and their people's sense of nationhood, and the larger issue of what shape the Arab world should take. This, they felt, was something to be decided by themselves, not the outside powers. But, as in earlier generations, outside forces would not allow them to do so unconstrained.

By 1951, officials from the members of the NATO alliance were visiting Arab countries trying to muster support against the Soviet threat. The first requests may have sounded reasonable enough to a Western ear. In Syria, they asked for the use of transport facilities in the event of war between the Western powers and the Soviet Bloc. Yet the fact that the requests were even made shows just how badly attuned the Americans, British, French and others were to the concerns of public opinion in an Arab country like Syria. Not only was the freedom of the Arab world from the colonial powers far from complete, but the urgent Arab need for defence against Israel and the demand for the restoration of Palestinian rights were completely overlooked when such requests were made. By no stretch of the imagination could America be described as even handed in its treatment of Israel and its Arab neighbours. During the period 1948–53, US aid to Israel reached $250 million, while all Arab countries combined only received $108 million.[40]

American politicians, no doubt chasing votes but genuinely mesmerised by an inspiring narrative of the creation of Israel, frequently praised the Jewish state in a way that swept the darker aspects of its history under the carpet. They could also, by either accident or design, be disparaging towards Israel's Arab neighbours when they did so. A good example was US Vice-President Barkeley's reference to Israel as "an oasis of liberty in the desert of oppression" in 1950.[41] This triggered massive anti-American demonstrations in Damascus organised by the Ba'thists, Muslim Brotherhood and Communists.

At this time Egypt was descending into a state of chaos. When suggestions were made to the Egyptian government that the British bases along the Suez Canal should be turned over to NATO, this was seen as adding insult to injury. Cairo adopted a policy of neutralism between East and West, but this did not save King Farouq's monarchy.

A coup by a group of army officers took control of the country in 1952 and restored order. Colonel Nasser, who emerged as the new leader of Egypt, had ideals of Arab unity which dovetailed in many respects with Ba'thism. He saw unity arising spontaneously through an instinctive sense of solidarity as the Arabs threw off the shackles of foreign rule. In 1954, he succeeded where all his predecessors had failed and negotiated a treaty with Britain under which British troops finally left Egyptian soil – although Britain retained the right for them to return in time of war.

In February 1955, a military pact was signed in Baghdad between Britain, Turkey, Iran, Pakistan and Iraq. Known as the Baghdad Pact, it was a kind of eastward extension of NATO to prevent Soviet penetration of the Middle East. The USA did not join but, in the words of the official historian of the US Department of State, it "signed individual agreements with each of the nations in the pact" and "participated as an observer and took part in committee meetings". But the pact had another objective which had little to do with Communism directly. On a very important level, it was an attempt by Britain in conjunction with its protégé, Hashemite Iraq, to recover some of the influence it had lost in the Middle East since its ignominious departure from Palestine. The Iraqi prime minister, Nuri Said, hoped to use it as a vehicle to make Iraq, rather than Egypt, the leader of the Arab world. Pressure was now applied for Syria and other Arab countries to join.

But time was running out, and it was soon too late for the West to bring Syria into its camp. Joining the alliance would have been a poisoned chalice for any ruler of Styria, as was the acceptance of American aid. American offers of arms were conditional on them not being used in a war with Israel, even though Israel was perceived by Syria as the aggressor who posed a major threat. The point of no return, as far as the battle for Syrian public opinion was concerned, was Israel's raid on Egyptian occupied Gaza on 28 February 1955 in which forty Egyptian soldiers were killed. Israel had taken advantage of its military superiority to humiliate Nasser. This led him to exclaim angrily to his aides, "We need arms at any cost, even from the devil himself!"[42] After the Americans refused his request, he turned to the Communist Bloc and received Egypt's first shipment of Soviet arms from Czechoslovakia in July 1955. The arrival of modern weapons in Egypt was greeted ecstatically in Syria. In October, Syria followed suit and signed a defence pact with Egypt. In April 1956, Egyptian troops were invited to join their Syrian colleagues for the march past in Damascus to celebrate the tenth anniversary of the final French withdrawal, and the Ba'th Party called for a full union between the two countries. This was a call that would steadily grow louder.

Two tugs of war were now taking place over Syria: the fight for supremacy within the Arab world between Egypt and Iraq, and the struggle of the Western powers to keep Communist Bloc influence out of the Middle East. Over the spring and summer of 1956, Iraq, with backing from America and Britain, encouraged exiled Syrian politicians and army officers to mount a coup. The attempts failed, to a large extent because the ambitions of the groups plotting against the Syrian government were too disparate and self-serving to be effective. They were also infiltrated by the Syrian intelligence services. Their failure exposed important political figures in Syria who were sympathetic to the West as traitors, and cemented the stance that Syria would henceforth adopt.[43]

In July, America retaliated against Egypt for its purchase of Soviet arms by refusing finance for the high dam at Aswan, which was Egypt's most important development project at the time. In response, Nasser nationalised the Suez Canal to raise the money and faced down the combined might of Britain and France, which were the major shareholders in the company that ran it. Together with Israel, the two powers invaded Egypt in October/November 1956 in an attempt to overthrow him, but were forced into humiliating withdrawals by American pressure at the United Nations.

This huge diplomatic success made Nasser the hero of radical Arab nationalists everywhere. He was already one of the leaders of the emerging Afro-Asian bloc of nations. He demanded that all Arab countries should adopt a position of neutrality between the USA and Western Europe, on the one hand, and the Soviet Bloc on the other. In Syria, this was music to the ears of Ba'thists and other radicals. Syrians saw the officers who now ran Egypt as having much in common with their own young officers, who were now rising up the ranks of the army and often engaging in politics. Like their Syrian counterparts, the Egyptian officers were fiercely patriotic. They were frustrated at the failure of their country's *ancien régime* and its elected politicians to reform and modernise. They were also vitriolic in their attitude to the Western imperialism which they saw as a prime cause for their country's retardation and its inability to save Palestine in 1948.

Syria's increasing closeness to the Egypt of Nasser was matched by an opening of the country to Eastern Bloc influence. The West was now paying the price for playing the role of Israel's "banker and armourer".[44] This was the time when Soviet penetration of Syria began in earnest. In August 1956, full diplomatic relations between Syria and the USSR were established for the first time. The following month, seventeen Soviet cabinet ministers toured Syria, even visiting people in their villages where they were given the chance to talk about their Communist ideology. Substantial arms shipments from the USSR began arriving, including, at long last, proper tanks. They passed cheering crowds as they were driven through villages on their way from Lattakia to Damascus. Syrian officers were soon going to the USSR for military training, rather than to the West as had previously been the case.

The friendship which developed so rapidly between Syria and the Communist Bloc from the first arms purchase onwards made America and Britain look at Syria with increasingly hostile eyes. Both powers feared that the Communists would do increasingly well in Syrian elections; they also had influential supporters in the armed forces. This fear demonstrated the gap that had opened up between Syria and the West, since each side had different views of what constituted a threat to security. For America and Britain, security in the Middle East involved keeping the area free of Communism and Soviet influence. For Arabs, on the other hand, it was primarily about liberating themselves from foreign domination, defending themselves against Israel and restoring the rights of the Palestinians, although the strength and cohesion of Turkey also cast a shadow.

American rhetoric described Syria as about to become a Soviet satellite. This caused America to lose the substantial goodwill it had acquired when it forced Britain and France to withdraw from Egypt during the Suez crisis. American and British intelligence services contemplated elaborate schemes to provide a bogus pretext for military intervention by Iraq, Jordan and Turkey in Syria. One idea was to arrange sabotage actions in Jordan, Iraq and Lebanon and border incidents, and then blame these on Damascus. Although the plans to overthrow the Syrian government never went beyond the design stage, the report in which they were set out was described by the British prime minister, Harold Macmillan, as "formidable".[45] They included the proposed assassination of Khaled Baqdash, the leader of the Syrian Communist Party, as well as the chief of Syrian military intelligence, Colonel Sarraj, and the chief of the general staff, General al-Bizri. These figures were perceived as a triumvirate who were moving Syria closer to Moscow. There were also threatening troop movements by Turkish and Iraqi forces near the Syrian border. The plans backfired and pushed Syria yet further away from the West. Although the crisis was defused by Saudi mediation, Nasser was able to pull off a master stroke. In October 1957, he sent Egyptian troops to Lattakia to show solidarity with Syria and offer tangible support. The response across Syria was ecstatic.

The talk of uniting with Egypt increased among Syrian politicians and army officers. Ba'thists and others on the self-defined progressive left considered unification to be the logical solution to Syria's dilemmas. On the one hand, Syria's identity was passionately Arab and it seemed right for it to be one of the founding units of what might one day be a state comprising the entire Arab homeland. On the other hand, Syria's experience since independence showed that it needed to be part of a larger unit for its own protection. Finding a majority in the Syrian parliament which would produce a stable government had never been easy and it was becoming ever harder. Now that the officer corps was irrevocably involved in politics, the views of generals and colonels were what really mattered. But the experience of army involvement in politics over nearly a decade had had its own corrosive effect. The officer corps was now fragmented. This was not just on ideological lines. Increasingly, important military figures were building up their own networks within the armed forces. These were composed of the people they could trust as individuals. Inevitably, regional, ethnic, sectarian and similar links made up important parts of these networks, which often reflected the rural roots of many officers.

While the politicians heatedly discussed the possibility of union, coordination on the issue in the Syrian government broke down. Without governmental authorisation, and merely leaving a note behind to tell the government what they were doing, the army chief of staff and a group of top officers flew to Cairo in January 1958 to meet Nasser. As fellow soldiers, they expected to be able to speak a common language of shared attitudes and values. They were also impressed by the position the army now occupied in Egypt, where they admired how Nasser had got rid of the divided, argumentative and frustrating politicians. Syrian officers, however, were also conscious of the rifts among themselves and knew how dangerous their own disunity was. Was not Nasser the ideal person to lead them, rather than risking further military coups, violence and possibly even civil war?

The idea of union had been poorly thought through. In his speech nationalising the Suez Canal in July 1956, Nasser had referred to the Syrian desire for unification as indicating how much the Syrian people supported his action. But now that the suggestion to unite the two states was actually made, he was taken aback. He had never envisaged a political programme to unite the Arabic-speaking peoples into a single state in the way that Bismarck had united Germany or Cavour had united Italy in the nineteenth century. His concept was more of Arab unity based on solidarity and cooperation among Arab states. This was what suited him best. As the ruler of the world's most populous and powerful Arab country, he would inevitably become the leader of the new Arab Bloc which that solidarity and cooperation would create.

Moreover, to Egyptians pan-Arabism was still relatively new. Egypt was the civilisation of the Nile Valley, and as such was one of the most homogenous states in the world, despite its sectarian split between the Muslim majority and the Coptic minority. Its borders were by and large uncontentious lines on the map, most of which ran through often waterless desert. Syria's, by contrast, were bitterly contested and the country was arranged around the competing centres of Damascus, Aleppo and a number of smaller cities. Sharing no frontier, having very diverse economies and physically separated by their arch-enemy, Israel, Egypt and Syria would not find union easy to implement.

Nasser had abolished political parties in Egypt and instituted a non-party national political organisation, the Arab Socialist Union, in their place. He had no intention of allowing the Ba'th, the Communists or any other political party to contest elections. Once the union was consummated, he would ruthlessly do all he could to stamp out Ba'thism and every other competing ideology. Political parties reminded him of the corrupt politics of the old Egyptian parliament before the revolution, which had had much in common with that of the Syrian notables. "I'm an honest and a decent man, so what need have we of parties?"[46] he would ask in all sincerity.

The Ba'thist Salah al-Din Bitar was Syrian foreign minister at this time, and the government despatched him to Cairo to find out what was happening. Like the officers, he had been given no authority to negotiate, but he did so nonetheless – and the actions of a foreign minister when reaching an agreement with another state are binding on his government. Nasser stated his terms and stuck to them. It would be a full union or nothing. Ba'thists were dismayed by the need to dissolve their party, but he tempted them with the idea that they would be able to enter the Arab Socialist Union to represent the people. He promised that they could continue the fight for their ideals within it.

Nasser's magnetism convinced the Syrians who had come to Cairo. When Bitar and the officers returned home, they carried everything before them. Some important figures, such as the minister of finance, had reservations but they could not make their voices heard. The Syrian cabinet cobbled together a suggestion for compromise, but Nasser would have none of it. Unification would be on his terms or not at all. On 1 February 1958, the treaty of union was agreed. Egypt and Syria now became officially the United Arab Republic. The name of the new state was an open-ended invitation for other Arab states to throw off the shackles of foreign domination and rule by their old elites, and to join. Syria ceased to be an independent state and member of the United Nations. Instead, it officially became the Northern Region of the United Arab Republic (the UAR).

This was the real end of Syrian democracy and of the old Ba'th Party. The disorderly democratic politics of Syria over the last few years had revealed strains in the party which may have persuaded Michel Aflaq that its dissolution was acceptable. It was the price for what he hoped would be a massive victory for Ba'thism's ideals. He may also have been conscious that the party had failed to win a single general election, and thus he saw the union as the best way to put its ideals into practice. The Ba'thist leaders had become accustomed to acting without consulting the membership, and the party was riven by factions. Many of those who had followed Akram Hourani into the party, for instance, remained at heart loyal to him personally as their leader, and had never become fully integrated into the new compound party. Now Aflaq went ahead and approved the union on his own initiative without calling a party conference to discuss it.

Other figures who might, perhaps, have been expected to oppose the union chose not to do so. Faris al-Khury, the highly respected veteran nationalist and liberal politician who had been appalled when Husni Zaim overthrew the constitutional order, was now in retirement. He supported the union. He felt there was no alternative and feared that, without it, Syria might indeed fall into the hands of the Communists. For anti-Communists, the union turned out to be beneficial. Nasser abolished the Communist Party along with all other political parties, and the Syrian Communists never recovered.

The story of Syrian politics in the period from independence to 1958 is the tale of a three-way clash. In one corner of the triangle was the established, ideology-free political class that had finally evicted the French. In the second were the new movements that dreamed of transforming society, of which Ba'thism was by far the most significant. The third corner was occupied by the army. Bit by bit, the old notable politicians lost out. The ideologically based parties took part in democratic politics, but they also recruited army officers who would use their positions of power in attempts to transform the nation. The officers would be the ones who ultimately came out on top.

As one Arab observer put it in 1958, "the Arab officer class has become the repository of self-conscious political power at a time when the traditional ruling class is bankrupt, the other growing forces and trends have not crystallised, and the general masses positively look to this class as a saviour."[47] This was particularly the case in Syria. The officers exemplified a brave new world. It was hoped that modern education, not privilege and the culture of deference which the age-old culture of patronage had engendered, would transform the nation in a way of which previous generations could only dream.

VI

Syrians soon found that the emotionally driven and hasty union had led to their country's absorption into a much larger entity dominated by the overbearing personality of Nasser. Egypt had a population four or five times that of Syria. It also had the Suez Canal and the River Nile. And it was already a leader of the Afro-Asian Bloc which aimed to represent the swelling number of new nations which were receiving their independence from the old colonial powers. Even without Nasser, Egyptian dominance was inevitable. As we have seen, the leaders of Syria had thrust the union onto him. His own instinct had been that union would require five years' preparation if it was to stick and be effective. This political union with another Arab state was a completely new departure for him, but he could not be seen to oppose it and quickly grasped the possible benefits. Vast numbers of people across the Arab world who listened to his radio station *Voice of the Arabs* responded to the union with enthusiasm. The hero of Suez who had ended the British role in Egypt and humiliated the imperial pretensions of Britain and France had now taken the first, tangible step to reunite the Arab world.

As the two states merged, Shukri al-Quwwatli, who had supported a federal union but had ultimately gone with the flow, ceased to be president of Syria. He was given the imposing yet meaningless official title of "First Arab Citizen". Two of the new United Arab Republic's four vice-presidents were Syrians (one was Akram Hourani), and it was intended that the national assembly of the UAR would be composed of 600 members, 400 from Egypt and 200 from Syria. Syria seemed to be well represented, arguably disproportionately so, but it soon became clear that this was a facade. All real decisions were taken by Nasser, and the Syrian members of the new state's leadership found themselves pampered in Cairo but cut off from their political bases. A close associate of Nasser's, General Abdul Hakim Amer, was installed in Damascus to run the Northern Region of the United Arab Republic. He was assisted by Colonel Sarraj, the former Syrian chief of military intelligence who was now minister of the interior of the Northern Region of the UAR. The enthusiasm for the union soon waned. Syrians who had positions which should have enabled them to wield power, such as the Ba'thists Salah al-Din Bitar and Akram Hourani, resigned. Colonel Sarraj eventually did so as well.

Before unification, the state was little involved in the Syrian economy, although there had been signs over the last few years that this might change. The French railways and utilities had been nationalised, and a World Bank report in 1954 had recommended major investment in agriculture and in transport – particularly a major expansion of the port of Lattakia. Most of the recommendations were implemented. In the first ten years or so of independence, the Syrian merchant communities, especially those of Aleppo, had much to be proud of. Private finance had carried out major land reclamation schemes in the valleys of the Euphrates and other rivers, and had also helped extend the cultivation of rain-fed cereals on Syria's eastern plains. This had transformed Syrian agriculture, giving the country a sizeable income from cereal exports and rendering the old corn-growing area of the Hawran uneconomic.

During the union with Egypt, by contrast, the state would interfere in an unprecedented way and follow policies which were being pioneered in Egypt. An attempt was made to reform the ownership of agricultural land on the Egyptian model: a change that had the ulterior motive of breaking the power of the 3,000 or so landowning families which provided the backbone of the notable class. In 1960 a Ministry of Planning was set up, and Syria was given its first five-year plan. Syrian private banks were included in the nationalisation programme of financial institutions which was getting underway in

Egypt. The old notable class and the business community were now being squeezed until the pips squeaked. They dragged their feet on the land sequestration measures (for instance, by allowing land to lie fallow rather than handing it over for redistribution). They also set out to end the union.

On 28 September 1961, Syrian officers staged a coup in Damascus. They said that they wanted to discuss reforms, but when Nasser refused to negotiate they ended the union. To his credit, when Nasser realised his choice was to seek to maintain the UAR by the use of force, or to reconcile himself to its end, he chose the latter. He said he was speaking "with a broken heart", but would not oppose the re-admission of Syria as a member of the United Nations. National unity in Syria, he said, should be the first priority of the new state.

VII

The officers who staged the 1961 coup were conservatively minded Damascenes who had the support of the business community. They also had the external backing of Jordan and Saudi Arabia, who were united by the threat which Nasser and radical Arab nationalism posed to the remaining monarchies in the Arab world. Some officers with suspected Ba'thist leanings were cashiered and transferred to bureaucratic jobs where they would not command troops. Elections were held on 1 December, and these produced an old-style parliament. This was the last gasp of the city notables who had run Syria under the Ottomans, who had led the independence struggle against the French, and who controlled parliament in the early years of independence.

Nasser did not forgive the "secessionist regime". He tried to undermine it with radio broadcasts and the other means of propaganda available to him, while his agents infiltrated the country and distributed largesse in the same way that other countries had always done whenever they tried to subvert Syria. While the Ba'th and other political parties attempted to revive their suppressed organisations, the country wobbled and lurched once again from crisis to crisis. In early 1962 a coup attempt was followed by a counter-coup, and then on 8 March 1963 a group of officers which included Ba'thists, Nasserists and independents took power. The Ba'thists were members of a secret military committee which had been formed by Syrians in Cairo who had been frustrated at the way Nasser had acted as a dictator. They were still committed to the idea of Arab unity and wanted to discuss with Egypt how the union between the two countries could be rebuilt, but this time in a way that would not merely make Syria a dependency of its larger partner. Syrian Nasserists, on the other hand, were prepared to restore the union with Egypt on the original terms dictated by Nasser. Of these groups, the Ba'thists soon came to dominate.

The coup of 8 March 1963 sounded the death knell of Syria's *ancien régime* and the end of the domination of the country by the Sunni notable families. But there were disturbing consequences for Ba'thism as an ideology when the Ba'th Party actually gained real power. Sami al-Jundi, a founding member of the party and now the minister of information, revealed these in a book published in 1969:

> Three days after my entering the Ministry [after the 8 March coup], the [party] comrades came to ask me for an extensive purge operation ... The measure of a minister's success [was determined by] the lists of dismissals, since party members as well as their relatives and the members of their tribes [came to] demand their campaign and kinship rights. From the time the party appeared on the stage, caravans of villagers started to leave the villages of the plains and mountains for Damascus. And while [rural accents] started to predominate in the streets, coffee houses and the waiting rooms of ministries, dismissals became a duty so that [those who had newly come] could be appointed.[48]

The Ba'th had chosen to override the elected politicians in government. Its revolutionary fervour had triumphed over its support for democracy. Now that power had been attained, the placing of relatives, friends and people who came from the same small town or belonged to the same tribe or sect in government jobs was a further step away from the party's founding ideals.

The countryside and the lower middle class now supplanted the old urban elite. The new arrivals included large numbers of Sunnis – especially among those who came from "the plains"– but many of those who got onto buses or climbed on the back of a pick-up truck to make the gleeful journey to Damascus and cash in their debt of obligation were Alawis, Christians, Druze or Ismailis. Minorities were displacing the Sunni majority in their influence. At the same time, many people now given positions in the bureaucracy were ill-equipped for their roles. Those placed in government departments dealing with commerce, for instance, often had little comprehension of private enterprise, and some of them felt hostile towards it because of the Marxist or socialist ideas they had absorbed. The foundations of the legendarily impenetrable bureaucracy that was almost to strangle commercial life in Syria had been laid. Meanwhile many were promoted in the army and the civil service because of blood ties to important individuals or friendships. This process, too, led to the disproportionate rise of members of minorities, especially Alawis. As in a Communist revolution, the old order was turned upside down and those who came to power were marked by their bitterness towards it. However, although Syria's friendship with the Soviet Union became closer, Ba'thists now controlled the army. They were Arab nationalists first and foremost, and they made sure that there was never any serious chance of Syria becoming a Soviet satellite.

Ba'thist control was tightened after an abortive Nasserist counter-coup in July 1963, in which gun battles took place in Damascus in broad daylight around the army headquarters and radio station. Several hundred people died in the violence. Afterwards, a further twenty-seven Nasserist officers were hauled before tribunals and summarily shot.[49] There had been no precedent for violence on this scale in any of Syria's previous coup attempts. Ba'thist officers were the rulers of the country, but they were ill-prepared for government. They were also preoccupied with struggles among themselves which they kept out of the public eye and had no thought-through programme for action. For their part, the merchant class detested the officers' left-wing leanings towards nationalisation and state ownership. As in many other authoritarian states, frustration was expressed on the street in demonstrations and riots which led to bloodshed and then repression. Much of Syria's commercial elite and many other talented people began to leave the country.

Taking advantage of widespread discontent, and also of the fact that mosques gave preachers a base for anti-government agitation, crowds took to the streets in many cities under banners attacking the Ba'th as "the enemy of Islam". The 1950s had proved to be difficult years for political Islam in Syria – and elsewhere in the Arab world. Islamists had flirted for a while with an Islamic form of socialism, but faced stiff competition for the socialist constituency from secular left-wing ideologies. The Syrian branch of the Muslim Brotherhood withdrew from party politics in 1954 and took no part in the major political events of the next few years – including the union with Egypt in 1958 and its termination in 1961. When they re-entered politics at the elections of December 1961 they performed well, but their movement had lost any chance of competing with Ba'thism as the dominant ideology in Syria. Now at last, popular discontent presented Islamists with a chance to reassert themselves.

Sunni religious elements organised a wave of demonstrations and shop owners' strikes across the country. The worst troubles were in Hama in 1964, where events turned violent and the army found itself putting down a full-scale uprising after demonstrators killed a Ba'thist activist. The government shelled a mosque in retaliation and a revolutionary militia was set up. The militia proved its worth the following year when opposition to a hastily implemented and rather arbitrary programme of nationalisation led to further strikes organised by merchants and supported by preachers.

An intra-Ba'thist struggle took place in February 1966 in the form of a second bloody coup. The purged included those who had been part of the original "secession" from Egypt and also signalled the end of the influence of the Ba'thist old guard led by Michel Aflaq. Activists in regional centres such as Lattakia and Deir al-Zour had secretly kept local organisations intact during the period of union with Egypt. Now they detested Aflaq because of his high-handedness in unilaterally dissolving the Ba'th Party in order to achieve the failed union with Egypt. Many army officers felt the same way about him, and inhabited a hard-nosed world which could not have been more different from the refined intellectualism of Aflaq's youth. His tactic was to resort to legalism, and he used the Ba'th's supreme body, the Beirut-based National Committee which supervised the regional Ba'th parties in all Arab countries, to assert control in Syria.

He won over to his side General Amin al-Hafez, the commander of the armed forces and apparent ruler of Syria in the eyes of the outside world. Hafez established a new government loyal to the National Committee, but when his defence minister ordered the transfers of three key officers to less sensitive posts, networks in the army under the control of the clandestine military committee which had carried out the 1963 coup struck. Amin al-Hafez was toppled from power. His position had already been weakened by his closeness to a man who, it was said, he was grooming to be a future defence minister. This man called himself Kamal Amin Ta'abet, a member of the Syrian community in Egypt which had lived in Cairo and Alexandria for several generations. He had come to Syria in 1962 posing as a Syrian from Argentina who had returned home because he was an ardent Arab nationalist. In 1965, he was caught red-handed and revealed to be an Israeli spy while transmitting military secrets to Tel Aviv. Eli Cohen (for that was his real name) was publicly hanged. The scandal did no favours to Amin al-Hafez. As with other instances when Israel recruited Arab Jews as spies, it also did no favours to Syria's small Jewish minority.

For his part Michel Aflaq was at home in Damascus when the coup took place. He could hear the distant gunfire and expected the imminent arrival of soldiers to arrest him. Instead, he found himself merely ignored.[50] He left for Beirut, travelled to Brazil, and ended his days in Iraq where he appeared in public from time to time to give legitimacy to the Ba'thist regimes of Hasan al-Bakr and Saddam Hussein.

The real leader of the regime installed by this coup was an Alawi officer, Salah Jadid. Nobody could shut their eyes to the fact that it was the army that now ran Syria, and that it was controlled by officers who tended to come from rural or small town backgrounds, and were often also from minorities. Except for military training, these officers had generally had no tertiary education, although three medical doctors of militantly left-wing views were placed at the top as "head of state" (the title of president was abolished because it might make the incumbent too powerful), prime minister and foreign minister. There were military purges throughout this period of turmoil. Many of these had the effect of reducing the number of Sunnis in key positions, although it is hard to tell the extent to which this was coincidental or the result of a deliberate policy. The abrupt dismissal of 104 senior officers on 3 March 1964 was only the first of many. Three days later, another 150 middle- and lower-ranking officers were retired.[51] Several further purges occurred in 1964 and 1966.

Salah Jadid's government was the most radical Syria has ever seen. It simmered with resentment against the old world of privilege and notables, and now set out to dismantle it with nationalisation and full- scale class warfare, making life hard for any member of the old notable elite. Ba'thism had now enabled many people to get ahead in Syrian society in a way that would once have been impossible for them. Thus, in Raqqa during the late 1960s, the head of the local branch of the Peasants' Union was the son of the slave of a local tribal chieftain. And the party secretary for the province was a school teacher whose father had been a vegetable seller.[52] But the regime had not learned from the uprising in Hama and the disturbances of 1964 that it had to co-exist with public expressions of Islam. Some of the officers who controlled it were indeed atheists. In April 1967, the gauntlet was thrown down when an article containing the following appeared in a Ba'thist-approved army magazine:

Until now, the Arab nation has turned towards Allah ... but without success as all [religious] values made the Arab man a miserable one, resigned, fatalistic and dependent. We don't need a man who prays and kneels, who curbs his head and begs God for his pity and forgiveness. The new man is a socialist, a revolutionary ... The only way to establish the culture of the Arabs and to build

Arab society is to create the new Socialist Arab man who believes that God, the religions, feudalism, imperialism, the fat cats and all the values that dominated the former society are nothing but mummies embalmed in the museums of history.[53]

Protests led to the dismissal of the author, who was put on trial for conspiring with America and Israel to sow dissension in Syria and split the people from the leadership – charges that were obviously trumped up. But the incident does tell us something about those controlling Syria at this time. They were arrogant, bitter, indifferent to public sentiment and unaccountable to an electorate. The "mummies embalmed in the museum of history" incident may well have been a contributory factor behind the eventual seizure of power by Hafez al-Assad in 1970.

This scandal erupted precisely when Syria desperately needed an effective military, since there were frequent tensions along the armistice line with Israel. By the time full-blown war with Israel broke out in June 1967, no less than a third of the officers in the army had been removed from their posts and replaced by under-trained reservists, who were disproportionately school teachers from a rural background. Leadership also revolved at the top. Over the four years since 1963, there had been no less than eight different ministers of defence and five chiefs of staff.[54]

VIII

Avi Shlaim has written that the Six Day War of June 1967 was the only one of the Arab Israeli wars that neither side wanted: "the war resulted from a crisis slide that neither Israel nor her enemies were able to control."[55] That said, war was probably inevitable at some stage. Neither side was content with the status quo. While the Arab states, led by Nasser's Egypt, were building up their armies in the hope that they would one day be able to establish strategic parity with Israel, many in the Israeli leadership wished to aim a devastating blow at Egypt if a suitable opportunity presented itself before this parity could be achieved.

Nasser gave them a golden opportunity to do this, and also to strike at Jordan and Syria. There were abundant causes of tension between Israel and its neighbours that increased the likelihood of war at some stage. An important one in the 1960s was the question of the headwaters of the River Jordan. These rose in Syria's Golan Heights and southern Lebanon, and since 1964 Israel had been channelling water off from the Jordan for irrigation projects. Israel let it be known that it would prevent by force any attempt by Syria or Lebanon to carry out similar projects which would inevitably have reduced the amount of water Israel could take.

Palestinian guerrillas, many of them dispossessed refugees, had been raiding Israel ever since the Jewish state was first established. The water carrier Israel had built to deplete the waters of the Jordan now became a target for sabotage, while the attacks on other installations and civilian settlements continued. In May 1967, Yitzhak Rabin, the Israeli chief of staff, argued for major retaliation against Syria, including the occupation of Damascus and overthrowing the regime.[56] From this point onwards, tension escalated. Israel was falsely reported to be massing troops on the Syrian frontier. Nasser, keen to retain his mantle of Arab leadership, had to be seen to take a stand. He was being taunted by other states for doing nothing, and was also bound by a defensive pact with Syria to go to its aid if Israel attacked.

What followed was a case study in the dangers of diplomatic brinkmanship. Nasser knew his army was in no position to fight Israel, but made belligerent noises which terrified the Israeli public and sent large forces into Sinai. He then exercised his right to demand the withdrawal of the UN peacekeepers who had been stationed along the border with Israel with Egyptian agreement since the ending of the 1956 Suez crisis. Nasser further announced that Egypt would blockade Israel's port of Eilat on the Gulf of Aqaba in the Red Sea. The military drums beat ever louder, and a wave of nationalistic fervour swept the Arab world. Fearing for his throne, King Hussein of Jordan rushed to Cairo and entered into a defensive alliance with Egypt, which meant accepting an Egyptian general as commander of his army. Nasser intended to take advantage of Cold War dynamics to show that he could force Israel to back down, thereby adding to his prestige. He played his cards in the hope of a diplomatic success similar to that of 1956, when he nationalised the Suez Canal and ended the last traces of Britain's special position in Egypt. It was a terrible blunder. On the morning of 5 June, Israel attacked. Nasser had been playing a game; Israel had been playing for real.

Israel's main objective was to destroy the Egyptian army and confirm its own military superiority so as to deter any future Arab attack. In the first day of the conflict, Israel virtually wiped out the Arab air forces, destroying most of their planes on the ground. Its armies then swept through Sinai in a classic blitzkrieg, before turning on the Jordanians who had begun shelling Israeli targets after the beginning of the Israeli aerial onslaught, and seized Government House on the 1949 ceasefire line in Jerusalem. Territorial objectives only emerged as the fighting progressed, but by the end of the first two days, Egyptian resistance east of the Suez Canal was militarily untenable. Likewise, resistance west of the River Jordan soon crumbled as the Jordanian army risked being cut off.

Apart from Israel's destruction of the Syrian air force on 5 June, fighting along the Israeli-Syrian border had been largely limited to artillery exchanges. The UN Security Council called for a ceasefire on 6 June, and this was accepted by Syria on 8 June. However, on 9 June the Israeli defence minister, Moshe Dayan, ordered his army to seize the Golan Heights even though he did not have cabinet authorisation to do so.

Over the last two days of the Six Day War, the Israelis attacked. On the first day, the Syrian army fought tenaciously but was overwhelmed. The inadequacy of its command structure and training was amply demonstrated. Incredibly, in some sectors of the front the Israelis were even able to take the Syrians by surprise and were helped by Syrian security which was lax with radio messages. The following day, rather than delivering the counter-attack the Israelis expected, the Syrians withdrew in panic after a false report was aired on Syrian radio that Quneitra had fallen. This town was a crucial strategic and psychological consideration, as it was the capital of the Golan governorate and was in the rear of the Syrian defenders. The defence minister, Hafez al-Assad, went on air to deny the report but it was too late. The Syrian army was fleeing, and most of it got away. When Quneitra fell undefended at 2.00 pm that afternoon, the Israeli invaders were staggered at the quantity of war booty they captured, including tanks and other vehicles in running order.[57] The war had humiliated both the army and the regime.

Naturally enough, recriminations followed. A fissure opened between Salah Jadid and the powerful defence minister, Hafez al-Assad. The two men were long-time colleagues from the days they shared building up the secret Ba'th military committee in Cairo, where they were both stationed during the UAR period. Now, though, Hafez al-Assad began to remove supporters of Salah Jadid from key positions in favour of colleagues whom he trusted as his own supporters. Some of them were men whom he believed had been wrongly purged, and would now owe him a particular debt of gratitude. The fissure widened into a gap between the armed forces – increasingly controlled by Hafez al-Assad – and the party apparatus in which Salah Jadid reigned supreme. In February 1969, Hafez al-Assad extended his empire, with the help of his younger brother Rif'at who was highly placed in the Ministry of the Interior. Tanks moved through the night-time streets as editors of newspapers, radio presenters and government and party officials were replaced by people Hafez al-Assad knew favoured him rather than Salah Jadid. The head of the party's Bureau of National Security, Abd al-Karim al-Jundi, whose loyalty was to Salah Jadid and who was meant to prevent such things happening, blew his brains out. Salah Jadid, together with the head of state and the prime minister, led the funeral procession. Hafez al Assad did not attend, but the Ministry of Defence sent a wreath.[58] He also took over control of the security apparatus which had been al-Jundi's fiefdom.

The final showdown between the two leaders occurred at a Ba'th Party conference at the end of October, 1970. Nasser had died from a heart attack on 28 September after returning home from Amman, where he had brokered a truce in fighting between the army of King Hussein of Jordan and the Palestinian nationalist guerrillas of the Palestine Liberation Organisation (the PLO) led by Yasser Arafat. This conflict had taken on the dimensions of a civil war in Jordan and put Syria in a very difficult position. Salah Jadid supported the PLO for ideological reasons and ordered Syrian military action against Jordan. However, Hafez al-Assad was only prepared for Syrian forces to intervene on the behalf of the Palestinians to a limited extent. It was a clash between idealism and pragmatism, not least because Israel and America would intervene on Jordan's behalf if necessary. If they did so, they would probably take the opportunity to smash the Syrian armed forces at the same time. Hafez al-Assad ordered the Syrians to pull back, even though this decided the outcome of the conflict in favour of King Hussein's army.

At the party conference, Salah Jadid tried to reassert control. Hafez al-Assad was accused of defeatism and kow-towing to imperialists. He and his deputy, Mustafa Tlas (an Assad appointee), found themselves isolated. The conference removed them both from their posts. But as soon as the conference had finished its proceedings, Hafez al-Assad made his move. Troops occupied the offices of the party as well as those of organisations belonging to it. The coup was bloodless. In fact, the Syrian branch of the Ba'th Party would maintain for evermore that it was not a coup at all, but rather *al-harakah al-tashihiyyah*, the "corrective movement" which was needed to put the Ba'thist revolution back on track, and to rescue the country.

Hafez al-Assad went to see Salah Jadid in his office. "If I ever attain power, you will be dragged through the streets until you die," is said to have been the latter's defiant retort when told to step down.[59] He was put in prison and remained there until his dying day on 19 August 1993.

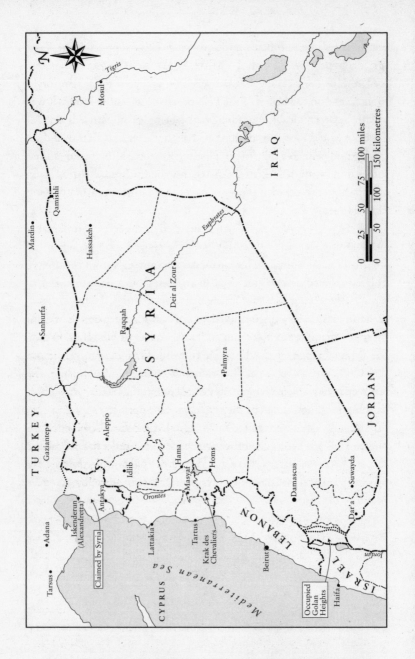

THE INDEPENDENT STATE OF SYRIA SHOWING MAJOR TOWNS

CHAPTER FOUR

Hafez al-Assad, 1970–2000

Foreign Policy Challenges

I

When Hafez al-Assad seized power on 13 November 1970, it was the start of a new era for Syria. He would stay in control of the country until his death on 10 June 2000. By then his rule would have lasted longer than that of the French, or of all governments since independence combined. Few at the time would have predicted that he would manage to remain at the helm for so long, but all would have agreed that Syria needed stability and that this required a very firm hand. Before Israel seized the Golan Heights, Syria had already been in chaos. Now it had its back to the wall. Anyone who stared up at the crest of Mount Hermon from a roof terrace in the old city of Damascus was looking at enemy-occupied territory. Not only was there a major threat to Syria unparalleled since independence, but stability and internal reconciliation were desperately needed after the upheavals of the quarter century since the French finally left. The price Syria was about to pay, as an observer has recently commented, was that it would be run by a regime with a heart that was made of lead.[1]

Indeed, the regime was perfectly prepared to use violence either in Syria or abroad when it deemed this expedient. This included assassinations and terrorism. The list of those whom Hafez al-Assad's regime is accused of assassinating is long and distinguished. It includes the co-founder of the Ba'th Party, Salah al-Din Bitar, General Muhammad Umran, who was one of Hafez al-Assad's colleagues on the Ba'thist secret military committee which carried out the coup of 8 March 1963 and became minister of defence before the 1966 coup, the Lebanese president-elect Bashir Gemayel, and Kamal Jumblatt, the left-wing Lebanese leader and Druze notable.

As with earlier periods of Syrian history, during the rule of Hafez al-Assad foreign challenges had an all-important impact on what took place inside the country. For that reason, this chapter will look at Syria's foreign policy during his thirty years in power, while the nature of his rule and the internal problems of Syria will be considered in Chapter Five. Two key foreign policy issues stand out. The first is the continuation of the Arab-Israeli conflict generally and Syria's struggle for the return of the Golan Heights. The other is Syria's involvement in Lebanon.

In 1970 Israeli tanks were poised little over thirty-five miles from Damascus, while Israeli radar and telescopes on the summit of Mount Hermon could observe planes taking off and landing at Damascus airport, and even the traffic moving in and out of the city. The recovery of the Golan Heights and justice for the Palestinians were non-negotiable, red line issues for any ruler of Syria. Syria's first priority was therefore to strengthen its armed forces so that, in partnership with the Egypt of Anwar Sadat, who became its president after Nasser's death, it could stand up to Israel in battle. This involved putting the country onto a semi-permanent war footing. As this situation continued indefinitely, it would lead to the long-term militarisation of Syrian society which would have its own, unwelcome consequences. Internal security was also vital. The country had already been under an emergency law since the coup of 1963. This would never be lifted so long as Hafez al-Assad lived. Another requirement was a reliable source of armaments and technical help. Because of the Cold War and the Arab-Israeli dispute, the USA, France and Britain were not prepared to offer these. By contrast, the USSR would do so but would expect to extract a price in the form of political influence. For the moment the dilemma this posed could be fudged, and Syria now rebuilt its armed forces with Russian equipment and support.

At 2.00 pm. on 6 October 1973 Syria and Egypt struck against Israel without warning, just as Israel had struck in 1967. Their objective was for Syria to retake the Golan Heights and for Egypt to take the areas immediately east of the Suez Canal. Syrian commandos in helicopters captured Israel's look-out posts on Mount Hermon, while armoured and mechanised units tried to punch three holes in the Israeli defences. In the south of the front, the Syrians achieved considerable success before they were turned back, and they forced the Israeli commander, General Eitan, to abandon his headquarters at Nafekh in the centre of the front. The attempt to break through north of Quneitra also came close to success but was bled dry with extremely heavy losses. By the time the Syrians had been driven back to their pre-war lines, they had lost 870 tanks and thousands of other vehicles. The Israelis then forged onwards, and added a big salient in the northern sector of the front where they pushed almost to Sa'sa'. They were some twenty miles from the suburbs of Damascus by the time of the ceasefire.[2]

In the first days of the conflict, Syria and Egypt had been able to neutralise the Israeli air force with their new Russian air defence missile systems, but their armies were exposed if they moved beyond the shield these provided and Israel soon reasserted its command of the skies. As the battle swung in favour of Israel, substantial Iraqi and Jordanian forces rushed to Syria's aid. These played a role in distracting the Israelis with a threat to their right flank which enabled the Syrians to regroup south of Damascus and end the war with their army intact. Syria had lost 3,100 dead and 6,000 wounded. The Israeli figures were 772 killed and 2,453 wounded.[3] Although Syria had incurred heavier losses, it was arguably better able to sustain them than Israel. Both sides would have been unable to continue the war beyond the first few days without airlifts of supplies from their superpower backers.

Israel was the party that would be considered in a conventional military analysis to have won the battle, but it was something of a Pyrrhic victory. The Syrian army had shown it was now very different from how it had been in 1967. It had performed bravely and competently even if, with some notable exceptions, most of its officers had shown themselves poor at adapting to rapidly changing developments on the battlefield. Still smarting from accusations that the army had run away in 1967, many units failed to retreat when that was the sound military course of action, and their men paid for it with their lives. The army had redeemed its honour and had every reason to be proud of its performance. It was also soon re-equipped.

Hafez al-Assad saw no reason to be obliging towards the victors. Israel's salient stretching towards Damascus might prove difficult to defend if full-scale hostilities broke out again, and would require Israel to maintain a degree of mobilisation that put its economy under strain. He began a low-level war of attrition using artillery duels and snipers. This was a war which he could always escalate when he chose, causing a corresponding increase in Israeli casualties on the Golan. He also rejected face-to-face meetings with the Israelis and refused to provide a list of Israeli prisoners of war. This was a very different approach from that of Anwar Sadat, his Egyptian counterpart, who quickly agreed to an exchange of prisoners and positively relished ceremonies in which Egyptian and Israeli officers met face to face and saluted each other. It was a sign of the rift that was developing between the two leaders.

The USA now used its good offices to mediate between Israel and its Arab foes. It had little difficulty minimising the Soviet role in the negotiations. In addition to its links with Israel, the USA had close relations at this time with Jordan, Saudi Arabia, the other Gulf States, Lebanon, Turkey and Iran (the October 1973 war was over five years before the Iranian revolution, and Iran was still a key US ally). If America had tried to use its power and these friendships in a skilful way to broker a comprehensive peace between Israel and all Arab parties, it might have succeeded. But under Presidents Nixon and Ford, and through the diplomacy of their Secretary of State Henry Kissinger, America developed a strategic objective that was more easily achievable but much more limited: to detach Egypt from its ally, the USSR, and bring it into the Western orbit. Once America had both Israel and Egypt as its allies, as well as its friendships with numerous other Arab governments, it would have conclusively gained the upper hand over the USSR in the Middle East. At the end of the day, America did not need Syria, while it considered that the Palestinian problem which was the origin of the entire conflict could be managed or contained.

This was Cold War thinking and has since proved to have been the sowing of dragons' teeth. The failure to achieve a comprehensive Arab-Israeli peace had knock on consequences which made reform in Syria even harder than it would otherwise have been. The same applied to solving certain other problems in the Arab world, notably those of Lebanon. At the time, America calculated with cold logic that Syria would be unable to do anything to regain the Golan Heights on its own once it had been shorn of its Egyptian ally. Syria was granted the bare minimum to force it to maintain a permanent ceasefire. This was the disengagement with Israel which was achieved in 1975 through the shuttle diplomacy of Secretary of State Henry Kissinger. Syria recovered civil control of the town of Quneitra and a strip of territory which ran the length of the front. These areas were made part of a demilitarised UN buffer zone.

Hafez al-Assad was slow to grasp the real direction of American diplomacy. Syria pressed at the UN for an overall solution to the conflict, including international recognition of Palestinian rights and the PLO as the representative of the Palestinian people.[4] He stressed the obvious point that the only way peace could be achieved was by involving all parties. As he put it in a speech on 26 February 1975:

> For our part we look upon peace in its true sense ... a peace without occupation, without destitute peoples, and without citizens whose homeland is denied to them ... Anyone who imagines that the peace process can be piecemeal is mistaken ... We say now as we have always said – that peace should be based on complete withdrawal from the lands occupied in 1967 and on the full restoration of the rights of the Palestinian Arab people.
>
> It is being said – and we might ask – what are these rights? Our answer is: let the PLO be asked. It is the PLO which will answer and we will support it in its reply.[5]

These were prophetic words. The day would come when Israel would have to talk to the PLO, and the principle that Israel could not annex occupied Arab land would be explicitly acknowledged by the international community.[6] In 1975, however, America and Israel were not interested in this Syrian olive branch and certainly had no intention of talking to the PLO. It seemed possible for them to disregard Syria, but Lebanon was about to provide a fresh arena in which Israel and America would encounter Hafez al-Assad.

II

At the start of the 1970s, Lebanon was considered the democracy of the Arab world. Its parliament elected its president who appointed its prime minister, and it was renowned for its relatively open society and free press. There was no other Arab country with this degree of political participation and internal freedom. However, it was an unstable, deeply divided country in which there was much corruption. Government authority was weak, and well-armed militias openly flexed their muscles. The root of Lebanon's instability lay in the manner in which it was originally established. A number of sectarian tribes with conflicting senses of identity had been thrown together as a sovereign state to suit the political purposes of just one of those tribes. Lebanon had thus been imagined on the basis of a predominantly Maronite vision of the country: Phoenician rather than Arab, Christian rather than Muslim, and capitalist and Western rather than socialist. The competing vision was of an Arab Lebanon in which the country was an integral part of the wider Arab world. This appealed to the Sunni and Shi'i Muslims, the Druze and also to many Orthodox Christians. By the 1970s, the proportion of Lebanese who held the Arab vision of their country definitely constituted a majority of the population.

Members of parliament were elected on a sectarian basis known as confessionalism, which had entrenched these rival identities and locked the country into tribal communal politics in which people looked first to their religious community and only secondly to the state. There was little shared sense of Lebanese nationhood. The structure of the Lebanese state had therefore always been precarious, and stability depended on delicate negotiations between the representatives of the different sects which made up the country's confessional mosaic. The system had already come close to breaking down in 1958. In the end, compromise prevailed but a prolonged civil war had only been postponed.

In the mid-1970s, the battle between the competing visions of Lebanon as an essentially Western enclave and an integral part of the Arab world was finally fought out with shells, bullets and bombs. On one level, this was a struggle between revolutionary forces such as Ba'thists and Nasserists who were pitted against those who backed the traditional, *laissez-faire* approach of the Lebanese commercial elite which dominated the country's economic life. It was thus a social conflict, which also happened to be between those who were partisans of the West and those who hoped for support from the Communist Bloc. Most of all, however, the strife followed sectarian lines. This stopped it developing into a revolutionary struggle focused on class conflict. The pro-Western forces were predominantly Maronite militias, while the revolutionary elements which called for the end of the confessional system were largely Muslim: Sunni, Shi'i and Druze. Up to that time, the state had been dominated by the Maronites, and the Maronite militias were determined to make sure that this remained the case. However, the Muslim sections of the population had now grown to be a majority and were demanding an end to this state of affairs. At the very bottom of the heap were the Shi'i peasants of the south and the Beqaa valley in the east of the country. They had a high birth rate. Poor and generally excluded by both the Christians and the Sunnis, this community would now finally begin to rise to prominence in Lebanese politics.

A further cause of instability was the intrusion of the Palestine issue into Lebanon's domestic affairs. Lebanon had played no part in the events of 1947–9 which had led to the establishment of Israel and dismemberment of Palestine except for a border skirmish or two, but it had been inundated with 135,000 Palestinian refugees.[7] Their presence became permanent and, like the Shi'is, they had a high birth rate. By the mid-1970s, their total was approaching 350,000.[8] They were placed in camps run by the United Nations Works and Relief Agency for Palestinian refugees in the Near East (UNWRA). Although some Palestinians made their way in Lebanese society, the overwhelming majority remained in these camps which stayed a world apart across the decades. They were predominantly Muslim, and their presence was bitterly resented by right-wing Maronites as an additional threat to their vision of Lebanon. No serious attempt was made to integrate them into the country, and legislation was even passed to ensure that the vast majority of them remained stuck in their camps. Lebanon was not involved in the Six Day War, but in its aftermath Palestinian guerrillas based in Lebanon made pin-prick attacks against Israel from southern Lebanon. These increased when the PLO was driven from Jordan in 1970, and Beirut became the centre of its political operations.

The weakness of the Lebanese government meant that it was in no position to stop these attacks on Israel, but they caused Israeli reprisals which often targeted the local population and seemed to have the primary objective of setting them against the Palestinian fighters. In doing this Israel had some success. It also took out its frustration on the Lebanese people and state by retaliating for hijackings and other acts of international terrorism. As early as December 1968, for instance, Israeli commandos destroyed thirteen civilian aircraft at Beirut airport as a reprisal for a hijacking in Athens. There was no connection between the airlines which owned these aircraft and the terrorists, and like many Israeli attacks on civilian targets across the decades one of the primary motivations for them was the appeasement of public opinion in Israel. The Lebanese government and its armed forces were too weak to reassert their control. It was the same when Israel arbitrarily devastated parts of the south of the country in retaliation for the massacre of Israeli athletes by a Palestinian group at the Munich Olympics in 1972.

The spark for the civil war was provided in March 1975 during a strike by Muslim fishermen in Sidon against the award of fishing rights to a Maronite consortium. When protesters were shot by the army, the violence took on a sectarian tone. After an unsuccessful attempt on the life of the Maronite leader Pierre Gemayel who was the founder of the right-wing Phalange Party, his militia slaughtered twenty-eight Palestinians on a bus in revenge for the three people killed by the assassins.[9] Barricades were soon going up in towns across the country and roads becoming unsafe. By the end of the year, tit-for-tat sectarian massacres were taking place on both sides of the Lebanese divide in which hundreds of people were killed for no reason except their religion. The Lebanese scurried back into their tribal identities. Thousands of young men joined militias which were often controlled by quasi-feudal notable families from the sect to which they belonged. The following March, the army split along confessional lines, and officers and soldiers alike joined the militias. The threads which stitched Lebanon together had unravelled.

Syria watched what was happening in Lebanon anxiously. This was only to be expected. As has been seen, for most Syrians and many Lebanese the split between the two countries had only come about because of the "divide and rule" politics of the French. Not only were there very extensive family, cultural and commercial links between their populations but chaos in Lebanon might cause Syria's own fragile mosaic of sects and ethnic groups to disintegrate. Syria also had another concern. It could not afford to allow Lebanon to fall under Israeli hegemony. This would have provided the Israeli army with a back route into Syria, which it might have used to encircle Damascus or even cut the country in two if hostilities ever broke out again.

Hafez al-Assad initially took on the role of conciliator. As Lebanon disintegrated, the revolutionary or leftist forces were clearly winning. He tried to persuade the Palestinian leader Yasser Arafat and Kamal Jumblatt, the Druze warlord who was also a key leftist leader, to compromise with the Maronites and end the conflict. However, when his efforts proved fruitless he accepted an unwritten set of understandings with Israel which Henry Kissinger arranged. Syria would intervene to bring the civil war to an end, but would not use its air force without Israel's consent or send its troops south of Sidon. Lebanon would thus be partitioned into spheres of influence. This led to the establishment of Syrian hegemony over the greater part of the country during the summer and autumn of 1976.

The Syrian forces had hoped that Palestinian and leftist forces would not resist them, but sometimes they had to use heavy weapons to crush opposition in important locations, such as along the Beirut-Damascus road. An ambush of Syrian tanks trying to enter Sidon led to casualties. There were also reports that Syrian anti-aircraft crew placed in Palestinian camps to defend them against Israeli aircraft were taken prisoner and beaten up. It may have been because of these incidents that Hafez al-Assad developed a strong hatred for Yasser Arafat[10] – a loathing that was fully reciprocated. Arafat's people suffered in consequence. The Syrian army now stood by while Maronite militias finished off resistance in Palestinian refugee camps and other hostile pockets. After a siege that began in late June and only ended on 12 August 1976, the Tel al-Za'tar refugee camp on the eastern outskirts of Beirut was pummelled into submission by militias operating from the Christian neighbourhoods which surrounded it. The camp was crammed with some 30,000 Palestinians as well as Shi'i refugees from the fighting. Ten per cent of the camp's population was dead by the time it was forced to surrender.

Although the Lebanese must carry the responsibility for the disintegration of their own country, it would be fair to add that what finally made the swollen dam break was the additional strain put upon Lebanon by the unwished-for presence of the dispossessed Palestinians. Once the civil war began in Lebanon, it became intrinsically linked with the Arab-Israeli dispute. By gaining a position of primacy for Syria in Lebanon, Hafez al-Assad had strengthened his position against Israel. His Lebanese adventure also had another aspect. He only mentioned the concept of Greater Syria occasionally, but strategically it was vital for Syria that Lebanon, the Palestinians and Jordan stood side by side with Syria to confront Israel. Needless to say, as far as he was concerned this had to be under his leadership. He feared they might make a separate a peace with Israel, or even cooperate with each other in ways that did not meet with Syria's approval. Over the coming years, he would use whatever means were at his disposal to coerce these smaller actors, and to keep them in line behind him, including on occasion assassinations, bombings and other acts of terrorism.[11]

III

In January 1977, Jimmy Carter was inaugurated as US president. In shining contrast to his predecessors, he did genuinely try to bring a comprehensive peace to the Middle East. He recorded a favourable initial impression of the Syrian leader in his diary after a three and a half hour meeting with Hafez al-Assad in Geneva on 9 May that year:

It was a very interesting and enjoyable experience. There was a lot of good humour between us, and I found him to be very constructive in his attitude and somewhat flexible in dealing with some of the more crucial items involving peace, the Palestinians, the refugee problem, and borders. He said that a year or two ago it would have been suicidal in his country to talk about peace with the Israelis, but they've come a long way and were willing to cooperate.[12]

In his autobiographical account of his presidency which was published in 1982, Carter would quote this extract from his diary then immediately add: "this was the man who would soon sabotage the Geneva peace talks by refusing to attend under any reasonable circumstances, and who would, still later, do everything possible to prevent the Camp David accords from being fulfilled."[13]

Carter was a scrupulously fair-minded man who would not have written such words lightly. However, his irritation and anger tell us as much about him – and about America – as about Hafez al-Assad and Syria. The die had already been rolled by Henry Kissinger, and would not be thrown again for over a decade. Kissinger had succeeded in his diplomacy and neatly detached Anwar Sadat of Egypt from his Syrian ally. Carter and Sadat were to find that their good intentions to bring overall peace to the Middle East would be ground down and frustrated by Menachem Begin, the Israeli prime minister who would not yield one jot on any issue other than the peace treaty with Egypt. Hafez al-Assad may have been prepared to trust Carter as an individual, but America had already shown itself duplicitous towards him. His sense

that Syria had been betrayed and his anger at the isolation into which
Henry Kissinger's diplomacy, and now that of Carter and Sadat, had
boxed it coloured his view of the world. This inevitably made him less
open to America and the West.

For his part, Carter was putting himself out on a limb with American
public opinion and would have felt that Hafez al-Assad needed an
education in the constraints he was under as US president. But Hafez
al-Assad could easily have retorted that the genuine efforts Carter had
made to understand the Palestine problem and the Arab world were
still inadequate, and America was not acting as an honest broker. What
is striking is that in the chapters in Carter's autobiography dealing with
his attempts to bring peace to the Middle East there are very few other
references to Hafez al-Assad. On the other hand, his ever-mounting
frustration with the Israeli prime minister's approach to his peace-
making efforts is burned onto almost every page. Carter and Sadat
had followed a course which damaged Syria's interests. It was therefore
scarcely surprising if Hafez al-Assad was uncooperative, and "did
everything possible to prevent the Camp David Accords [which led to
the separate peace between Israel and Egypt] from being fulfilled".[14]

When Egypt's treaty with Israel was finally signed in 1979, it shocked
the rest of the Arab world and led to Egypt's expulsion from the Arab
League for a decade. While Israel withdrew in stages from occupied
Egyptian territory as envisaged under the treaty, Syria was left facing
Israel across the demilitarised UN buffer zone on the Golan Heights
without an ally. It seemed to have no possibility of ever again achieving
a balance of power to level the playing field. Israel took advantage of
this to give its occupation of the Golan an increasing air of permanence,
and formally annexed the area in 1981. This was a grotesque breach
of international law. By then, Ronald Reagan was US president. The
USA voted for the UN Security Council Resolution condemning
the annexation, but Regan took no further action and tolerated this
behaviour by America's proxy. Israel and America had made their
strategic calculations and assumed that there was nothing Syria could
do in reply.

IV

Henry Kissinger had intended that the unwritten understanding which he had arranged between Syria and Israel would make Hafez al-Assad responsible for the behaviour of the fractious militias in Lebanon. However, the limitations Hafez al-Assad had accepted on his freedom of action meant he could not be held liable for Palestinian attacks against Israel from southern Lebanon. These continued. Eventually, Israel decided to deal with them once and for all. When there was an attempt on the life of the Israeli ambassador in London by Palestinian gunmen in early 1982, Israel used this as a pretext to invade southern Lebanon and flush out the Palestinian guerrillas.

The Israeli minister of defence, Ariel Sharon, had a secret, wider objective which was not approved by the cabinet: to drive the Palestinian leadership from Beirut and destroy the forces and, indeed, the very idea of Palestinian nationalism. His dream, and that of his prime minister, Menachem Begin, was to recreate Jordan as a Palestinian homeland, leaving Israel free to subdue and colonise the West Bank and Gaza. The Lebanese part of this strategy was to conquer the southern part of Lebanon as far north as the suburbs of Beirut and then to install the leader of one of the main Maronite militias, Bashir Gemayel (the son of Pierre Gemayel who had survived the assassination attempt in 1975), as a president who would be friendly to Israel and sign a peace treaty with it. The Palestinian leadership would be forced to find a refuge far away in another Arab country that did not have a border with Israel. At the same time, the Palestinian refugees would be put under the full control of the Lebanese army, Syrian forces would be removed from the country, and Hafez al-Assad humiliated.

This Israeli project was to ratchet the violence in Lebanon up to unprecedented levels. At first, the plan went well. Israeli forces drove through the south, crushing Palestinian resistance. They were often greeted as liberators by the Shi'i peasants who had resented Palestinian domination of their villages and the suffering they had endured during the years when they had been caught in cross-fire. As the Israelis drove further north, they ignored Kissinger's understanding with the Syrians, and pushed them back from the Beirut-Damascus road. They also isolated a substantial Syrian force in Beirut and shot down large numbers of Syrian aircraft which Hafez al-Assad desperately threw into the battle.

The Israelis now linked up with the Phalange militia of their allies as planned. But then things became more complex. West Beirut and the city's southern suburbs were still held by Palestinians, left-wing Lebanese allies and the Syrian units which were now cut off in the city. All these groups had shown themselves to be determined fighters. It soon became apparent that bombardment was not enough to cow them into submission. Infantry attacks would be needed to tame Beirut, and that would lead to casualties as the troops went in. Israel had anticipated that this would be a role for Bashir Gemayel's Phalange militia, but now discovered their allies were unwilling to take on the task.

Israel turned to siege warfare. Supplies were cut off, and the city was subjected to fierce bombardment by land, sea and air. The number of civilian deaths mounted well past the 10,000 mark and shocked the international community. The Lebanese tragedy now sucked in the great powers. America and the Europeans intervened to negotiate the evacuation of the PLO by sea to Tunisia and other Arab states, while Russia resupplied the Syrians with new and more advanced equipment. The USSR had been displeased by Syria's support for the West-leaning Maronites, and arms deliveries had been slowed down. But the dynamics of the Cold War were such that the Soviets could not allow their protégé to be further humiliated. Soon Syria's forces were back at a level of credibility: they could not defeat Israel in a war, but Israel could not crush Syria without massive and politically unacceptable casualties. Israel had lost the chance to drive Syria from Lebanon.

Bashir Gemayel was elected president of Lebanon by the Chamber of Deputies. There were indications he would not be the puppet which Israel had hoped for, but we will never know because he was assassinated on 14 September before he had even taken office. Israel's Lebanese adventure now went very badly wrong. Further international criticism of its invasion increased after massacres in the Sabra and Shatila refugee camps, where Phalangist militiamen took revenge for the perceived Palestinian role in Bashir Gemayel's death. They systematically murdered Palestinian women, children and elderly who were defenceless after the departure of the PLO fighters. Israel was in control of the area where the massacre was carried out. It knew what was going on and made no attempt to stop a very foreseeable atrocity. The events caused massive protests and a public enquiry in Israel. Although the Palestinians in the camps were those who suffered as a result of Bashir Gemayel's death, the assassin was a Maronite Christian who had connections with Syrian intelligence. If it is asked who benefited from the assassination, it is indisputable that Syria did.

Israel's replacement nominee for the Lebanese presidency was Bashir Gemayel's brother, Amin. He was duly elected by the Chamber of Deputies, but the full peace Israel had hoped to squeeze out of him proved a mirage. There had always been Maronite leaders who felt sympathetic to Israel (and before that to the establishment of a Jewish state in Palestine), as Maronites and Zionists shared common ground against pan-Arab nationalism. However, Maronite interests were not identical with those of Israel. The full peace treaty Israel hoped to extract might not have been forthcoming from Bashir. Both brothers knew a consensus among Lebanese would be needed for such a momentous step.

Amin Gemayel saw advantages in a good relationship with Syria. Yet after he had been placed under remorseless pressure, Israel extracted an agreement from him that was effectively a treaty of surrender. Lebanon would cease to be a belligerent and would allow Israel to control a security buffer zone extending forty-five kilometres into Lebanese territory. However, the agreement did not deliver the results for which Israel had hoped, and in any case Amin Gemayel eventually repudiated it. The Shi'i villagers of the south resented Israel's control and its use of a Maronite proxy militia which called itself the South Lebanese Army to enforce it. Lebanon became an ever less welcoming place for the Israeli army which found itself under attack within its buffer zone from Shi'i militias, including a new organisation called Hizbullah. This, in time, would show itself to be a very potent force indeed. Syria remained firmly in occupation of most of the rest of Lebanon, while the competing militias controlled various enclaves. Israel's Lebanese dream had gradually turned into a nightmare, and was an increasingly expensive and fruitless project.

Inside Lebanon itself, the war smouldered on, sometimes reigniting to frustrate attempts at reconciliation. Eventually, it came to an end in 1989–90 on terms very advantageous to Syria. When Amin Gemayel's term of office ended in September 1988, the Chamber of Deputies failed to agree his successor. He therefore appointed the head of the army, General Michel Aoun, as prime minister to run the country when he stepped down. But Aoun was a Maronite. This made his appointment unconstitutional, since the prime minister had to be a Sunni Muslim. Michel Aoun's premiership was accordingly rejected by the Muslim majority who backed Selim al-Hoss, the Sunni prime minister, as the next president. Selim al-Hoss had ambitions to dismantle the confessional system, but his appointment was equally unconstitutional, since only a Maronite could be president.

This deadlock was ended after an agreement between the factions was brokered in the Saudi Arabian mountain resort of Taif in September 1989 and approved by the Lebanese Chamber of Deputies. The Taif Accords, as they became known, provided that the Christians lost their majority in the Chamber which would henceforth be divided equally between Muslims and Christians, while the power of the Maronite president was reduced. There were also provisions dealing with the regaining of control over the south of the country from Israel and recognition of Syria's strategic needs in Lebanon. Neither Lebanon nor Syria, the accords stated, would be allowed to pose a threat to the security of the other. The practical consequence of this was that the Syrian army remained in most of Lebanon – as Lebanon's official "ally".

General Aoun rejected the Taif Accords. This led to the final, bloody stage of the Lebanese civil war. Aoun had been backed by Saddam Hussein's Iraq. But when Saddam Hussein occupied Kuwait in August 1990, and found his country threatened by the steady build-up of the military might of a US-led coalition to free Kuwait, he could no longer spare the resources to support his proxy. Syria, by contrast, had the military means at its disposal to deal with Aoun. In October 1990, the Syrian army drove him from the presidential palace at Ba'bda.

The rebuilding of shattered Lebanon could now proceed, although it was interrupted from time to time by more trouble with the Israelis in the south. In 2000, shortly before the death of Hafez al-Assad, Israel finally cut its losses and withdrew unilaterally. Since then, Israel has returned to bomb and devastate Lebanon several times, but a kind of balance of power – or, as it is sometimes called, a balance of terror – has been achieved between it and Hizbullah, which has shown on a number of occasions that it can retaliate effectively against Israel with rockets fired over the border. Hizbullah also sometimes provokes confrontations itself.

By playing his cards skilfully after the Lebanese state broke down in the mid-1970s, Hafez al-Assad would almost turn Lebanon into a Syrian protectorate. Yet the role Syria played in Lebanon can only be understood if it is put in the context of Syria's continuing struggle with Israel. The reasons for that struggle and the bitterness behind it become clear if seen in the light of the original partition of Greater Syria by Britain and France – of which the incorporation of the Balfour Declaration into the Palestine Mandate had been an important element. The Arab-Israeli dispute and the politics of the Cold War had made the wounds caused by that partition fester. This distracted Syria from the most urgent tasks before it: confronting the problems in its own society, developing a clear sense of nationhood, and creating an economy that would make its people prosperous and part of the modern world.

V

While Hafez al-Assad's troops were evicting General Aoun from the Lebanese presidential palace and occupying Lebanese ports to make sure that no fresh munitions reached him, the Syrian president was also given an opportunity to rehabilitate himself with the West. In August 1990, the Iraqi dictator Saddam Hussein occupied Kuwait and claimed it as an Iraqi province. As a US-led coalition was put together under

UN auspices to evict him from this small but very rich land, Hafez al-Assad offered his full support. It was a prudent hedging of bets since the Soviet Union, the source of Syria's weaponry and diplomatic and much other support, was in the process of collapsing. Benefits followed for backing the right horse. These included the discreet reassertion of Syrian hegemony over Lebanon.

Once the Iraqis had been driven from Kuwait in January 1991, President George H. W. Bush and his Secretary of State James Baker made America's first concerted effort to bring peace to the Arab-Israeli dispute since the days of Jimmy Carter. However, the new diplomacy did not succeed in achieving peace between Syria and Israel. The divisions between Arab parties enabled Israel to succeed in one of its major tactical objectives in negotiations with the Arabs: all Israel's significant dealings with its Arab neighbours were to be bilateral. This enabled the Israeli government to pressurise its negotiating partners by switching its engagement from one party to another whenever it found this convenient. In this way, it dangled the prospect of a settlement (on Israel's terms) before Syria or the Palestinians, but with the implicit threat that even this might be lost if it was rejected.

Two sets of bilateral negotiations led to results. The first was the Israeli-Palestinian Oslo Accords which were negotiated under Norwegian auspices in 1993. The other was the peace treaty between Israel and Jordan the following year. No serious territorial issues were at stake between Israel and Jordan, so the negotiation of that treaty proved fairly unproblematic. In the case of the arrangements between Israel and the Palestinians, however, there was a structural weakness in the Oslo Accords which became ever more apparent as time passed. Although the Palestinians had accepted the existence of Israel, Israel made no corresponding acknowledgement of Palestinian rights. That is the underlying reason why, for the next twenty years, the deadlines for the process Oslo initiated came and went.

On the other hand, nothing came from the negotiations between Israel and Syria – although they were the first face-to-face peace negotiations conducted between the two countries since 1949. The first set of negotiations seems to have been triggered by an approach from Hafez al-Assad which was communicated through the Americans and Egyptians. Talks took place between 1992 and 1995, but there was a hiatus starting in September 1993 when Israel slowed progress down while it turned its attention first to the Palestinian, and then to the Jordanian, track. Hafez al-Assad was all too conscious of the perils of weakening his position without being sure that he would gain something in return. This also meant that he was reluctant to negotiate at all if his position was weak, since this might enable his adversaries to wring something out of him.[15] Syria's position was therefore that full withdrawal and full peace should be reciprocal, and that it was necessary for this to be agreed as the starting point for negotiations. This meant that Israel would have to prepare to return all the territory occupied in 1967 and make a prior commitment to this effect.

Return of all the occupied territory would have allowed Syria access to the eastern shore of the Sea of Galilee. The Syrians believed, on the basis of discussions relayed to them through Warren Christopher, the US secretary of state, that Yitzhak Rabin, the Israeli prime minister, had agreed to this in principle. However, if he did so it seems he had not informed the Israeli negotiator, the chief of staff, Ehud Barak, with the result that the Syrians became suspicious of Israeli intentions. The public Israeli position was that the border between the two countries should reflect the old line between the French and British Mandates which, they maintained, would have run just east of the lake and not allowed Syria access to it. There were also other matters to be agreed: security, normalisation of relations between the two countries, and transitional arrangements. But the negotiations did not run their full course, and ended only a little over a month after they had begun when Rabin was assassinated by a Zionist militant on 4 November 1995.

Shimon Peres took over as Israeli prime minister after Rabin's assassination. Talks resumed at the end of December 1995, but there was no progress before the Israeli election of May 1996 in which Benyamin Netanyahu replaced Peres as prime minister. Netanyahu's position was absolutist: there should be peace talks, but these should start from the assumption that Israel had sovereignty over the Golan Heights. His position was strengthened when the Israeli parliament voted in July

1997 to reiterate the annexation of the Golan. Although it was a private member's bill, Netanyahu and most of his cabinet voted in favour. Unsurprisingly, a period of military tension between the two countries ensued. But chances for peace had not yet died. In 1999, the government of Netanyahu fell in its turn and Ehud Barak replaced him as prime minister. In early 2000, the Clinton presidency made a final effort to reach peace.

Hafez al-Assad was terminally ill with leukaemia, but in March 2000 he made his way to Geneva to meet President Bill Clinton and Ehud Barak. Barak had not adopted Netanyahu's extremist position, but neither was he prepared to make the concessions Hafez al-Assad expected to hear. Ehud Barak did not think the Israeli public would accept the Syrians being on the eastern shore of the Sea of Galilee. Instead, he suggested a form of wording to negotiate "a commonly agreed border" which would be based on the pre-1967 armistice lines but would not allow the Syrians access to the lake. When he heard this, the Syrian president wearily concluded that Ehud Barak was not ready to make peace, and returned home.[16]

Three months later he was dead. Peace with Israel was as distant as ever.

VI

Although complete consistency can be seen in Hafez's al-Assad's attempts to regain the Golan Heights, there are other aspects of his foreign policy which raise questions – and which led to much consternation among Arab nationalists both in Syria and elsewhere. When he decided to throw Syria's weight behind the Maronite militias in 1976 to save them from the leftist forces of Kamal Jumblatt and the Palestinian revolutionaries of Yasser Arafat, he took a decision which involved defeating the forces which should have been the natural allies for a Ba'thist. But their victory would have posed major problems for him. If he had let them crush the Maronites, the result would have been an unstable Lebanese entity which provided a base for attacks on Israel and might well preach subversion against his own rule. It would only outrage Western opinion against the Arab cause and sooner or later invite Israel to launch a full-scale invasion aimed at conquest. Syria would then have found itself facing Israeli troops on another front along the Lebanese border to the west of Damascus, very probably preceded by the traditional avalanche of refugees.

Although he had first showed patience and caution by going to great lengths to persuade the leaders of the left-wing forces in Lebanon to come to a compromise, Assad acted ruthlessly when that policy was unsuccessful. That ruthlessness made him appear to many Ba'thists and other Arab nationalists as completely unprincipled. He had sent his army into Lebanon to protect the reactionary, sectarian elements in the country who did not have the interests of the Arab people at heart. Hafez al-Assad's apparent cynicism led to whispers. Was his support of the Maronites in 1976 influenced by the fact that he came from a religious minority himself? Was there some unspoken alliance between the Lebanese Maronites and the minorities who seemed to be favoured by the Ba'thist regime against Syria's Sunni Muslim majority?

With hindsight, Hafez al-Assad's involvement in Lebanon created almost as many problems as it solved. He prevented Lebanon falling under Israel's hegemony and instead placed it under his own. He showed that there were ways in which Syria could still fight back, and that Israel could never expect to live in peace so long as it coveted the Golan Heights and other occupied Arab land. Hizbullah, Syria's ally, gradually emerged as one of the major political forces in Lebanon and by far the strongest of the militias. It is now the only surviving Lebanese militia of that era, since the rest were disbanded when calm finally descended after 1990. It is not an exaggeration to say that Hizbullah has come to have almost the function of a professional army in the way it has defended Lebanon's border in the south. It has often provided a genuine deterrent to Israel (although it has also sparked its share of confrontations). It has been a very valuable ally for the Syrian regime. It would come to the aid of the embattled government of Hafez's son, Bashar al-Assad, when civil war came to Syria in 2011–12.

But there were limits to what success in Lebanon could achieve and there were downsides. Hafez al-Assad died without regaining the Golan Heights and without achieving peace. Indeed, his sponsorship of Palestinian groups which conducted operations against Israel including terrorist attacks on civilian targets made peace more distant. In addition, it made a genuine rapprochement with America, as opposed to a temporary alliance based on convenience, much harder. Syria's role as a kind of suzerain over Lebanon angered many Lebanese. Its meddling in Lebanese politics was as self-seeking as that of Israel. This added to the growing disillusion of Arab nationalists with Hafez al-Assad. There has also been another price to pay. Smuggling across the Lebanese border had first become profitable when the customs union between Syria and Lebanon was ended in 1950. Over the subsequent decades, luxury goods reached Damascus with help from the smugglers' associates in the customs, security and intelligence services. When Hafez al-Assad sent the Syrian army and intelligence services into Lebanon, such activities increased exponentially. Many officers and soldiers engaged in racketeering, hashish smuggling and other corrupt activities. Dirty money soon trickled back home, and added to the growing moral dissatisfaction with the Ba'thist regime.

Moral dissatisfaction also grew because of Hafez al-Assad's handling of relations with two other countries that were key for Syria: Iraq and Iran. As has been seen in earlier chapters, Syria's relations with Iraq had always been, at best, delicate. Iraq had always harboured Syrian dissidents. It was now governed by its own branch of the Ba'th Party, but this faction was at daggers drawn with the Ba'th of Hafez al-Assad in Syria. Hafez al-Assad had genuine reasons for bitterness towards the Iraqi dictator Saddam Hussein, who used fears of Syrian plots as an excuse to carry out purges when he seized power in 1979. But many across the Arab world were surprised and dismayed when Syria supported Iran during the war which began when Saddam Hussein invaded it in September 1980. This conflict would last until 1988, by which time both parties would have fought the other to a standstill in the most blood-stained conflict in the Middle East since 1918. It may have killed a million people or more – we will never know the exact figures. What was Syria, the home of Arab nationalism generally and Ba'thism in particular, doing backing a non-Arab power which had its own hegemonic ambitions over the Gulf? Whatever the many evils of Saddam Hussein's regime might be, it was an Arab nationalist one. Hafez al-Assad's support for Iran was another issue which raised doubts about him in many people's minds, just as his backing of the right-wing Maronites against the Palestinians and the revolutionary forces had done in Lebanon.

Ideologically, Ba'thist Syria and the Islamic revolutionaries in Iran could not have been further apart. One was Arab, the other Persian; one was militantly secular, the other preached a revolutionary Shi'i message which aimed to rouse the Muslim masses across the Islamic world. That message was hostile to Arab nationalism. Nevertheless, the alliance was less surprising than at first glance. The Iranian revolution had overthrown the nationalist regime of the Shah who was a friend and backer of Israel, Syria's arch enemy, as well as one of America's closest allies. While the Shah ruled, Hafez al-Assad had sheltered important Iranian opposition figures who had been exiled. Now that they were back home occupying key positions, he had friends in high places in Tehran. Another point of commonality was the links both regimes now had with the Shi'is of Lebanon. They were a natural constituency for Hafez al-Assad: a poor, downtrodden and excluded peasantry from a religious minority. Now, they were receiving help from the new authorities in Tehran, including arms and training by Iranian revolutionary guards, and had set up militias which were cooperating with the Syrians in Lebanon. Why should the Lebanese Shi'is have to choose between their friends in Tehran and Damascus? For the moment at least, all three were on the same side. History would ensure that they would remain so.

Iraq's attack on Iran had also meant that Iraq's military might could not support Syria against Israel. It ended any possibility – however remote – of establishing a new balance of power with the Jewish state. For Hafez al-Assad, Saddam Hussein's war on Iran was thus a betrayal of Arab nationalism. It is small wonder if he grinded his teeth in frustration while his dislike of the Iraqi dictator turned to positive hatred. He also had little doubt that if Saddam Hussein won his war, he would seek to dominate Syria as well as the oil states of the Gulf. His alliance with Iran was thus very understandable even if it put him, once again, on the receiving end of bellicose rhetoric accusing him of being a traitor to the Arab cause.

For his part, Saddam Hussein waged a brilliant propaganda campaign to justify his own position when he occupied Kuwait. He said that he would put Kuwait's oil wealth at the disposal of the "disinherited" and tried to link progress on a political solution to the "Palestine problem" to simultaneous progress on the "Kuwait problem". This may have been highly cynical, but it resonated with broad masses of people everywhere in the Arab world outside the Gulf. Some rulers, such as King Hussein of Jordan, had no realistic alternative but to remain neutral and call weakly for an Arab solution, while Yasser Arafat flew to Baghdad to offer his services as mediator. Once again, Hafez al-Assad's position would have seemed to many Arabs to be a betrayal. The confusion of ends and means in his pragmatic foreign policy helped take any sparkle that still remained out of Ba'thism. Although his policies gave him moments of great popularity – as when Syrian troops fought against the Israelis in Lebanon – cynicism, that great enemy of any true revolution, grew. This applied not only to the attitude of the Syrian people towards him and his regime, but to the way in which the Ba'thist elite came to see the Syrian people. No longer were the masses to be liberated and their consciousness raised. Instead, they were to be controlled. It is unsurprising, therefore, that as time passed the regime of Hafez al-Assad became increasingly conservative and steadily less revolutionary. This is one of the topics we will examine in the next chapter.

CHAPTER FIVE

Inside the Syria of Hafez al-Assad,
1970–2000

I

Hafez al-Assad was born in 1930 in the village of Qardaha in a predominantly Alawi area of the mountains above Lattakia. He grew up in a house with a dirt floor and no indoor plumbing or electricity (indoor plumbing and electricity would have been unknown in the mountains – and in much of urban Syria – at that time). He was tall (a characteristic inherited by his son, Bashar), and was the grandson of a formidable wrestler. In Qardaha and its neighbouring villages his family were the leaders of a small clan. They counted as fairly important locally, but they were medium-sized fish in a very small pond indeed. He was a peasant and would always remain proud of this. He saw the peasantry as his natural constituency, and those whom it was his primary duty to look after. This was undoubtedly a factor behind his success in staying in power.

As an Alawi, he came from a minority on which many other Muslims looked with suspicion – often openly doubting whether Alawis were Muslims at all. When he was growing up in the 1930s and 40s, Alawis were a clannish and secretive group at the very bottom of Syrian society. Most of them scratched a living from the poor soil of the mountains east of Lattakia where they were a majority of the population, but some of the most ruthlessly exploited peasants in the countryside of the

Orontes valley around Hama were also Alawi. A consequence of their poverty was that some Alawis sent their daughters to work as domestic servants for prosperous Sunni families in the major cities. Sometimes, girls were sold for life. On other occasions, they were indentured for a term of years. This would have been seen as shameful by all Syrians. Sending a daughter to live and work in another household risked her being taken into concubinage which would compromise the family honour.

In the words of one respected scholar of current Syrian affairs, "being Alawite is more about cultural and social behaviour than adherence to a set of religious tenets and obedience to religious hierarchies. Indeed, power in the Alawite community resides in clans rather than in clerical institutions."[1] If this is so, it may be the reason why many Alawis in the mountains believed they were members of a large tribe, rather than a sect.[2] Whatever the case, the important point for our purposes is that Alawis have an identity which sets them apart. Doctrinally, Alawism springs from Shi'ism and incorporates elements of Neo-Platonism. The name of the original teacher of Alawism was Ibn Nusayr, and Alawis are therefore sometimes called Nusayris. The appellation may have originally been dismissive, and it certainly is today when it is used in the polemics of firebrand Sunni preachers attacking the Syrian regime. A fierce anti-Alawi polemic was written by the Damascus-based scholar Ibn Taymiyyah, who died in 1328, and has remained all too accessible. Such preaching may have contributed to a marginalisation of Alawis and sometimes caused them to be persecuted. Like more mainstream Shi'i groups, Alawis have responded to fears of persecution by teaching that it is permissible to hide their true beliefs through the practice of a form of dissemblance known as *taqiyya*. Inevitably, this would have increased the suspicion Sunni Muslims felt towards them, and marginalised them even more.

Hafez al-Assad had been taught by his parents to value literacy, and he appreciated the education he now had a chance to receive but which had been denied to them. He had the good fortune to go to the government secondary school in Lattakia – in his day the only such school in the whole province. As he was the son of an Alawi peasant, boys from the local notable families in the town looked down upon him. They wore smart clothes and expected deference in the playground. Some notable families would intimidate teachers if their son did not get outstanding marks which he had not deserved, forcing the teachers to bow to their wishes. One day he saw a teacher walk out. "You can't buy my dignity for a few liras," he snapped at a well-dressed boy who refused to sit down when told to. For Hafez al-Assad, that teacher would be a life-long hero and possibly the beginning of his political consciousness.[3]

He was exactly the kind of bright boy from a rural background who had few avenues of advancement open to him apart from the armed services. His profile made him a natural, in fact an archetypal, recruit to the Ba'th Party which he joined in 1946. As a Ba'thist student activist, he took part in the campaign to nationalise the infamous tobacco monopoly. He also engaged in street fights in Lattakia with youths from Islamist groups, and was knifed in the back during a brawl. His dislike and fear of religious militancy thus sprang from lived experience. His family could not afford the fees for him to study to become a doctor, which had been his first choice for a career, so he joined the air force as a pilot cadet while remaining politically active. His progress was based on merit and he was sent for ten months' training in the Soviet Union. On his return, he was posted to Egypt during the period of union with Syria. In 1960, despairing of the way in which Syrian voices and interests had been sidelined by Nasser, he joined the secret military committee of Syrian Ba'thist officers in Cairo. Five of the fourteen members of the committee were Alawis. These five included the three top figures: Muhammad 'Umran, the commander of the 70th Armoured Brigade, Salah Jadid, the army chief-of-staff, and Hafez al-Assad himself.[4] When the union with Egypt collapsed in 1961, the Syrian authorities put him on indefinite leave and then transferred him to a bureaucratic job in the Ministry of Economics. This did not prevent him remaining a member of the secret military committee. Together with Nasserists and other elements, the committee was to lead the coup of 8 March 1963 which overthrew Syria's last elected government.

During the coup, he played an important role by negotiating the surrender of a key air base which had been inclined to resist. He now began his rise to the very top. In December 1964, he became commander of the air force. After the February 1966 coup, in which Michel Aflaq was finally sent packing and Salah Jadid became the real leader of the country, he was made defence minister. Together, he and Salah Jadid purged the officer corps after another attempted coup was planned by a Druze officer. Hafez al-Assad narrowly survived the aftermath of the 1967 war, probably because of an instinctive closing of ranks within the regime. Nevertheless, as defence minister he was a natural target for the recriminations which followed that military and political disaster. The war was the turning point of his political life. A cautious, pragmatic man who lacked obvious charisma but combined a will of steel with a perfectly pleasant manner, he had been a trusted lieutenant of Salah Jadid up to that point. Now, in the aftermath of the defeat, things looked rather different to him.

He was angry at the mistakes that had been made and which continued to be made – and about which some key people seemed to be unaware or in denial. He had no illusions about Israel's military strength. The trio of left-wing doctors who occupied the very top offices of state at that time made public utterances which showed a woeful ignorance of military and political realities. He despaired of their pointless, bellicose rhetoric as well as that of so many other Arab leaders, including Nasser. The rulers of both Syria and Egypt had inflamed the feelings of their citizens. By raising tensions in the spring of 1967, they had handed Israel a golden opportunity to strike.

Quietly, almost imperceptibly, he began to build up his own base of patronage through the appointments he made as defence minister, in exactly the same way that so many other Syrian politicians and military officers had done before him. In the meantime, he kept his counsel and was known for his self-control. He observed, but did not speak his mind. If he had a low opinion of a colleague, he would remain silent rather than indulge in gossip. Disciplined and with a very cool head, he was absolutely ruthless when he needed to be. This could only indicate a degree of coldness, the lack of compassion that has often been remarked upon in men who become dictators. As was explained at the end of Chapter Three, when the time came Salah Jadid would find that he had picked a very dangerous man as his subordinate. Those who crossed swords with Hafez al-Assad once he was the ruler of Syria encountered a formidable antagonist.

II

Hafez al-Assad was able to take control of Syria in 1970 because he had the armed forces behind him. His first internal challenge was to reshape the Ba'th Party and make sure it could pose no challenge to him. Old Ba'thist figures like Michel Aflaq, who was in exile in Iraq but potentially still dangerous, were tried for treason *in absentia*. The party was now transformed into a movement that existed to support the leader – a complete contradiction with the ideals of its founders. It became the vehicle every ambitious person had to join in order to get ahead and an instrument with which to control the country. It also became impossible to challenge Hafez al-Assad within the party, although debate on the country's direction and policy issues still took place at party conferences behind closed doors.

A workaholic with a reclusive streak (once his power was consolidated his favourite method of communicating with subordinates was by telephone), he paid great attention to detail and had a tendency to micro-manage. He surrounded himself with hardworking staff whose loyalty was to him personally. Trusted advisers from his early days in power remained in place for decades, controlling access to him and adding to the sense of stability of his regime. He did not make the error of some of his predecessors by neglecting the armed forces. When he took power, the army needed to expand and he made sure that it did. Israel's occupation of the Golan Heights and the general threat to Syria which it posed were justification enough for this expansion, but it also made it much harder for a small group of conspirators to mount a coup. Nevertheless, Hafez al-Assad left nothing to chance. The different army commanders reported to him directly as commander-in-chief, while the number of security agencies began to grow. They, too, were responsible to him alone. Things had changed. For the first time in the history of Syria there was a leader whose position could not be challenged. There seem to have been few large-scale purges of the military during his rule, with the notable exception of that concerned with the showdown between himself and his brother Rif'at in 1983, and possibly in connection with the Islamist insurgency which had preceded it.[5] This can only mean that his control of the armed forces was such that he did not need to carry out frequent purges. Gone were the days when power was divided between an unstable coalition of army officers, old-style notable politicians and fervent, demagogic revolutionaries. In 1971, a referendum in which Assad was the only candidate made him president for a seven-year term. Although some non-Ba'thist parties were tolerated and even given cabinet seats, they could not threaten the Ba'th's position. An article was inserted into the Syrian constitution in 1973 to make the Ba'th "the leading party in the society and the state".

In some respects, Hafez al-Assad modelled his rule on the ways of a traditional Arab monarch. He met delegations to listen to their problems, and made quasi-royal progresses round the country to find out what was happening from the lips of the people in their own locality. This was a sharp contrast to his feuding predecessors, who had preferred to devote their energies to bombastic rhetoric pumped out over the radio from Damascus. He was generally more flexible and much better organised than they had been, and initially tried to heal the rifts in Syrian society which might threaten his rule. At first, this made Syria a slightly freer place. He made overtures to the business community and members of the old Sunni notable elite, enticing some of them back to Syria to join in the rebuilding of the country. In an innovation for Syria, he established locally elected councils. These were set up in the governorates into which the country was divided and advised the governor who was sent from Damascus to administer the governorate in coordination with the local Ba'th Party chief and head of the security services. In his early years in power Assad took considerable care to consult the people – but only ever up to a certain point. He knew that a leader has to ensure that the people follow, but it was for him, and for him alone, to decide how that would be achieved. On social and economic matters his instinct was always to build a consensus whenever he could. On the other hand, as we have seen, in the perilous worlds of foreign policy and external defence, the need for firm leadership and secrecy made him act autocratically throughout his rule. The same applied to internal security.

The degree of repression during his rule varied. It depended on the seriousness of the threats which the regime perceived to its own survival. But the repression also had an arbitrary quality. The police and the intelligence agencies, the feared *mukhabarat*, were exempted from any form of judicial oversight by the 1963 Emergency Law. In practice, the *mukhabarat* could generally hold people for as long as they liked and torture or even murder them. Ordinary Syrians knew that if they ever fell into their hands, they would be completely at their mercy. Not accountable to the public, *mukhabarat* officers were often corrupt, with the consequence that bribery or the use of important connections – what is called *wasta* – were the only ways to secure the release of a family member or friend. Everyone knew that the regime was brutal when it needed to be. Individual *mukhabarat* officers often behaved as they liked and got away with it if their victim was defenceless and lacking in connections. This was in contrast with the use of violence in the international arena, which only ever occurred when the regime judged it to be in its interests.

III

The repression and corruption of Hafez al-Assad's rule are what are focused upon today, and with very good reason. However, this must not obscure the very real transformation that took place in Syria during his years in power. He completed the Ba'thist revolution which had begun in 1963. There was much that was positive in this. It brought education, electricity and piped water to virtually the entire country for the first time. Infant mortality was reduced and life expectancy increased.

Some of the statistics speak for themselves. In the thirty years from 1963–1993, the mileage of standard gauge railway lines in the country quadrupled, while the length of all-weather asphalted roads increased five-fold.[6] In 1960, two thirds of the population over the age of ten (the age at which most of those children lucky enough to attend school would have left the classroom for good) was illiterate. The position was worse among girls, 84.2 per cent of whom were illiterate, while only 49.1 per cent of boys were. By 1990, the figures had improved substantially, and four out of five ten-year-olds could read. The gender gap still existed: nearly nine boys out of ten could read, but only seven out of ten girls. This progress in schooling should be seen against the background of a population growing at 3.3 per cent annually. By 1993, virtually all boys in the countryside were attending school, although there were still a number of girls who were not.[7] However, rapid expansion of education sometimes led to a slipping of standards and the Ba'thist education system in Syria, like that of many other Arab countries, tended to produce compliant rather than questioning minds. Nevertheless, the spread in literacy was a considerable achievement. Progress in literacy was paralleled by that in rural electrification. By 1992, 95 per cent of villages had electricity, which was provided by the great Tabqa dam on the Euphrates which Hafez al-Assad constructed in the 1970s, and was renamed after him. Before this project came on stream, only approximately 5 per cent of Syrian villages had electricity.[8]

Another Ba'thist achievement was the ending of the exploitation of the peasantry by usurious landlords and money lenders. Farmers needed to borrow to tide themselves over from one harvest to the next or to purchase seed. In 1932, the loans they were forced to take out from their landlords or money lenders were generally at a rate of about 30 per cent. At times rates of up to 50 per cent or higher were charged. It is no exaggeration to say that this forced many peasants to live in a state near to slavery. An agricultural bank was established by the Ottomans as early as 1888, and was replaced by a specifically Syrian one in 1918. The interest rates it charged were reasonable, and fluctuated between 4 and 10 per cent depending on economic conditions and the market. Yet what happened in practice was that it lent to the large landlords, who then proceeded to lend on to the small peasants at the traditional, usurious rates. It was only under Nasser, during the union with Egypt, that the power of the landlords over the peasants began to weaken. But it was the Ba'thist revolution that ended usurious lending and brought affordable credit to the countryside.[9]

Despite such achievements, the Ba'thist revolution also stored up problems for the economy. The Ba'thists nationalised big business in 1964, and many more enterprises were brought into the public sector the following year. The number of state employees (outside the army and police) grew exponentially: from just under 34,000 in 1960 to nearly ten times that figure a decade later and to over 700,000 in 1992.[10] The country Hafez al-Assad left behind him at his death was choking with bureaucracy. His successor also inherited many problems on the economic front. In May 1991, an investment law was passed that was intended to encourage private investment.[11] Tax holidays of five years were offered to private sector investors, and this rose to seven years if the investment was in partnership with a public sector entity that owned 25 per cent of the project, and to nine years if the project earned hard currency by exporting more than 50 per cent of its produce. This was all very well so far as it went – but each investment under the law had to be approved by the Supreme Investment Council. Ba'thist Syria was not about to lose control of its economy. The economy would continue to be rigidly planned and would often be a cash cow to be milked by the elite. Indeed, one could say that control was the watchword of the Syria of Hafez al-Assad.

IV

Within a few years of Hafez al-Assad taking power, inflation was once again worsening and the economy slowing. Commissions were being earned on government contracts by the cronies of powerful people, something that made corruption increasingly obvious. There was therefore opposition to his rule from many quarters. Despite his attempts to reach out to the country's Sunni Muslim majority, it would be militant Sunni Islamist groups that capitalised on this discontent.

Islam provided the most convenient rallying cry against the Ba'thist revolution which had ended the old order. There were several strands to this revolution. The most important was the transfer of power from the old, Sunni notable elite to the ambitious, newly educated sons of the countryside. The parents of the new elite had often been illiterate, but their children were now running the country as the backbone of the Ba'th Party. Nationalisation and redistribution of land had deprived the great families of their power. Islam's support for rights of property and entrepreneurship were stressed by the revolution's opponents, and religious opposition to the restructuring of the nation along socialist lines was strong. There were many people who had lost out in consequence of the revolution: not just those who had previously run the country and controlled its wealth, but the far greater number of ordinary people who depended on them. It was also a huge cultural shock; the seemingly unchanging ways of the centuries had been turned on their head.

Another reason behind the success of Islamism in becoming the rallying point for opposition stemmed from the inevitable consequences of the way Hafez al-Assad had taken power. These forced him to play by the same rules as other Arab military men who had done the same. Ultimately, his power depended on personal ties and, beyond that, patronage. Members of his family became indispensable figures, the most prominent of whom was his younger brother Rif'at. Patronage was also extended to many fellow Alawis, especially in the armed forces and security services. The Alawis already had a tradition of serving in the military. This had dated back to the Mandate, when the French had deliberately encouraged members of the religious minorities to join the *Troupes Spéciales* which provided the nucleus for the Syrian army after independence. Because of the poverty of their community, a higher proportion of Alawis than members of other groups were forced to do military service, since they could not afford to buy themselves out of it. After independence, the proportion of Alawi officers increased until it reached 42 per cent in 1970, and was paralleled by a growth of Alawi members in the senior echelons of the Ba'th Party, reaching nearly a quarter in the same year.[12] This was not a case of sectarianism in the sense of an attempt to recreate Syria as an Alawi nation or state, and certainly not a sectarian privileging of Alawis by law, but a very traditional use of patronage to extend the influence of the ruler and ensure his survival. That is the simple reason why Hafez al-Assad relied on so many Alawis in key positions. Of the thirty-one officers whom he picked himself for key roles in the army and intelligence/security services, nineteen were Alawis. Eight of these nineteen came from his own tribe, and four from his wife's.[13]

In 1973, only two of the five divisions in the regular army had been commanded by Alawis. By 1992, seven of its nine divisions had Alawi commanders.[14] Sunnis remained in prominent positions. His Sunni friend General Mustafa Tlas was Defence Minister from 1972 onwards and commanded the Syrian Armed Forces during the October 1973 war. This was because Tlas's position – like those of his Alawi counterparts – stemmed from his relationship with Hafez al-Assad himself. Nevertheless, it is sometimes possible to see a pattern of Alawis being put into posts where they "shadowed" powerful Sunnis. Thus, although the head of the air force was a Sunni, the head of air force intelligence was an Alawi, while the defence companies of Hafez's brother Rif'at guarded the Mezze airbase outside Damascus and another Alawi was in charge of the Missile Corps.[15] Such arrangements were paralleled by the "partnerships" between Alawi generals and Sunni businessmen which dominated much of the private sector.

All this bred resentment. Hafez al-Assad was aware of the dangers. Although he was an Alawi, as a Ba'thist he was an opponent of separate sectarian identities and was extremely successful at winning over the Sunni merchants of Damascus to his regime.[16] Over the first half of the 1970s, he increased the number of Sunnis in the cabinet. They were put into key posts such as foreign minister, defence minister and first vice-president, but he achieved this by reducing the representation of other minorities while leaving his Alawi base intact.

Although many Alawis reached high rank under his rule and constituted a disproportionate segment of the elite, there is little to suggest that the majority of his co-religionists or fellow tribesmen were privileged over other Syrians.[17] They were also politically marginalised like everybody else – a point made by Salah al-Din Bitar, the Sunni co-founder of the Ba'th who was eventually assassinated on Hafez al-Assad's orders (or with his connivance) in 1980. Bitar spoke of the "necessity" of distinguishing between the regime and the "great body of Alawis who had no role in establishing it and are part of the silent majority of the people who resist its crimes at least with their hearts".[18]

Hafez al-Assad always stressed that he was a Muslim. He declared, for instance, that the corrective movement which had brought him to power was "necessary to preserve the Islamic identity of the country" against Marxist "deviances".[19] There is no reason to doubt his sincerity in making this statement, although at the same time it should be stressed that it was highly expedient for him to adopt this course. He made a point of being seen on major Muslim feast days praying with leading Sunni religious leaders. Aware of the inhibitions many other Muslims had about an Alawi becoming head of state, he obtained an opinion from Musa al-Sadr, a leading Shi'i scholar in Lebanon, to the effect that Alawis were indeed true Muslims of a Shi'i persuasion. A statement was also made by eighty Alawi religious leaders confirming the same. One eminent Alawi scholar, Sheikh Badr al-Din Jawhar, also helpfully disassociated the sect from some of the superstitious practices of the Alawi peasantry.[20]

Hafez al-Assad would have preferred a constitution for the country that was completely secular but, was prepared to compromise. The Muslim Brotherhood and other Islamist forces did not achieve their greater objective of cementing Islam as the religion of the state, but they were granted an article in the constitution providing that the president should be a Muslim. That was something Hafez al-Assad could easily live with. He went to Mecca as a pilgrim to perform the rites of *Umrah*, the lesser pilgrimage, and set up a prize in his own name for recitation of the Qur'an.

V

Hafez al-Assad's attempts to reach out to the Sunni majority while retaining power in his own hands did not work. In 1976, a campaign of assassinations of prominent Alawi figures and bomb attacks against government targets began against a backdrop of violent religious rhetoric and continued over the next few years. This rhetoric was inspired by the militant ideology of the Egyptian Sunni Islamist intellectual Sayyid Qutb who had been executed by Nasser ten years earlier. His ideology included *takfir,* "the accusation of unbelief", against alleged apostates who had left the Muslim community and were therefore worthy of death. This would have been problematic enough as an idea in any circumstances, but was made infinitely worse by the absence of any objective criterion for deciding who was an apostate. Now it was used to target the Syrian Ba'thists because they were allegedly seeking to dismantle a Muslim society and turn it into an atheist one.

There is much talk today of the Sunni-Shi'i divide, which has been exacerbated in particular over the last decade or so following the US-led invasion of Iraq and the toppling of Saddam Hussein. The background to it is the power struggle between the revolutionary Shi'ism of Iran and the literalist form of Sunni Islam loosely referred to as Wahhabism or Salafism which is preached and financed by Saudi Arabia. This power struggle developed as the 1980s wore on. Nevertheless, at the time of the Iranian revolution, which overthrew the secular and nationalist regime of the Shah in early 1979, this divide was much less pronounced – or even non-existent. The Sunni militants in Syria who were armed with the ideological tools of Sayyid Qutb now took the Shi'i revolution in Iran as an inspiration. They were determined to push aside what they saw as a godless order in their own country in the way the Iranians had done. Because of the Alawi domination of the regime, and helpful factors like the existence of the *fatwa* (scholarly religious opinion) by Ibn Taymiyyah that Alawis were enemies of Islam, it became easy for Islamists to respond to genuine grievances by tapping into the resonances of the warrior rhetoric of their religion and casting their opposition to Hafez al-Assad in sectarian terms.

Major disturbances began in 1979 and were centred on Aleppo, the Orontes valley and the areas between them. In this part of Syria, much rich farmland had been distributed to peasants at the expense of old landowning families, which began to provide finance to the Muslim Brotherhood to stir up opposition to the regime. Traders in the *souqs* (markets), another constituency with traditional values which had suffered as a result of the Ba'thist revolution, shared their frustrations at government economic policies. Public expenditure had quadrupled in the early years of Hafez al-Assad's rule. Much of it was spent on creating government jobs to employ the new society the Ba'th were creating. Inflation reached 30 per cent in 1976 and ate away at the livelihoods of ordinary people.[21] As mentioned in the last chapter, the regime's Arab nationalist credentials had also been compromised. Its policies in Lebanon seemed to put expediency over principle and it was engaged in clamping down on the inspirational but disorderly Palestinians there who, when all was said and done, were struggling to win back their country. There were plenty of reasons for the public to feel confused and angry.

There were demonstrations in many cities, but those in Aleppo and Hama were the largest and were led by the local branches of the Muslim Brotherhood. Aleppo was Syria's citadel of private enterprise and had been marginalised and excluded by the revolution, while the landowning families of Hama had been targeted by it and lost their rural estates. In June 1979, a Sunni captain who was a disaffected Ba'thist let militants into the artillery school in Aleppo, where at least thirty-two officer cadets who were predominantly, if not exclusively, Alawi were shot dead and many more wounded.[22] A wave of repression inevitably followed in the city and several hundred people were killed. Fifteen imprisoned members of the Muslim Brotherhood were executed as a reprisal.[23]

In Aleppo, over time, Hafez al-Assad was also able to defuse matters by compromise, which included sacking the governor and replacing him with a respected local architect from the city itself. On the other hand, the destabilisation caused by the artillery school massacre led to a purge of Sunni officers from the army and leading positions in the party. In June 1980, there was an Islamist assassination attack on Hafez al-Assad who very nearly succeeded. He was waiting to receive a visitor outside the Guest Palace in Damascus when machine guns opened up and two hand grenades were thrown. He kicked one grenade away, while a guard sacrificed his life for the president by throwing himself on top of the other one.[24] Hundreds of Islamist prisoners detained at Palmyra were executed in cold blood as a reprisal.[25] As so often, it is not clear at what level in the regime authorisation for this was granted. Damascus and the south of the country remained fairly quiet, but an Islamist bombing campaign in the autumn of 1981 aimed at regime targets in the capital included attacks on the prime minister's office and the air force headquarters.[26]

The climax of the rebellion was in Hama in February 1982, when militants from an organisation called the Fighting Vanguard backed by the local leadership of the Muslim Brotherhood rose up with the intention of sparking uprisings across the country to topple the regime. The Fighting Vanguard had been preparing this uprising for three years, and was probably responsible for the nakedly sectarian artillery school massacre.[27] When the uprising itself began in Hama, over seventy Ba'thists were killed, many in their homes. Calls for the uprising and for jihad against the regime were shouted from the megaphones of the city's mosques. According to Abu Mus'ab al-Suri, a member of the Fighting Vanguard who subsequently travelled to Afghanistan and joined al-Qa'ida, the insurgents had secretly stored weapons such as heavy machine guns and rocket-propelled grenades. Eight thousand Russian-made sub-machine guns were distributed on the morning the insurrection started.[28]

The rebellion did not spread and revenge was brutal, thorough and indiscriminate, and must be a matter for speculation. No reliable casualty statistics were ever drawn up. Estimates of the number killed vary from 5,000 up to 25,000 while figures which go as high as 40,000 are also bandied about. Only one journalist, Robert Fisk, managed to witness some of the fighting. His presence in the city was entirely by accident as the government had made certain there was a complete media blackout. Fisk was travelling by taxi from Damascus to Aleppo when his car was flagged down by an officer who instructed the driver to make a diversion to Hama in order to take two soldiers back to their units.[29]

Fisk saw the regime reacting to the rebellion with, to use his own words, "a ferocity born of fear".[30] His account resonates today because it is so reminiscent of what we can now see of the fighting in Syria when it reaches our television screens. As the taxi reached its destination by the side of the Orontes across from the old city, he saw a curtain of brown and grey smoke rising from it. T-62 tanks pumped out shells. "Every minute or so", he wrote, "one of the barrels would shake, the tank would pitch backwards with the vibration and a shell would go hissing over the river and explode amid the walls."[31] Women and children, who had not been able to wash for a week, were being taken out of the city, some of them clearly starving. Soldiers he spoke to reported that comrades had defected to the "fanatics"[32] on the other side, while he heard a conversation between two officers who both came from the city. "Why don't they let us fight on Golan instead of this?"[33] Fisk heard one of them plaintively ask the other.

Two days later, Fisk's "mischievous lies" were attacked on Syrian state radio. He went to see the minister of information, Iskander Ahmad Iskander, who disputed the facts of his report for the record, but denied calling him a liar. When Fisk then mentioned that he had been called a liar on Syrian radio, the minister was sceptical. "The radio? I have not heard this broadcast," he said with a smile, and offered Fisk a Havana cigar.[34]

VI

It was by relying on Alawis that the regime of Hafez al-Assad survived. It has been suggested that, rather than bringing them prosperity in a way that would move them up into the middle classes, he cynically kept them apart from the rest of Syrian society. Evidence for this is the poor but fortress-like suburb Mezze 86, which stands on a hill on the fringes of Damascus. It is just behind the presidential palace, and has something in common with some of the illegal Israeli settlements deliberately built in East Jerusalem to cut the city off from its West Bank, Palestinian hinterland. Mezze 86 is overwhelmingly inhabited by Alawis who had been encouraged to move to Damascus after 1982, and many of whom were given jobs in the security services.[35] Yet, as his Sunni friend Abdul Halim Khaddam, who served him as foreign minister and first vice-president, pointed out, Hafez al-Assad's regime "should not be seen as the rule of one confession over others but rather of one man over others".[36] The dominant position Alawis now occupied in the army and security services could not be challenged, but that was solely because Hafez al-Assad depended on them.

With the fading of Ba'thist ideals, the elite that ran the country behaved like its predecessors. Syria became an increasingly "soft state", to use the expression of Gunnar Myrdal. Laws existed, but they were not invoked against the rich and powerful. They were there to be used for the benefit of the regime, not to hold it to account. Leading figures in the Ba'th Party and close relatives of the president amassed fortunes, and in practice were immune from prosecution. They would expect preference when it came to the awarding of government contracts and disposal of government land and other assets. Economic opportunities were seen first as largesse to be shared out in a bid to build and retain loyalty, and only secondarily as chances to expand the country's wealth and bring prosperity to its people.

After the Hama massacre of 1982, the *mukhabarat* were everywhere. Fear would now stalk the land for so long as Hafez al-Assad lived. There were genuine threats to his state, both external and internal: the dangers of another Islamist rebellion or even a rival Ba'thist or Nasserist faction backed by another Arab country. Ever-hostile Iraq, which welcomed Syrian Islamist militants and exiled Ba'thist dissidents alike, hoped one day to overthrow him. Yet the rival Ba'thists in Baghdad were not the only potential supporters of sedition. Saudi Arabia and Jordan also took in ambitious political refugees, and these monarchies, too, had no compunction about providing Syrian revolutionaries with military training. Then there was the Lebanese cauldron: a kaleidoscope of armed conflict where Syria had many enemies, to say nothing of Yasser Arafat and his Palestinians whose hopes of turning Lebanon into a base had been dashed by Hafez al-Assad. Antagonism with the PLO continued throughout Hafez al-Assad's life, and he did his best to build up rival factions to Arafat's PLO, including its great rival the Islamist group Hamas. And what of Israel and its patron America, for whom he was a thorn in the side? The CIA had intrigued in Syria before. Had it renounced its bad habits?

There was nothing irrational about fearing subversion or worse from any of these quarters. In a rather plaintive anecdote, when nervous-looking colleagues entered Hafez al-Assad's office to tell them his son Basil had been killed in a car crash, he could tell they were the bearers of bad news. But what he expected them to tell him, when they opened their mouths, was that he had been overthrown.[37] The possibility of a coup was never far from his mind. Fear is self-feeding. It corrodes from within. It is a sign of Hafez al-Assad's robustness that he does not seem to have descended into paranoia after the manner of, say, Stalin. Instead, his regime became paranoid on his behalf. Perhaps the man at the top needed it to be so and deliberately encouraged it. That paranoia, thirty years after Hama and more than ten years after his death, would play a large part in its finally losing its grip on Syria.

In neighbouring Iraq, there was a Soviet-style attempt to repress religion during the dictatorship of Hassan al-Bakr in the late 1970s. This was triggered by indications that the Sunni and Shi'i religious leaderships of the country might be about to line up against the regime. Hafez al-Assad's realism and flexibility ensured that he attempted no such thing in Syria after the crushing of the Hama rebellion. Instead, he continued to make efforts to reach out to the large and increasing number of Syrian Sunnis who focused a major part of their identity on their faith, and wished to lead devout lives.

The Islamic revival, which had perhaps first been sparked by the Six Day War and alienation from the West, was now in full swing across the Arab world and beyond. In Syria, the form the revival took was connected with the spread of literacy, which enabled many more people to study and explore their religion. Islam and Arabism flowed closely together. There was nothing intrinsically incompatible between the Ba'thist nationalism which the state was officially promulgating and a desire to live a more devout life as a Sunni Muslim. An ever-increasing number of young professional people, most of whom owed their education to the regime, thirstily sought out the paths of piety. As literacy rippled out from the towns and into the countryside, it was followed by an earnest quest to learn how to live the life of a good Muslim.

Hafez al-Assad set out to co-opt the religious revival. He persuaded many Sunni merchants in Aleppo to line up behind him, in the same way as their brothers in Damascus had done. He was helped by the support of some noted religious scholars, such as the Kurdish Sheikh Ahmad Kuftaro who proclaimed his admiration for Hafez al-Assad's "dedication and ... steadfastness on the principle of faith". Kuftaro also asserted that:

> Islam and the regime's power to enforce the law are twin brothers ... It is impossible to think of one without the other. Islam is the base and the regime's power of rule is the protector; after all a thing without a base is destined to collapse and fail, and a thing without a protector will end in extinction.[38]

Another religious scholar who supported him was Sheikh Sa'id al-Buti, who sided with him over the Hama massacre, pointing out that the Muslim Brotherhood and the Fighting Vanguard had brought *fitna*, civil strife, to Syria. This was an endorsement of the regime's crackdown, since the stirring up of *fitna* in the population is against the principles of Islam. He was also a firm opponent of allowing political parties with a religious basis to contest elections in Syria, because he believed they would be taken over by militants.[39] On an occasion in the early 1990s when thousands of Islamist prisoners were released as a Ramadan gesture, Sheikh Sa'id al-Buti addressed Hafez al-Assad at a reception. The following words, which are as masterful as they are unctuous, illustrate the rewards for a deference which simultaneously reinforced the status of the speaker and the personage at whom the words were directed:

> Mr President ... I wish that God makes your extraordinary wisdom (I choose my words carefully), your great calm and the dedication your family and friends know well, into a solid pillar for the protection of religion ... I am convinced that those who have been released these days are the vanguard of those who burn to be always behind you ... and I know that the small number of those who still await their release are impatient to stand with their brothers in this trench in order to be devoted soldiers behind you.
>
> As for your soldiers outside this country, they are our Syrian brothers who ... perhaps have been prevented from seeing the truth in the past ... perhaps have been deceived by conspirators ... but today – I can personally testify to that – they repudiate their old ideas and raise their heads, proud of this country and its leadership.[40]

Hafez al-Assad's "soldiers outside this country" were exiled Islamists in Saudi Arabia whom the sheikh had visited, and on whose behalf he was pleading that they be allowed to return home. In some cases he succeeded, and Hafez al-Assad graciously permitted the return of a number of Islamists to Syria provided that they supported – or at least did not criticise – his regime.

VII

It transpired, however, that the greatest internal challenge to Hafez al-Assad after 1982 came not from Islamists or any other political group but from within his own family. This was a reflection of where real power in Syria was now located. In November 1983, while a complex collection of crises in Lebanon required especially firm leadership in

Syria, heart problems brought on by exhaustion threatened his life, and it was far from certain that any recovery would be full. Suddenly the risks inherent in the concentration of all power in the hands of one man focused minds. The most powerful person in the country after the president was his brother, Rif'at. Rif'at al-Assad had been at his brother's side during his rise to power and had played an important role in the coup in which he had ousted Salah Jadid. He was the only person "who could genuinely claim to have shared power with the president".[41]

Seven years younger than his brother, Rif'at had risen in his shadow but was a person of considerable talent in his own right. He was much more familiar with the West than Hafez al-Assad and argued, sometimes in public, for greater freedom for private enterprise. He also took a leading role in many development and education projects, and advocated foreign and defence policies which did not tie the country so closely to the Soviet Union. He was thus used to questioning his brother's policies, and asked whether it was right to go so far down a road that alienated Syria from Europe and America by supporting terrorist elements and engaging in an arms race with Israel it could never win. He was also an advocate of greater democracy within the Ba'th Party.[42] He came across as one of the more "pro-Western" voices in the inner counsels of the regime, sometimes a lone one. This aroused suspicion among the president's inner circle. Moreover, he had also managed to acquire, in a way that was not immediately obvious, considerable wealth. This included an extensive portfolio of property in Syria, Europe and the USA. His value to his older brother lay in his control of the defence companies he had established to protect the regime. The troops in these units were largely Alawi, but they have been described as "lacking discipline, indifferent to human life, and beyond the restraints of the law".[43] They were also resented by the regular army because of their privileges and better pay. Rif'at al-Assad was at the heart of the regime, but controversy surrounded him.

From his sickbed, Hafez al-Assad appointed a kind of regency council to manage the country until he recovered his strength. It had six members, who all happened to be Sunnis[44]: the prime minister, foreign minister and minister of defence, the chief-of-staff and two top Ba'th Party officials. Although those listed did not include the president's powerful brother, some in the inner circle and a number of influential Alawi generals considered that he should not have been excluded from it. Rif'at al-Assad was persuaded to take part. Contrary to the president's instructions, in late 1983 the country came under the control of the twenty-strong regional command of the Ba'th Party, in which Rif'at was a prominent member. His influence in the regional command increased. It even looked as though he might be about to become the de facto ruler.

When Hafez al-Assad began to recover, a strange situation emerged. Rif'at al-Assad commanded a substantial proportion of the armed forces, including many elite units, and received adulation from young soldiers to whom he had clearly been inspirational. For a while the atmosphere was tense. It seemed as though the country might dissolve into a civil war with commanders of military units declaring for one or other of the brothers. This would have had incalculable consequences, not least the probable destruction of Damascus, but in the end Rif'at decided not to oppose his brother – although he is said afterwards to have regretted the decision[45] – and left the country on the pretext of leading a delegation, comprising his closest supporters, to Moscow. Although he returned to Syria at various times and for considerable periods, he was never again to be close to power. He eventually settled in Paris.

The story of the stand-off between the brothers reveals how closely power was kept within the entourage of the president, as well as how the bonds of the Assad family were ultimately the most important. But if a talented brother might be a threat to Hafez al-Assad, the same was not the case with a son. Roger Owen conjectures that it may have been as early as the time of the Rif'at affair that Hafez al-Assad's thoughts first turned to the option of making his son Basil his successor. Owen also stresses that it would have been consistent with his caution to keep the option open to see how matters developed, rather than making an irrevocable commitment.[46] But by 1991, banners and posters were affectionately referring to the president as "Abu Basil", "father of

Basil", putting the son, who had hitherto had a reputation mainly as a playboy, in the public eye. Basil was also appointed commander of the presidential guard. We will never know how matters might have developed subsequently. Basil al-Assad died in 1994 in an accident caused by his own negligence while driving a sports car far too fast through fog on the Damascus airport road.

Hafez al-Assad's second son, Bashar, was summoned back from London later that year to join the army, interrupting his training as an ophthalmologist at the Western Eye Hospital. Yet it was only in 1998, when his father's health went into terminal decline, that public signs of a campaign for him to succeed his father became apparent. An anti-corruption drive was launched which just happened to target certain prominent people who were thought likely to oppose the dynastic succession from father to son. A bid by Rif'at al-Assad also seems to have been feared, and individuals deemed to be his potential supporters were arrested. At the same time, the constitution was changed so that a person of Bashar's relatively youthful age of thirty-four could become president. Nevertheless, when Hafez al-Assad died in June 2000, power under the constitution passed to the first vice-president, his old friend and trusted lieutenant Abdul Halim Khaddam. If those who held power in the regime had wished otherwise, Bashar al-Assad would not have become president. The fact that no one opposed him demonstrates two things. The first is that the elite at the top stuck together and would not risk a battle over the succession. The other was that the Assad family had become the guardians of their interests.

VIII

Hafez al-Assad was often inscrutable. "We do not know where he really stands," said the PLO leader Abu Iyad. "He is an enigma," was the verdict of Ilyas Sarkis, the former president of Lebanon.[47] Did power corrupt him? His propaganda machine identified him with the Syrian people and the state, and built a massive personality cult around him:

"Our Leader Forever, the Faithful Hafez al-Assad"; "Loyalty to him is loyalty to the party and to the people and their cause"; "A breach of this loyalty, in whatever form ... constitutes a grave deviation which the party and the masses reject."[48]

Some of the choices he made were very murky indeed. Perhaps he lost his way somewhere between pragmatism and ruthlessness. He exacted a terrible price from the people of Hama when the rebellion against his rule occurred in their midst. This has been contrasted with the "largely elusive and indirect character" of his response to Israel's 1982 invasion of Lebanon, which was how his handling of that crisis was perceived by many Syrians.[49] Perhaps. Yet in Lebanon he had no alternative to strategies of indirect approach. Anything else would have been military and, therefore, political suicide.

By 1987, there were credible reports that the share of the Syrian GDP that comprised the "black" economy was 30 per cent.[50] There are few reasons to suggest it may have declined over the following years. Concerns about corruption had been expressed as early as 1975–6. Hafez al-Assad sometimes reacted with a nod and a wink. Many of those around him grew rich in this way. It has been suggested that irregular transactions sometimes took place with the explicit connivance of the state. Thus, it is alleged that revenues from oil fields near Deir al-Zur were kept out of the state budget and controlled by the Republican Guard instead.[51]

As Hafez al-Assad lay on his deathbed, it was obvious to anyone who cared to look that the corrupt and repressive regime over which he presided was an obstacle to progress for Syria. It was also running out of money while, as always, impoverished people from the countryside, albeit now often literate, continued to flock to the cities in the desperate hope of finding work.

CHAPTER SIX

Bashar al-Assad, 2000–

From Succession to Civil War

I

Bashar al-Assad was aged just thirty-four when he took power in June 2000. He was the youngest ruler of an Arab country at that time. Fluent in English (and educated in French), he had been eighteen months into his studies in London to qualify as an eye doctor when he was called home after the death of his brother Basil. This choice of career was a sure sign that he did not anticipate that, one day, he would take over from his father. While in London, he met his future wife, Asma, who was a native of the city but ethnically Syrian. A person of considerable ability in her own right who worked in London's banking and financial services industry, Asma was a Sunni and the daughter of a cardiologist who came from a Homs notable family. Both she and her husband shared an interest in technology, and one of Bashar al-Assad's first appointments when he arrived home was to succeed his deceased brother as president of the Syrian computer society. The pair were a stylish and even glamorous couple who seemed to bridge the Sunni-Alawi divide, to be deeply rooted in Syria while at home in the West, and who aspired to transform their country for the better. Bashar's brother Maher also married a Sunni, as did other children of leading Alawi Ba'thists.

On 17 July, a mere thirty-seven days after his father's death, the new president gave his inaugural speech to the Syrian parliament. The speech was well structured and it is safe to assume that its words were chosen with great care. It paid tribute to his father's achievements and contained much of what would be expected in an inaugural speech by any new president of Syria, such as a demand for the return of the Golan Heights in exchange for peace with Israel. What is more interesting for present purposes is the criticism it contained – sometimes implicit, sometimes rather more direct – of Syrian society and institutions, and the failure of some government policies.

The speech pleaded for a kind of national dialogue. A recurring theme was the need to establish transparency and a culture of constructive criticism which had been absent in the Syria Bashar al-Assad had inherited:

> We should face ourselves and our society bravely and conduct a brave dialogue with both in which we reveal our points of weakness and talk about our customs, traditions and concepts which have become a true impediment in the way of any progress ...
>
> We have to shake off the attitude of evading the sense of responsibility. We have to give up reliance on others ... You should not rely solely on the State nor should you let the State rely solely on you: let us work together as one team.[1]

Tucked away in the speech were frank admissions that some officials were dishonest and a plea for more accurate statistics. It also contained appeals for the encouragement of the free market (which, it was conceded, had only been opened up in a haphazard fashion under his father), improvements in the position of women, the need for the rule of law, and a call for "democratic thinking".

His words about "democratic thinking" suggest he had an understanding of what true democracy was, as well as an appreciation of the obstacles to building a democratic society in Syria. After a plea for strengthening institutions, in which he called for "institutional thinking" in which the building of institutions would be a joint endeavour for all by "putting the mentality of the state above the mentality of the tribe", he moved on to the closely connected topic of "democratic thinking":

> [Institutional thinking] is the logic of cooperation and openness to others, and it is inseparable from the democratic thinking which has many things in common with it in various places ... To what extent are we democratic? And what are the indications that refer to the existence or non-existence of democracy? Is it in elections or in the free press or in the free speech or in other freedoms and rights? Democracy is not any of these because all these rights and others are not democracy, rather they are democratic practices and results of these practices which all depend on democratic thinking. This thinking is based on the principle of accepting the opinion of the other and this is certainly a two-way street. It means that what is right for me is a right for others but when the road becomes a one-way road it will become selfish. This means that we do not say I have the right to this or that; rather, we should say that others have certain rights and if others enjoy this particular right I have the same right.
>
> This means that democracy is our duty towards others before it becomes a right for us. Democratic thinking is the building and the structure ... [E]ach building is designed in a way and has a foundation appropriate to the weight it is expected to carry. Hence, we cannot apply the democracy of others on ourselves. Western democracy, for example, is the outcome of a long history that resulted in customs and traditions that distinguished the current culture of Western societies. In order to apply what they have we have to live their history with all its social signification. As this is, obviously, impossible we have to have our democratic experience which is special to us, which stems from our history, culture, civilisation and which is a response to the needs of our society and the requirements of our reality ...[2]

The above is a typical example of Bashar al-Assad's rather convoluted style when making a political speech, but the thrust of it is clear enough.

If he was making an oblique statement of intent to turn Syria into a genuine democracy which would be based on Syria's own culture and reflect the needs of its society, then he had allowed himself plenty of ways to slow down or even abandon this path if he deemed it appropriate. All he would need to say was that the time was not yet right, or the circumstances not appropriate. However, his acknowledgement of the hard realities of what was involved in building Syrian democracy was not necessarily cynical. Arab critics have noticed how Western democracy can be abused. The role played by media moguls in shaping Western public opinion and the influence of big money at election time spring to mind. But if a uniquely Syrian form of democracy was to be grown, this would take time. It would also need plenty of consultation in which people could speak their minds freely, and a strong guiding hand provided by a government that was reasonably transparent and free of vested interests.

It was just such a government that Bashar al-Assad was never able to provide, but he did take steps which he may have genuinely hoped would eventually lead to one. During the period from his assumption of office until the early months of 2001 there was a trickle of liberalisation measures. These included the release of political prisoners of all persuasions, the granting of government licences for new, independent newspapers, the encouragement of an atmosphere of discussion and debate in which the government could be criticised, and the establishment of civil society groups aimed at working for human rights and related goals. Intellectuals drafted declarations calling for freedom and democracy, while organisations like the Muslim Brotherhood and the Communist Party (which reinvented itself as the Popular Democratic Party) issued manifestoes calling for a pluralist society. The Muslim Brotherhood dedicated itself to dialogue and a "democratic political framework". It officially renounced violence and called for the protection of human rights.[3]

Yet the hopes raised by the Damascus Spring, as it was called, were soon crushed. Official newspapers and the Ba'th Party, as well as heavy-weight figures from Hafez al-Assad's day such as the defence minister Mustafa Tlas and vice-president Abdul Halim Khaddam, attacked it.

The *mukhabarat* chiefs told Bashar al-Assad that if he continued on this path of political reform then they could not guarantee that he would remain in power. By the summer of 2001, restrictions on political freedom were reappearing. Whether by chance or because it was a good day on which to bury bad news, many activists were arrested on 11 September 2001. Some of them, such as the writer Radwan Ziadeh, now look back on the period with a considerable degree of cynicism and see the reforms as essentially a public relations exercise by the authorities and little more.[4]

II

Whatever the truth about the Damascus Spring, many Western governments and commentators wished to give Bashar al-Assad the benefit of every possible doubt. They sympathised with the dilemma faced by a son taking over the presidency of a police state on his father's death. But they sometimes overlooked two crucial points. The first was that he, like everybody else, was a product of the world in which he had grown up. As David Lesch has put it, he was a child of the Arab-Israeli conflict and the Cold War, as well as of his strongman father.[5] A sign of the pressures that would be placed on the shoulders of this young doctor occurred shortly after his return to Damascus in 1994, when the file dealing with Syria's interests in Lebanon was thrust into his hands. This was almost certainly given to him as a test: the cautious Hafez al-Assad was not going to procure the nomination of his son as his successor unless he was satisfied he had the necessary skills to take over.[6] Bashar al-Assad would have to learn very quickly about the hard-nosed realities of power in the Middle East. He would also need to maintain continuity with his father's rule, since it was his father who had dealt him the cards he would hold in his hand.

The second often overlooked point is closely related, but deserves to be stressed because it is so frequently forgotten. Like every other ruler, Bashar al-Assad inherited the burdens of the past. In his case, these were not just the events that had occurred in the thirty years since his father took power. They also included all that had happened during the fifty-three years since the partition of Palestine, the fifty-five years since Syria became fully independent and, indeed, the eighty or so years since Britain and France had arbitrarily partitioned Greater Syria. He would have to play his rather mediocre hand very skilfully while tied up in the straitjacket of history. Events would soon show just how dangerous was the environment in which Syria was located. The foreign policy challenges which confronted him almost from the day he took office would bear this out.

In late September 2000, less than four months after the death of Hafez al-Assad and before the new president could be said to have had a chance to find his feet, Ariel Sharon, at that time the leader of the opposition in the Israeli parliament, visited the Esplanade of the Mosques in occupied East Jerusalem accompanied by 1000 security guards. The Israeli prime minister, Ehud Barak, had given his consent to him making this visit.[7] Ariel Sharon's visit confirmed what Palestinians had long feared and what had become increasingly apparent to many observers since early in the Oslo Process. It showed that, despite everything, Israeli governments were still unprepared to acknowledge Palestinian rights and were light-years from preparing Israeli public opinion to do so. To Palestinians, Ariel Sharon's visit was a deliberate provocation, a symbolic act of contempt.[8] Demonstrations were greeted with violence by the Israeli security forces, and the occupied territories exploded. The Second Intifada had started and would cause much bloodshed over the next few years. A campaign of suicide bombings against civilian targets in Israel was part of the Palestinian reaction. This terrorism led to the melting away of the very substantial Israeli peace camp, while at the same time public opinion in Syria and other Arab countries was outraged at the bulldozing of large areas in Palestinian cities by the Israeli army and the numerous civilian casualties.

While the Intifada was raging, Osama bin Laden's suicide team crashed their hijacked airliners into the Twin Towers and the Pentagon on 11 September 2001. Some 3,000 innocent victims perished. For Americans, the surprise and the shock were all too reminiscent of the

Japanese attack on Pearl Harbour, and their instinctive reaction was the same: to destroy the enemy which had assailed them. This time, the enemy were the Islamist militants of al-Qa'ida. President George W. Bush declared a "war on terror" against them, and set out to track them down wherever they could be found. In the short term, this enabled Bashar al-Assad to achieve a certain rapprochement with America, since he was able to provide information about Islamist terrorists gleaned by his intelligence services. This even led to an admission by officials of the US Administration that Syria had helped to save American lives.[9] But would this be enough? As a stunned and angry US administration went round the world asking its allies and other countries "Are you with us or against us?" Syria was put in an impossible position. How could it be expected to give a simple answer in response to this question when Syrians were angry about the pictures they could see almost every night on their television screens from next door in Palestine? Their own country, too, had been a victim of America's Middle Eastern policies for many decades.

The American-led invasion of Iraq in March 2003 was an event which, like Israel's reoccupation of the West Bank during the intifada, Syria had to be seen to oppose. It also put an end to a lucrative source of income for Syria: trade with Saddam Hussein's Iraq in breach of UN sanctions. Since Bashar al-Assad took power, Syria had received several billion US dollars in this way. Trade included not just cheap oil and transit dues on pipelines but, it was calculated, 70 per cent of the weapons which entered Iraq illegally during this period. Turkey and Jordan had also traded with Iraq, but in the run-up to the invasion they scaled back their activities. Syria did not do so, even though this could only be calculated to embitter relations with America and the other countries making up the coalition that was about to enter Iraq.[10]

It was therefore small surprise that, with American troops suddenly on Syria's long, eastern border and bellicose rhetoric emanating from Washington, another question was asked as the initial combat operations in Iraq came to what seemed a successful conclusion after only two months. "Will Syria be next?" There were plenty of Neo-Conservative voices in the USA which hoped that it would be. 9/11 had unleashed a wave of anger and jingoistic fervour in the USA which, when coupled with the unprecedented absence of a superpower rival, enabled influential lobbies to dream dreams which ought to have been seen as implausible as conquering Russia. These were the reshaping of the Middle East to suit America and Israel. For the hawks of the Bush administration, there was no place in that Middle East for a regime like Syria that still proclaimed a passionate Arab nationalist ideology.

The US-led invasion of Iraq would put yet further strains on Damascus. Syria became a destination for those fleeing the violence in Iraq. A trickle became a flood until the number of refugees reached 1.2 million.[11] Those with money caused a boom which inflated rents in the Damascus property market and excluded many young Syrians from it, while the poorer refugees competed with the shoe-shine boys of Syrian cities and their children put additional strain on Syria's education system. Such matters seemed often to be barely noticed in the West. America and its allies, which had lit the fuse that ignited the dissolution of Iraq along sectarian lines, shut their eyes to the effects of their policies on Syria.

Stung by Syria's toleration of Islamist fighters travelling across its territory to join the growing insurgency in Iraq and hoping to end Syria's grip on Lebanon, President George W. Bush signed the Syria Accountability and Lebanese Sovereignty Restoration Act into law on 12 December 2003. The Act blocked all US exports to Syria except food and medicines, and proscribed all US investment there. However, a close reading of the Act shows that it was not just concerned with punishing Syria for allowing infiltration across its border into Iraq by volunteers going to fight the US-led forces. It was actually aimed at pushing Syria to accept the entirety of the hegemonic vision the Bush administration had developed for the region.

The Act denounced Syria as a sponsor of terrorism and called upon it to withdraw its forces from Lebanon. The "terrorist offices, training camps and facilities" in Syria which it had to close were not just the offices, camps and facilities of groups supporting the growing insurrection in Iraq. They included those of groups resisting Israel such as Hamas, Hizbullah and the leftist Popular Front for the Liberation of Palestine. There were no reciprocal obligations on Israel – a nuclear power – to match other requirements imposed on Syria, which was called upon to halt production of rockets and weapons of mass destruction. In the same way, the Act called on Syria (and Lebanon) to "enter into serious unconditional bilateral negotiations with the government of Israel in order to realise a full and permanent peace". The Golan Heights were not mentioned in the Act. The implication of the wording would seem to be that the failure to achieve peace lay at Syria's door, rather than at that of Israel, and that Syria should seek peace even if Israel was not prepared to return the Syrian territory it occupied.

Israeli maps showed the Golan Heights as an integral part of Israel, and Israeli citizens and tourists who entered the occupied area were often not even aware that they were leaving Israel. Syria had every reason to fear that it would never regain its land if it had no means to put pressure on Israel. Moreover, with Hizbullah disbanded and the Syrian army withdrawn from Lebanon, Israel would once again be able to outflank Syria militarily by sending an army into Lebanon whenever it chose to do so.

Bashar al-Assad dug his heels in with the same stubbornness his father would have shown, although perhaps with a lesser degree of skill. Sunni Islamist fighters and supplies continued to pass through Syria on their way to Iraq. The insurgency against the Americans there gathered pace, and the problems America was now facing in Iraq soon reduced the likelihood of it invading another Arab country. But then, on 14 February 2005, another crisis began. A bomb which weighed a ton and was hidden inside a parked van killed Rafiq al Hariri, the former Lebanese prime minister, as his six-car convoy drove through downtown Beirut. A Sunni billionaire with his own construction empire and good contacts with investors in many countries, especially in Saudi Arabia, he had first been appointed to this office in 1992. He had held it for most of the time since then and had facilitated the rebuilding of Lebanon after the civil war. His own construction enterprises had played a major role in this, and there was no doubt that he had benefited personally by exploiting conflicts of interest. Hariri was a controversial character, but without him Lebanon would probably not have been rebuilt. He was seen by many Lebanese as their best hope for the future.

Once there may have been justification for Syria to have a special position in Lebanon and to have an army stationed there, but times had changed. The Lebanese civil war had ended in 1990 and Israel had withdrawn from the south of the country ten years later. Nevertheless, Syria still interfered in Lebanese politics as it saw fit. This was bitterly resented by many Lebanese. In 2004, Syria had used its influence over parliamentarians to re-elect President Emile Lahoud for a further three years, even though this required a constitutional amendment. The president was Syria's man, but Rafiq al-Hariri, when prime minister, had opposed the extension of his term. Rafiq al-Hariri had the confidence not to vary his motorcade's route as often as security advisers would have been likely to suggest. It can be inferred from this that he did not see the assassination coming. Yet was Syria directly or indirectly involved in his assassination? This is believed by many well informed observers as well as many Lebanese. Fingers are also pointed at Syria's ally, Hizbullah. Hariri's death led to an immense welling up of anger against the Syrian presence in Lebanon and its undue influence over Lebanese politics. This culminated in a demonstration on 14 March in which a million people participated. The "Cedar Revolution", as it was quickly dubbed, took its name from Lebanon's national symbol. As it was backed by international pressure, especially from the USA and France, Syria had no option but to withdraw its forces.

Bashar al-Assad ensured that his soldiers left rapidly. The last had crossed back over the border within a matter of seven weeks. But that was not the end of the story. Hizbullah now flexed its muscles in a clever way. It organised its own massive demonstrations to thank the departing Syrians for their role in bringing the Lebanese civil war to an end and helping to resist the Israelis. The scale of these demonstrations made it clear that the country was split and that not all Lebanese supported the Cedar Revolution. A number of prominent anti-Syrian activists, including members of parliament and journalists, were assassinated over the next two years, while Syria maintained its ties with Hizbullah which had retained its competent and battle-hardened militia.

Developments in the various crises in the Middle East did not come to a halt. While the fighting between US-led forces and Sunni insurgents in the provinces of Iraq immediately across from the Syrian border was still at its height, and the Americans were also facing Shi'i militias further south, yet another military campaign took place. This was the Israeli invasion of Lebanon in the summer of 2006. On 12 July, Hizbullah forces crossed into Israel, killed several Israeli soldiers and captured a further two who were taken back to Lebanon. Unable to find the two soldiers or procure their release, Israel devastated southern Lebanon and systematically destroyed much of Lebanon's infrastructure which had been painstakingly rebuilt since the end of the civil war, to a large extent with European aid. Lebanese refugees numbering 400,000 flooded into Syria,[12] many of them put up in their homes by Syrian families. The attack temporarily united Lebanese of all sects against Israel and in support of Hizbullah. For its part, Hizbullah showed that it, too, possessed a deterrent and showered northern Israel with indiscriminate rocket fire. Like the Israeli bombardments, this was a war crime.

The USA, with the support of the government of Tony Blair in London, seemed to be intent on slowing down the diplomatic wheels at the United Nations which soon started rolling to achieve a ceasefire. Many Arab rulers such as Hosni Mubarak in Egypt and the monarchs of the Gulf appeared to go along with this approach. They would not mind at all if Israel destroyed Hizbullah, or at least mortally wounded it, but now it was Israel's turn to overreach itself. As Lebanese civilian casualties mounted towards 1,000 dead and many more injured, Hizbullah showed itself still able to resist with efficiency. A groundswell of admiration for the Shi'i warriors broke across the Arab world, temporarily bridging the growing Sunni-Shi'i divide. The diplomatic push for a ceasefire could no longer be resisted, and left Hassan Nasrallah, the religious scholar who was leader of Hizbullah, a national hero not just among Lebanese of all sects but in other Arab countries. At last the Arab world had found a figure in whom, at least for the moment, virtually all could take pride. Fanciful claims were even made that he was the new Nasser. In Damascus Bashar al-Assad was able to bask in the glory won by Syria's ally for whom he had been the cheerleader. There were other, more tangible, benefits. Hizbullah's influence in Lebanese politics was enhanced, and Syria re-established some of the influence which it had appeared to lose after the assassination of Rafiq al-Hariri.

It seemed that, by a combination of caution, pragmatism and obstinacy, Bashar al-Assad had stepped straight into his father's shoes. He had weathered these storms, each of which had blended into the next during the first six years of his rule. By standing up to Washington and to Israel, he became more popular at home – as well as in other Arab countries. Rewards would now come his way. In 2007, the ice of Syria's isolation seemed to be melting. US parliamentarians, including Nancy Pelosi, the speaker of the House of Representatives, visited Damascus. Syria exchanged ambassadors with Iraq and was invited to attend the Annapolis process, at which America launched a road map to achieve peace between Israel and the Palestinians that November. Bashar al-Assad seemed to be able to build on these successes. In 2008, Turkey facilitated indirect talks between Syria and Israel, but these were ended because of Israel's particularly brutal invasion of Gaza in December that year in response to rocket attacks. The following February, the Obama administration even lifted a few of the sanctions in the Syria Accountability Act to supply spare parts for Syrian Air's Boeing aircraft. Then, in 2009, King Abdullah of Saudi Arabia visited Damascus and a military cooperation pact was signed with Turkey.

III

Foreign policy issues were not the only problems lurking in Bashar al-Assad's inbox when he came to power. As has been seen, he inherited a corruption-ridden state which was run by a nomenklatura and dominated by an inefficient public sector. The economic situation was deteriorating. As ever, the numbers of urban unemployed and underemployed were growing. Sixty-five per cent of the country's population was below the age of twenty-five, and the population was still growing at 2.4 per cent per annum. Many of the young people coming onto the job market every year were university graduates. They owed their education to Ba'thist policies, and had had their expectations raised, but they could not find work. Their expectations could not be met unless the system changed.

In the last two years of his life, Hafez al-Assad had shown signs that he realised the economic status quo in Syria could not go on. In the speech he gave when he was sworn in for another seven-year term on 11 March 1999, he called for a revision of the investment law and modernisation of the country's administration and banking system which had both clogged up its development.[13] He acknowledged the poor economic performance and crumbling of the country's infrastructure a year later, just a few months before his death, when he described the government of Prime Minister Mahmoud al-Zu'bi who had held office since 1987 as "the worst in the country's history". This neatly transferred the blame for economic decline away from himself,[14] and followed a year in which the economy had actually recorded negative growth.[15]

Although it was easy to make a list of economic problems facing the new president when he took office, the question of how to tackle them was much harder. The solution to the shortage of investment capital would be to free up the banking system, particularly by allowing private banks. But as Asma al-Assad commented a year or two after her husband took power:

> We have not had private banks in Syria for fifty years. Our public banks are not functioning ... We have staff who do not speak English, who do not have computers. So we are on a very, very basic level ... We had no idea how to do this. We don't have the experience.[16]

In the first years of the new president's rule, there was discussion of economic reform and talk of producing a Syrian social market economy. To some extent progress towards reform may have been slowed by the negative effects of the US-led invasion of Iraq on any programme which might radically transform Syria,[17] but the regime also seems to have been inspired by the Chinese model of economic liberalisation without a loosening of the political system.[18] Private banks did arrive in Syria in

2004, followed by insurance companies the following year. There were reforms to the laws governing investment, companies and taxation, and a competition or anti-trust law was promulgated in 2008 with the intention of combatting monopolistic practices as the economy liberalised.

A stock exchange was established in 2009. The currency passed through many gradual stages from unconvertible to freely convertible, but in 2010 the economy was still predominantly cash based. Syria remained in the bottom quartile (number 143 out of 183) in a World Bank Index of economies in terms of ease of doing business. There was a very long way to go. Although GDP growth occurred, it tended to be up to a maximum of around 5 per cent or 6 per cent.[19] Sometimes it was considerably less. In 2010, the IMF estimated it was merely 3.9 per cent (although, of course, this was after the world financial crash of 2008). This erratic progress was well below that being achieved at the time by the tiger economies of the Far East or next door Turkey, where rates of around 10 per cent per annum were far from unusual. It was also below that of Mubarak's Egypt, which had similar problems and challenges in many ways.

Particular problems of the Ba'thist state which Hafez al-Assad had created stood in the way of reform.[20] The cadres who ran it were still soaked in the Marxist and socialist ideas of an earlier generation. Many civil servants and political appointees had served for long periods, leading to the growth of a culture of vested interests. They were self-seeking and jealous of losing what they had, although over time Bashar al-Assad succeeded in placing a number of able technocrats into key positions. Few Ba'thist functionaries had previously had any experience of a Western economy or society. Some had been trained in Eastern Europe before the collapse of Communism, or might have lived in Saudi Arabia or the Gulf. Theoretically, the Gulf States were citadels of free enterprise but they were also strongholds of monopolistic practice and cronyism. Oil revenues and the relatively small size of their populations shielded them from the cold economic winds to which Syria was exposed. The idea of a comprehensive plan to turn Syria into a market economy was gradually dropped in favour of piecemeal changes which were often carried out almost surreptitiously.[21]

Although the limited opening of the economy benefited many ordinary people, the reforms skirted anything that threatened the position of Bashar al-Assad's most important supporters. This slowed the spread of prosperity. There was an expansion of crony capitalism of the most extreme kind. This was exemplified by Bashar's cousin Rami Makhlouf who was frequently cited (not least in the London *Financial Times*[22]) as controlling 60 per cent of the country's economy. He represented over 200 foreign companies operating in Syria, and controlled what should have been the showcases for a new, open Syrian economy: the free trade zones and both the country's mobile phone operators.[23] Everybody knew that the new competition law was not going to be used to split up his business assets or those of other key supporters of the regime. The small group of wealthy people in the uppermost echelon of society grew, as did the numbers of poor at the bottom. Those in the middle found themselves squeezed.[24]

One big difference from his father's time was that Bashar al-Assad's rule was never that of one man. When he took power, he had to negotiate with those at the very top of the regime in order to get his way. Initially, these were men close to his father such as Mustafa Tlas and Abdul Halim Khaddam who, it will have been noted, opposed the brief period of liberalisation immediately after Bashar al-Assad came to power. Over a few years many of them retired or were removed, and the new president became dependent on a clique of family members and other close associates in a way that narrowed his power base when compared with that of his father.[25] These included his younger brother Maher, who became commander of the Republican Guard and other special forces, his brother-in-law Assef Shawqat, who was deputy defence minister and deputy chief-of-staff at the time of his death in a bomb attack on 18 July 2012, and his businessman cousin Rami Makhlouf who has already been mentioned, and whose brother Hafez was put in charge of internal security in Damascus.[26]

Whether Bashar al-Assad was (and is) able to exercise complete control over these figures is uncertain. There has been speculation that he is not abreast of all the activities of the security services and that other powerful figures in the regime act without his approval. Whatever the case, it seems that the destinies of those at the top of the regime are bound together and that they will survive and fall as one.

There was now a rich and increasingly sophisticated elite in Damascus, Aleppo, Homs and Lattakia that was strongly behind him and contained members of all the different Syrian sects and ethnic minorities. It would have been very easy for him to fall into a complacency encouraged by their adulation. The existence of this elite which seemed to be pushing the country forward may also have masked him from the gap between the very wealthy and the poor. This was constantly widening, and was the antithesis of everything Ba'thism was meant to stand for. Many people believe that Bashar al-Assad was essentially corrupted by power.

He neglected rural areas in a way that his father, with his strong self-consciousness as a peasant, would never have done.[27] Spending on social services and projects in rural areas was cut back as a result of attempts at economic reform, and private charity – funds often raised by Islamic NGOs – was allowed to fill the gap.[28] This took place during the years of drought which lasted from 2006–10, when many penniless families and unmarried young men left the land to gravitate to the ever-swelling cities. It may be no coincidence that the area around Der'a in the south would be the place where the discontent which evolved into the Syrian civil war first manifested itself. Once Der'a had been a stronghold of the Ba'th Party, but those Bashar had put in charge of its administration and security were now perceived locally as outsiders.[29] Nevertheless, many Syrians from all walks of life had been prepared to give Bashar al-Assad (if not the regime itself) the benefit of the doubt.

He may also have felt that he had survived the challenge from political Islam. He continued his father's policy of reaching out to religious scholars who were willing to coexist with the regime, allowing them freedom to preach and teach. Like his father, he was to be seen in public praying at Muslim festivals. He also defused the battle over the hijab, the female headscarf that covers the hair and neck, and which generations of secularists and feminists in Syria and other Arab countries had attacked as a symbol of backwardness and female oppression. The

Islamic revival, on the other hand, had portrayed it as a positive symbol – a sign of a woman's determination to stay true to the traditions of her country and to practise her religion while entering the modern world. In 2002, girls were given the freedom to wear it in schools if they wished. On one level, this was a retreat from secular values but there was another side to it. The girls who wore it (and they were a substantial majority) were receiving a modern education, something that was a triumph for the values of secular Ba'thism. It underlined the message Bashar al-Assad desperately hoped the people would accept: that there was no conflict between Islam and the regime. In 2006, the Ba'th Party officially started to observe Muslim festivals for the first time, and even called for an alliance with Islamists against external pressures.[30]

But there was no progress on two key fronts: fighting corruption and starting moves towards freedom, democracy, the rule of law and the dismantling of the security state.

As Syria slid down the spiral which ended in civil war, Rami Makhlouf would issue a statement which indicated that he realised the harm his activities had done to the regime's image among ordinary people. He announced that he was going to divest himself of his riches and devote the monies to helping the people. This, an observer commented acidly, was as implausible as if Saddam Hussein had suddenly decided to repent and model his life on that of Mother Teresa of Calcutta. Whether the conversion was sincere or not was beside the point: by then it was too late.

IV

The Arab Spring, which started in Tunisia in December 2010, caught most commentators by surprise. The fall of the regime in Tunisia was closely followed by that in Egypt. Disturbances rocked Libya, Bahrain and Yemen and appeared likely to spread further. For a time it was widely assumed that history was on the side of the leaderless protesters. What they wanted was human rights, democracy and jobs: three demands which they summed up with the one word "dignity". It was a call that was self-evidently just, and for that reason it was hoped tyrants were destined to crumble. But there was much wishful thinking, and we now know from the hindsight of only four years that it would turn out to be much more complicated than that.

As of December 2014, only Tunisia still seems to be making the transition to democracy. After lengthy negotiations within a constituent assembly elected after the fall of the dictator Zine El Abidine Ben Ali, it has hammered out a new democratic constitution and held elections which have led to a change of government at the ballot box.

In Egypt, by contrast, when elections for a new president were held in June 2012, they led to a government dominated by the Muslim Brotherhood, whose Freedom and Justice Party had also received by far the largest share of the vote in parliamentary elections. But the Brotherhood appeared intent on using its democratic credentials to replace an old elite with a new one, and on refashioning society in its own image rather than uniting it. This was all too reminiscent of so many earlier Arab revolutions, except this time the beneficiaries would be Islamists. A year after its assumption of power, the Muslim Brotherhood government under President Mohamed Morsi was removed by the army, following massive opposition demonstrations. A bloody crackdown ensued in which a thousand people or more may have been killed. In May 2014, Abdul Fattah al-Sisi, the former head of the military, was elected president. No Islamist was allowed to stand against him, and the Brotherhood was banned.

In Libya, there was armed intervention by NATO with the backing of the Arab League to protect the rebels. This led to the collapse of Muammar al-Gaddafi and his regime, but that had not been the ostensible purpose of the intervention. It had been intended to be humanitarian in nature and to prevent the regime massacring its opponents. By taking sides in the civil war, the intervention led ineluctably to regime change in October 2011. Since then, state building in Libya seems to be proceeding at a snail's pace. Tribalism has reasserted itself, armed militias still roam the streets and the country seems to be dissolving into civil war.

The Arab Spring was late in reaching Syria, although the high- and low-level corruption and the arbitrariness of the security and intelligence services vexed everybody who was not directly or indirectly on the regime's payroll. The regime appeared confident, if not cocky, because of the differences between it and its counterparts in Tunisia and Egypt. The regimes running those countries had placated the Americans and the Israelis, creating a sullen resentment. Bashar al-Assad emphasised that he had held Syria's head high, and was now being rewarded by a gradual normalisation of relations with Europe and America. This counted in his favour so far as it went. There was also another factor which made Syrians initially reluctant to come out on the streets in large numbers. They were only too conscious of the turmoil in Iraq, and had vivid memories of the fifteen years of the Lebanese civil war. They did not want to risk the same in their own country. Bashar al-Assad, helped by the nasty reputation of his security services, looked as though he would survive.

What changed everything was an incident which threw into sharp relief the untackled problems of his security state. At the beginning of March 2011, children aged between nine and fifteen wrote graffiti on the walls of their school in the depressed southern town of Der'a calling for the fall of the regime – a slogan which echoed from Tunis and Cairo to San'a and Tripoli – or, according to some reports, just "freedom". They may have been copying events in other Arab countries which they had seen on television, or perhaps they were repeating the discontent which they had heard their parents voice in the privacy of their families on countless occasions. In any event, they were school children, not adults. But twitchy security officials overreacted in a way that showed they had no qualms about brutality and felt no accountability to the people.

The children were arrested and taken to Damascus for interrogation where they may have been tortured. Their families were still unable to obtain their release after two weeks. On 15 March, a protest in Der'a calling for the release of the children and an end to such arbitrary behaviour swelled to several thousand. Four demonstrators were shot dead by the security forces. The next day the numbers demonstrating had risen to 20,000. They attacked the governor's office, the local Ba'th

Party headquarters and the premises of the security forces: the three pillars of the regime's control at a local level in each province. The protests were now repeated every day. On 23 March, the security forces raided a mosque which had become a temporary hospital to treat those now being injured in the ongoing disturbances. On that day, fifteen people were reported killed and hundreds injured.

The grievances in Der'a were local but resonated throughout Syria because of their underlying causes which affected all Syrians. Other protests which seem also to have been sparked by local issues occurred elsewhere, notably in Homs, Lattakia, Banyas, Hama, some suburbs of Damascus, and among the Kurds in the north-east of the country. But they all reflected the same underlying problems and ultimately voiced the same demands: an end to the unaccountable security state and the absence of freedom; policies to tackle the lack of jobs and opportunities; and a drive against corruption. The regime's response seemed confused. At first the president was absent from public view, but the government tried to placate the demonstrators by promising a commission to examine the 1963 Emergency Law, an offer of staggering pay rises of 20 per cent to 30 per cent for government employees, and a general promise to look at legitimate grievances.

On 30 March, Bashar al-Assad addressed the nation from the podium in the Syrian parliament where he was guaranteed an adulatory audience. His silence up to this point had been noticeable. Seemingly emulating his father's legendary caution, he said that he had held back until he had been able to investigate the situation. Now that he had done so, he could tell the nation with confidence that Syria was the victim of a foreign conspiracy. This tone was set very early in the speech:

Our enemies work every day in an organised, systematic and scientific manner in order to undermine Syria's stability. We acknowledge that they have been smart in choosing very sophisticated tools for what they have done; but at the same time we recognise that they have been stupid in choosing the country and the people, because such conspiracies do not work with our country or our people.[31]

Israel and America were mentioned once or twice as the source of the conspiracies, but for the most part the foreign countries conspiring against Syria were not named – leaving the possibility that, as so often in the past, other Arab countries might also be involved. He suggested that the ripple effect of demonstrations in many parts of the country was evidence that the conspiracy was spreading its tentacles. He said that the government would respond in a firm and well thought-through manner: there would be reform – he acknowledged the need for it – but it would be in accordance with the government's programme. He reminded the viewers that from the first days of his rule he had been intending to carry out reforms, but gave reasons why they had been delayed, namely the many crises that his regime had survived. He referred specifically to the Second Intifada in Palestine, 9/11, and the invasions of Afghanistan and Iraq. He also hinted at the events following the assassination of Rafiq al-Hariri and mentioned the Israeli wars in Lebanon in 2006 and Gaza in 2008–9. He added to this list the drought which had blighted the country over the last few years. The point was, he tried to reassure the viewers, that the intentions of the government were good. It had been planning reforms for many years, but the time had never been right to proceed. Now it would do so, but it must not be pressured.

Having made his promise that reforms were on the way and that the people were being listened to, he returned to his rhetoric about conspiracies against Syria for the remainder of the speech. In essence, it was a plea to the people to trust him. But could they? Now he would find himself the victim of his own failure to introduce transparency into the government's workings and tackle the security state and corruption. The speech was made in self-justification, not in a spirit of apology. It did not contain the specific and targeted programme of reform, which many people had been hoping it would announce. It left most Syrians apart from his core supporters deeply disillusioned.

The government's reaction to events as they continued to unfold did not suggest a coordinated approach to the developments. The president established a committee to examine the Emergency Law and indulged in some gesture politics: he replaced the unpopular governor of Der'a, announced that many Kurds who did not have full Syrian citizenship would now receive it, and repealed a ban on women teachers veiling their faces when they taught in schools. These measures were all aimed at placating diverse but very specific groups – the people of Der'a, the Kurds and Wahhabi Islamists. They were signs of a government trying to buy popularity rather than reform. Yet rather than die down, the protests continued to intensify and spread. This was especially the case when crowds of men gathered together after the Friday noon prayers and the mosques disgorged their congregations onto the streets: an obvious time for protesters to give vent to their demands. Even the lifting of the Emergency Law and abolition of the State Security Courts on 21 April was aptly described as "prestidigitation"[32] by one analyst. All Syrians knew that there were other laws in force, some of them only recently passed, which meant that the repeal made little practical difference.

The inadequate response by the government nudged the country onto a downward slope. This accelerated into a vicious spiral, as the security forces showed that many of their members did not know how to handle peaceful demonstrations without responding brutally. Snipers on rooftops targeting individuals in the crowd provided a striking contrast to crowd control in Jordan around the same time, where police politely martialled the protesters and even provided them with bottles of water. The regime probably thought it could afford to behave in the way that it did. Many areas were quiet, with life continuing as normal. Large-scale demonstrations had not yet spread to Damascus and Aleppo, which when considered together probably contain over a third of the Syrian population.

There were certainly many regime supporters in the two cities as well as many other people who were dependant on the government pay roll, but the security services were active, too. They feared above all else the opposition rallying in a major square of the capital, congregating there in their hundreds of thousands and refusing to move as had happened in Cairo's Tahrir Square, forcing the Egyptian regime from power. The security services succeeded in preventing such an occurrence in Syria, but now the regime was feeling the heat. The slogan "the people want the fall of the regime", which epitomised the revolutions in other Arab countries, was now chanted as the security forces used violence to drive the protesters from the streets. By the end of April, there were reports of soldiers being shot for refusing to open fire on crowds.

V

Whatever goodwill many in the broad mass of the Syrian public may have still felt for Bashar al-Assad as an individual melted away. Although the government continued to make statements about reform and tried to set up dialogue with approved activists, the brutal crackdown on demonstrations continued. This was something on which those in the regime with direct responsibility for security did not seem willing to compromise. Different parts of the regime appeared to be acting with open disregard for each other but displayed a rock-solid unity to the outside world. A propaganda war developed, fuelled by the new technologies of cameras on mobile phones, Facebook and YouTube. The stream of images posted on the Internet by protesters could not all be verified but everyone knew that, for its part, the regime was perfectly capable of lying. Its denunciations of the protesters as terrorists carried no conviction, especially as it also banned foreign journalists from reporting, thus adding to the anger. Mass protests in support of the regime were organised and the media invited, but these marches were obviously stage managed, at least in large part.

It is hard to say when the point of no return was passed, after which Syria became predestined to descend into chaos and civil war. It may have been as early as the particularly grisly story of Hamza al-Khateeb. He was a thirteen-year-old boy from the village of Jeezeh near Der'a who was last seen alive on 29 April 2011 when security forces opened fire on a demonstration in which he and his family were taking part. The crowd scattered and Hamza was separated from his family. A month later, his grotesquely mutilated body was returned to them. The government denied that he had been tortured, and Bashar al-Assad even visited the family to offer his condolences. But few Syrians outside the regime's core supporters believed the government's story. It was all too plausible that the security services had tortured the boy and returned his remains to the family as a grim warning. An autopsy report which the government commissioned claimed to show that the wounds on the corpse were not consistent with torture. This was simply not credible to most Syrians. Even if the government had been innocent, it paid another instalment of the price for its failure to establish an effective system to bring accountability to the activities of the security services, as well as for its lack of transparency. The leopard had spots it could not change.

As the hot Syrian summer began, there were more reports of gunfire directed at the security forces. The government claimed that 120 soldiers had been killed by armed gangs in the town of Jisr al-Shughour in Idlib province, south-west of Aleppo. Refugees began to flee to safer places near family and the strongholds of their ethnic or confessional communities. Others escaped abroad. Ten thousand had already crossed the Turkish border by June. Ramadan coincided with a boiling August, during which the protests and the violence intensified. Although the regime was desperately trying to start a national dialogue on reform – or doing everything to give the impression that it seriously wanted to do so – there was no sign that it would be willing to relinquish power if the popular will called on it to do so. Besides, the anger that its repression had unleashed created new obstacles to it stepping down. Would not many of its key figures, including the president, now find themselves on trial? Was there not just too much anger? The regime battened down the hatches, repeating ad nauseam its mantra that it was fighting extremist Islamist terrorism, and using a sectarian narrative that was aimed at alienating secularists and the minorities from the opposition. There were sectarian attacks which often involved the regime's shadowy, Alawi-dominated militias known as *shabiha*, or "ghosts".

By the end of July, 2,000 people were reported to have died in the disturbances, according to UN human rights organisations.[33] An opposition Free Syrian Army was established by officers who deserted. Initially it was led by Colonel Riyad al-As'ad. On 29 July he called on soldiers to defect and "to stop pointing their rifles at the people's chests, join the free army, and to form a national army that can protect the revolution and all sections of the Syrian people with all their sects."[34] Although it was hard to see – at least initially – how the Free Syrian Army could coordinate its activities on the ground, and armed opposition groups were generally local, it was a sign of how the regime seemed to be losing its grip. However, desertions from the ranks of the regime by top officials were rare: a very noticeable contrast to what was then occurring in Libya during the death throes of the Gaddafi regime. This was an early sign that if a full-blown armed conflict developed in Syria, the regime would not easily be swept away and the fighting would be bitter and lasting.

Opposition groups tried to organise and rally Arab and international support. In October, an opposition Syrian National Council (SNC) was established in Istanbul. It was intended to bring politicians in exile and activists on the ground together in a common front, but there was doubt as to how realistic it was for the SNC to coordinate effectively. Many opposition figures had been forced to live outside Syria for years, while communication with those fighting on the frontline in Syria would not be easy. In November, Syria was suspended from the Arab League in protest at the violence of the government clampdown. The League imposed political and economic sanctions, but stopped short of any military action. Nevertheless, this was a massive humiliation for the Ba'thist state. Although the League sent observers in the hope of damping down the fighting, they soon left because of the deteriorating security situation. On 4 February 2012, the regime demonstrated that it still had crucial international support. Russia and China jointly vetoed a UN Security Council resolution condemning it.[35]

The regime made certain that chaos (or worse) would be the only alternative to its survival. Sometimes it did things that could only be calculated to add to the disorder, or presented itself as the only solution to problems which it had created or exacerbated. Thus, it set up a website in the name of the Syrian Muslim Brotherhood and posted on it claims of responsibility for terrorist attacks in Damascus on 23 December 2011 which killed forty-four people.[36] Then, in February 2012, it released Abu Mus'ab al-Suri, the former member of the Fighting Vanguard and of al-Qaʿida, from prison.[37] It was scarcely surprising if many Syrians suspected that the regime was itself behind atrocities, especially those of a sectarian nature.

The situation grew ever uglier. In Homs, where many Alawis, Christians and others lived as well as Sunnis, the protests had been particularly vigorous and the response correspondingly brutal. Opposition fighters took control of much of the city. The regime responded with tanks and artillery in the way it had done in Hama in 1982. It recaptured the rebel-held neighbourhood of Baba Amr in March 2012 after lengthy bombardment. But if it was trying to teach the people a lesson it seemed to be a failure, since armed resistance continued to infect new areas while attempts through the UN to establish a ceasefire were frustrated on the ground. UN monitors were despatched pursuant to Security Council Resolution 2043 which was adopted on 21 April, but they were soon forced to suspend their work because of an intensification of fighting in June. Fighting spread to suburbs uncomfortably near the centre of Damascus. By the end of July Aleppo, too, became a war zone. This was also the month in which the Red Cross officially declared that, in its view, the fighting had reached the proportions of a civil war.

Splits became visible in the opposition as time wore on. There were attempts to make it more coherent and to give it greater legitimacy. In November 2012, the Syrian National Council joined with other groups to set up the National Coalition for Syrian and Opposition Forces (the National Coalition), but important Islamist groups which were fighting in the Aleppo area, Jubhat al-Nusra and the Tawhid Brigade, refused to join. They even denounced the National Coalition as a conspiracy. In December, however, the National Coalition won recognition from the Western powers, Turkey and the Gulf States.

In March 2013, rebel forces seized control of the town of Raqqa in the Euphrates valley. The regime's response was to bomb it. This was now an established pattern. If the regime lost control of an area, its people would be punished. This was the first and, as yet, only time a provincial capital has fallen to rebel forces. It was a symptom of how thinly stretched the regime was on the ground. Its priority was to retain

– or regain – control of the artery linking Aleppo and Damascus. It could survive if it lost control of the relatively sparsely populated areas east of this corridor. It gradually became apparent that in many areas in eastern Syria, the regime was quietly withdrawing most of its forces and administration. Yet it had a trump card up its sleeve. It knew that if it pulled out the rebels would be left in control. They were already vulnerable to factional infighting, and the regime might be able subtly to promote this.

In that same month, there was disarray in the National Coalition. Its chairman, Moaz al-Khatib, resigned. The reason he gave was that it was not possible for him to "work freely ... within the official institutions". But other reasons lay behind these diplomatic words. He was frustrated at the failure of the international community to give full support to the Syrian uprising and at the tendency of important players including the USA, Saudi Arabia and Qatar to back different factions. He also stood for negotiations with the regime to bring an end to the fighting, a position that was seen as tantamount to treachery by some other opposition leaders and factions.[38]

His resignation was an immense loss to the credibility of the rebel cause. Moaz al-Khatib was an imam who was a walking antithesis of sectarianism. A distinguished Islamic scholar, he had succeeded his father as imam of the Umayyad mosque in Damascus. But he was not the inhabitant of some cloistered world. Born in 1960, he had studied geophysics at university and worked as a geologist for an oil company in Syria. He was the kind of Islamist who actively strove for democracy and pluralism for many years. He had been jailed by the regime several times, and finally fled abroad in July 2012. In his speech accepting the position of chairman of the National Coalition he had said "we demand freedom for every Sunni, Alawite, Ismaili, Christian, Druze, Assyrian ... and rights for all parts of the harmonious Syrian people."[39] He meant every word. He was a leader who was acceptable to Syrians well beyond the Sunni community, but who also had the credentials to represent that community.

Over May and June 2013, the regime retook the town of Qusayr near the Lebanese border with the active help of detachments of Hizbullah fighters from Lebanon. But if it was winning in some areas, the rebels were still advancing in others. In July, Islamist groups including the al-Qaʻida-affiliated Nusra Front took the government base at Khan al-Asal to the west of Aleppo and were reported to have executed fifty-one prisoners. Their Islamism could not have been more different from that of Moaz al-Khatib. The National Coalition, which had rejected an alliance with these groups, condemned the atrocity but by now the Western powers were increasingly wary of granting rebels on the ground any support which went beyond humanitarian aid.

On 21 August a major chemical attack took place at Ain Tarma and Zamalka in the Damascus suburbs which killed hundreds of civilians, including women and children.[40] There had been allegations of the deployment of chemical weapons before. Both sides had accused the other of using them at Khan al-Asal, but this time their use was proven. The regime was the only credible culprit, although the reason it carried out the attack has not been established and it is not known at what level the attack was authorised. Paradoxically, the international condemnation of the attack seemed to rebound to the regime's advantage. It swiftly undertook to renounce its chemical weapons, allowed inspectors to visit the sites where they were stored, and agreed a programme for their transport to the coast and subsequent destruction at sea. These events gave the regime a new lease of diplomatic life which even appeared to nudge it closer to respectability, despite the fact that the National Coalition had achieved much diplomatic success and now represented Syria on the Arab League. President Obama had hinted strongly that the use of chemical weapons would be a "red line" which would prompt immediate US intervention, but votes on Capitol Hill and at Westminster showed that there was no public backing to send armies to Syria to save lives under the international law doctrines of humanitarian intervention or responsibility to protect. Any other form of military intervention was blocked because of the Russian veto on the UN Security Council. Many observers said that Syria and its people were now paying the price for the botched intervention in Iraq.

As 2013 drew to a close, Islamist groups were fighting against the Free Syrian Army and capturing some of its bases near Aleppo. This added yet further to Western reluctance to support the Free Syrian Army in any tangible way. In December, the USA and the UK suspended even non-lethal support. The Syrian opposition was proving to be fluid. Fighters defected from one faction to another, and there was little way to check what happened to any aid they received. The presence of increasing numbers of foreign fighters, many of whom joined one of the hardline Islamist groups, was widely attested. Their presence led to justifiable worries that a new Afghanistan or Somalia was in the process of formation and might provide a base for destabilisation elsewhere.

This was no baseless fear. In April 2013, a group that started calling itself the Islamic State of Iraq and Shaam (ISIS) took over Raqqa. It had grown out of the remnants of an insurgency in Iraq originally linked to al-Qa'ida which expanded into eastern Syria as the government of Bashar al-Assad lost control of the plains east of the Euphrates. It would grow steadily stronger, uniting disaffected Sunnis in eastern Syria and north-west Iraq. It also showed that it possessed military expertise (chiefly acquired from former soldiers in the Iraqi army) and high-tech public relation skills which would enable it to attract large numbers of fighters from other countries. Its militants combined discipline with a ruthlessness that crossed the boundary of psychopathic cruelty. Behind the facade of the reinstatement of ancient interpretations of Sharia, the reality was that non-Muslim men such as Christians and Yazidis often faced extermination at the hands of ISIS if they did not convert to Islam, while young women and children were considered war booty and enslaved. Shi'is and others deemed to be heretics suffered in the same way.

Bashar al-Assad may be reaping the whirlwind he has sown as militants whose transit to Iraq was facilitated by the regime return to fight it. However, a curious thing about ISIS in its early days is that it seemed rarely, if ever, to fight against regime forces. Strong links must have been forged between *mukhabarat* officers and Sunni Islamist fighters who travelled through Syria on their way to Iraq during the insurgency which began soon after the US-led invasion of 2003. To many Syrians it seemed perfectly plausible that there was some kind of alliance between groups such as ISIS and the regime, or at least a relationship which might be described as a form of mutual manipulation. These groups benefit the regime in some ways, since they discredit the opposition in the eyes of the international community and distract other rebel groups from their fight against it.

In January and February 2014, the UN brokered talks in Geneva in which representatives of the National Coalition sat down face to face with representatives of the regime for the first time. However, the regime would not countenance discussion of a transitional government and the meetings ended inconclusively. It appeared to prefer to fight on in the hope of ultimate victory.

As of December 2014, there is no sign of an end to the conflict. The human suffering it has caused beggars belief. Over 200,000 Syrians have already died; 3.2 million have fled the country; 6.45 million have been internally displaced and a further 4.6 million are under siege or in areas which the fighting has made difficult to reach. Some parts of Syria are under complete government control, while in others no government presence is left. It is still perfectly possible for a Damascene to pick up a taxi and travel to Beirut and back in the same day, progress only being slightly impeded by a couple of regime checkpoints and queues at the Lebanese border. On the other hand, within a few miles of the centre of Damascus parts of the Ghouta, the once rural area which is now a sprawl of concrete and breeze-block buildings, are under siege by the government. The inhabitants of these suburbs cannot travel freely into the city. The same applies to Yarmouk, once a camp of tents housing Palestinian refugees outside Damascus but now well inside the city and indistinguishable from the other built-up areas around it. The regime has been deliberately starving these enclaves in the hope of forcing the rebels to leave. This, like so much else happening in Syria at the moment, is a war crime. Government artillery on Mount Qassyoun and other strategic high points pounds rebel-held areas, while the rebels retaliate when they can. They occasionally succeed in firing mortar rounds into central Damascus – even into the old city.

The regime has reasserted control over most of the corridor stretching north along the motorway from Damascus to Aleppo. In Homs itself, most of the city's urban sprawl is now back in government hands. The coastal cities of Lattakia, Tartous and Banyas are firmly controlled by the government, as are most of the mountains behind them. This, of course, includes the Alawi heartland and the small Christian area of Wadi al-Nasara.

Further north, much of Idlib province (like Der'a, once a Ba'th Party stronghold) and other areas in the Orontes valley are in rebel hands, and the frontline sometimes runs between Sunni and Alawi or Shi'i villages. Aleppo is cut in half, and much of its unique medieval city is in ruins. The government has also lost control of the countryside extending up to the Turkish border. In the Euphrates valley, Raqqa remains in the hands of ISIS which also dominates the province of Deir al-Zour. In the plains east of the Euphrates, the government has withdrawn its forces, leaving Kurdish militias who are fighting for autonomy within Syria to battle it out with ISIS. In the south, control is also disputed, although the Druze heartland around Suwayda remains quiet.

There are few predictions for a military victory for either side. In fact, it is no longer accurate to speak of the conflict as two sided. There has been serious fighting between rebel groups, as well as kidnapping and brigandage by criminal elements who are sometimes attached to one or other party in the conflict. The regime has resorted to ever more indiscriminate forms of violence, including dropping crudely made barrel bombs from helicopters, and its use of chemical weapons in August 2013 should not be forgotten. There is a voiceless silent majority stuck in the middle, and the dearest wish of the mass of the Syrian people is for the war to end and life to return to a state which is as near to normal as possible. The regime is too strong to be dislodged, but its forces are stretched thinly and seem to lack the capability to reconquer all the areas it has lost. The situation on the ground is unstable and the economy a shambles. The focal points of the fighting change regularly and often indecisively, while diplomatic attempts to reach a solution have been repeatedly unsuccessful.

The Syrian civil war has become a proxy conflict or, rather, two proxy conflicts. The government is firmly backed by Russia which has a naval facility at Tartous. Determined to show that it can no longer be pushed around, Russia has resisted attempts by the USA, Europe and much of the international community to broker a deal under which President Assad will step down. Russia has been dogged in its support for the regime, and repeats the regime's narrative that the rebels are all Islamist terrorists. So long as Bashar al-Assad retains Russian support, the record after four years of rebellion suggests that his regime can continue to fight more or less indefinitely.

The other proxy war taking place in Syria is partly internal to the Arab world, but is also a sectarian war within Islam. There are foreign fighters on both sides. Sunnis have come to aid the opposition. They are drawn from many Arab countries and from across the Muslim world – including small numbers of individuals from the Muslim communities in France, Britain and other Western countries. The fear that they might return home one day after being radicalised rings alarm bells in the West. This does not help the opposition acquire a positive image abroad.

Sheikh Muhamad al-Ya'coubi, one of Syria's most respected Sunni Muslim scholars, issued an appeal to young Muslims tempted to fight in Syria at a fundraising dinner for a relief charity in London in January 2013. He was addressing a predominantly Muslim audience. While calling on the British government to arm the rebels, he urged young Muslims to fight jihad against their own egos, not to indulge those egos by taking up arms to fight in a conflict that is for Syrians and not for them. As a Sufi, Sheikh Muhammad was doing no more than repeat and apply to the Syrian conflict one of the ancient insights of his tradition which is shared by authentic representatives of all religious traditions across the world: pride corrupts, and is the root of all evil.

Shi'i volunteers also travel to Syria to support the government side, especially from Iraq. But the main sources of Shi'i support are not individuals but the Islamic Republic of Iran and the well-organised and highly effective militia of Hizbullah. Their support for him is not because his regime is Alawi dominated (it will be recalled that Alawis are distinct from more mainstream Shi'is) but because of a straightforward political alliance which they see as the axis of resistance against American and Israeli hegemony. This also pits them against the oil-rich Sunni monarchies. They fear the Salafi or Wahhabi trends in the Syrian opposition. There is a long history of Wahhabi devastation

of Shi'i places of pilgrimage. In 1802, Wahhabi warriors swept out of
Arabia and sacked one of the most important Shi'i shrines in the world:
that of the Imam Hussein at Karbala in Iraq. Since the invasion of Iraq
in 2003, there have been numerous attacks on Shi'is in Iraq by Wahhabi
elements, including the massive act of calculated sacrilege when the
shrine of Askariyya was blown up in February 2006. Damascus, too,
has a major Shi'i shrine: the tomb of Sayyida Zainab. The defence of
this shrine has provided a potent rallying cry for Shi'is against the
Sunni Islamist forces which seem to have become the strongest and best
organised groups on the rebel side.

The last few years have been disastrous for Syria. It is as though the
country has been thrust into a torture chamber and pulled to pieces by
men wielding pliers. The agony continues, and there is no sign of when
the door will open and the traumatised prisoner be allowed to stagger
back into the daylight, to feel the sun and the breeze on his face. This
book has tried to show how the current situation arose. Although
Syrians are the only people who can bring the fighting to an end, their
country has, as so often before, become the plaything of foreign interests.

But the agony is not confined to Syria. It is spreading out across
what was once Greater Syria, into Turkey and Iraq, but especially into
Lebanon and Jordan.

Jordan remains stable for the time being, but as of late 2014 it is
hosting more than 618,000 Syrian refugees among a host population
of nearly eight million. In Lebanon the situation is even grimmer, as
the number of refugees has now touched 1,133,000 amongst a host
population of under five million.[41] Lebanon has stability problems
of its own, without another massive influx of refugees. It has still not
absorbed those who arrived from Palestine in 1947–9, and the Syrian
incomers – some of whom have now been there for nearly four years –
will upset the sectarian balance once again if they do not go home soon.
After the end of the Lebanese civil war, all militias except Hizbullah
were disbanded. Now they are all too likely to reappear. If the tensions
cannot be contained it is almost inevitable that the Christians, as well
as the Sunnis, will rearm.

There has already been tension between Sunnis and Shi'is in

Lebanon, as members of both communities travel to Syria to take part in the fighting on opposite sides. There have been bomb attacks in Shi'i neighbourhoods of Beirut and in the Beqaa valley by Sunnis enraged at Hizbullah's support for Bashar al-Assad. The Sunni strongholds of Tripoli and Sidon are tinderboxes. There have been a number of occasions when the army has had to keep Alawis and Sunnis apart in Tripoli, while demagogic preachers stir up fear and hate. Sidon's rural hinterland is Hizbullah country, and the tension in its old city seems palpable. Hardly anyone comes to visit its historic souqs and mosques or to stay in its hotels. Its people fear a siege.

If the Syrian conflict cannot be ended, it seems only a matter of time before it engulfs the rest of Greater Syria.

CHAPTER SEVEN

Drawing the Threads Together

I

What does Syria's history over the last hundred years tell us about how the present tragedy occurred and whether it could have been avoided? Does it provide any clues as to how the current conflict may end?

Faisal's short-lived attempt in 1918–20 to set up a decentralised constitutional monarchy seems to have been the best chance the people of Arabic-speaking Greater Syria ever had to develop their own nationhood, or to choose another form of self-determination.[1] That chance was dashed because of French and British ambitions. The two great powers carved up the territory under their control and gave the area now known as Syria arbitrary borders. Yet there is no point in walking down the road of history's "what if's?" and "might have beens". Instead, a crucial historical fact should be emphasised: what happened in the immediate aftermath of the Great War created a legacy of mistrust of the West which subsequent history would repeatedly compound. Today's inability of the West to prevent Syria descending into the darkness of civil war – and its failure to find a way to bring the civil war to an end – will only have increased that mistrust yet further.

Faisal was followed by other moderate Arab politicians. They, too, would also be expected to compromise perfectly reasonable demands made on behalf of their people. Concessions were demanded by Western powers acting for their own selfish interests. The policy of honourable cooperation by the National Bloc under Jamil Mardam is a good example. A democratically elected government in France frustrated the treaty which would have given Syria independence and even preserved a degree of French influence. It then heaped further humiliation on Syria by transferring the province of Alexandretta to Turkey even though, overall, it had an Arab majority.[2] France's motive was to seek Turkey's support, or at least neutrality, in the looming European war. However, the transfer broke the terms of the Mandate and was yet a further breach of the sacred trust of civilisation which France had taken upon itself when it accepted the Mandate.

Although the French Mandate should never have been set up in the first place, it also became a missed opportunity. Instead of trying to bring Syria's people together so that they were "able to stand by themselves under the strenuous conditions of the modern world",[3] the French did their utmost to make the establishment of a successful, independent Syrian state as hard as possible. After the occupation of Damascus in 1920, Millerand, the French prime minister, proclaimed that Syria henceforth would be held by France: "The whole of it, and forever."[4] The destruction of the Syrian parliament building in 1945 was a potent symbol of French determination to thwart Syrian independence.

For very good reasons, democratic governments today are seen as having much more legitimacy than dictatorships and other authoritarian regimes. Yet when it comes to the history of the peoples of Greater Syria, it has been the democracies of the West – and, since 1948, also of Israel – that have, time and again, refused to acknowledge the full rights of these peoples, or demanded that they waive those rights. During the Second World War, the Allies tried to pressurise Shukri al-Quwwatli and the other leaders of the National Bloc to compromise with France over Syrian independence. This was important for the Allies because of the battle for French public opinion which was then raging between the fascists of Vichy and the Free French of General de Gaulle. But the retaining by France of an imperial presence in Syria had no conceivable benefit for Syrians, was detrimental to their interests, and was not something the Allies had a right to demand. In terms of the fight against the Nazis, the French position may seem understandable, but it was also counterproductive. It was only too likely to alienate Syrians from the Allied cause (as was the transfer of Alexandretta to Turkey in 1939) and drive them into the hands of the Nazis.

The destruction of Palestine in order to create Israel must be seen against this already embittered background. Palestine was the only predominantly Arab territory under a Mandate which was never granted a parliament. If one had been created, it would have passed legislation restricting Jewish immigration from Europe. This was unacceptable to the Zionist movement. From an Arab perspective, the fact that the territory of Palestine sheltered refugees from Hitler did not give those refugees the right to establish their own state at the expense of the indigenous population – especially when Western countries were simultaneously slamming their doors in the faces of many of the same refugees. Once again, moderate Arab demands were rejected by a European power because of the pressures of public opinion in the West. The trampling underfoot of Palestinian rights made the task of moderate Arab nationalists who wished to find an accommodation with the West infinitely harder. The same applies to the West's subsequent struggle to prevent the Arab states from gaining military parity with Israel: something that was always Hafez al-Assad's great ambition. If the Arab states had been able to achieve that parity, it might well have led to the negotiation of a peace based on the equality of the parties.

Husni Zaim made an offer of peace to Israel in 1949. The story of that offer illustrates the point just made. Israel was only prepared to enter into peace negotiations with Husni Zaim if he first made concessions (a Syrian withdrawal from the strategic fragments of land its army was occupying in the territory of the former Mandate of Palestine). This pattern of Israeli behaviour may explain why later leaders such as Hafez al-Assad hesitated when they attempted to negotiate with Israel. In a nutshell, while Israel has always insisted that Arab states acknowledge its legitimate rights, it has refused to make a reciprocal acknowledgement of Palestinian or Syrian rights in international law. In the case of Syria, the Golan Heights are Syrian sovereign territory, and Israel is obliged to recognise this.

For much Western public opinion, the Cold War blended with the Arab-Israeli dispute until the two conflicts seemed almost seamless. Israeli victories in 1967 and 1973 were celebrated in the West as defeats for the Soviets, and the fact that Israel's conquests in 1967 added new injustices to old was all too frequently overlooked. The West left Syria to whistle in the wind for the return of the Golan Heights. To this day, Israelis take Western visitors to the crest overlooking the Galilee and tell them how the Syrians shelled their settlements below. It is perfectly true that the Syrians repeatedly shelled those settlements, but the visitors are unlikely to be told by their guides that many of the artillery exchanges were deliberately initiated by Israel,[5] or that Israel repeatedly shelled, bombed and dynamited Arab towns and villages. In 2013, Israel granted a company in which Rupert Murdoch and a member of the Rothschild family are shareholders a licence to explore for hydrocarbons on the Golan Heights. Although any hydrocarbons eventually extracted will be the property of Syria and will therefore have been pillaged, the licence has attracted barely a flicker of interest in the West. Some Jewish organisations in Western countries sometimes respond to criticism of Israeli expansionism in a mealy-mouthed way. In March 2014, for instance, the Board of Deputies of British Jews issued a "Jewish Manifesto for the European Elections". This document speaks of the need for peace, but refers to EU guidelines which seek to exclude Israeli settlements from EU funding programmes. Those settlements are illegal and therefore fly in the face of international law. Yet, to the Board's shame, it expresses concern "that the European Union is, in effect, thereby trying to dictate [Israel's] borders".[6]

Throughout the Cold War the USSR was able to manipulate public opinion in Syria – and all other Arab countries outside the oil-rich Gulf – against the West, while the voices of pan-Arabism seemed to Western observers to be parroting the words of the Soviets. In countries such as Britain and France there were those on the right of the political spectrum who still mourned the loss of empire and therefore cheered Israel from the columns of conservative newspapers, while for Syrians the wounds of Arab humiliation were reopened by Israeli victories. The period after the collapse of Communism shows how hard it has been to repair the damage, despite the fact that Hafez al-Assad lined Syria up with the West and the Gulf States against Saddam Hussein in 1990. What has happened since 2011 shows that the alienation that has characterised the relationship between Syria and the West was something that neither party could easily afford.

II

The police state of the Assads might be compared with a crumbling block in a curved arch that is held in place by the adjoining blocks. During the Arab Spring, the cries for freedom, democracy and the end of corruption and repression looked for a while as though they were going to shake the stones in the arch free, so that the entire edifice would collapse. As it was, the tremor loosened the Syrian block so that now it hangs precariously. We still do not know if or when it will come crashing to the ground – and, if so, whether it will shatter on impact. Those cries for freedom were not enough on their own. Today there are forces which still prop the regime up, despite its corrosion.

One of the principal pillars of the regime is patronage. This tendency is deeply rooted in Arab societies. In the distant past it was exercised through the tribal system which provided the only form of security. Those with no blood links to a tribe needed to find one which would accept them as its clients in order to be safe in the perilous world of the Arabian desert. The tribe would defend them and, if it came to it, extract revenge from anyone who harmed them. This social structure has survived into living memory among the Bedouin and others. Whenever the state is threatened by lawlessness the importance of such tribal relationships reasserts itself, and they become necessary for self-protection. This happened in Iraq after the decapitation of the Iraqi state following the US-led invasion of 2003, but the process had already begun under Saddam Hussein during the long years when the Iraqi economy was devastated by sanctions after the 1991 Gulf War. The same process will unquestionably be happening in Syria at this moment.

But patronage in Arab countries takes many forms and extends well beyond tribal societies. In Ottoman Greater Syria, under the French and during the early years of independence, it was exercised by the notables. The oligarchies they formed in the major cities inevitably looked after themselves. The members of these oligarchies were joined by bonds of mutual obligation to their clienteles, whose interests they would look after provided they respected the status quo. There was therefore a reciprocation of obligations between patron and client in the cities under the Ottomans and the French. That relationship extended out onto the landed estates in the countryside. It also existed in one form or another among the religious minorities, who had their own notable classes. The patronage of the notables really only decayed after independence when this echelon was put under pressure by forces such as the Ba'th and the rural followers of Akram Hourani.

When Ba'thists acquired power, initially as partners with others in an elected government and subsequently as the result of military coups, they never really managed to find a way to gain support except by setting up their own system of patronage – something which plunged Syria into class and, to an extent, sectarian conflict. Having grown up with the exercise of patronage by the notables and its deep roots in Arab society, Ba'thists may just have seen it as the natural basis for their own rule.

It is hard to exclude an element of patronage from even the most democratic politics anywhere. But for Ba'thists starting off in a society still dominated by a social system which they wished to overturn, rewarding those who would benefit from their reforms would have seemed the obvious way to gain support. Peasants, they hoped, would look to the Ba'th to secure themselves a fair deal. Ba'thists sought to benefit their followers: not just by arranging for schools, electricity and running water in the countryside, but by finding them government jobs. Many of these were located locally in the nearest small town, as well as in the great cities. A wheel then turned full circle. Just as the notables had once controlled society, and resisted attempts by others to loosen that control, so, too, did the Ba'th. In time the Ba'thist elite took the place of the notables and, later still, neglected the poor who had now become dependent on them. They also found themselves forced to rely on quasi-tribal solidarity. That was the story of the Assads and the Alawi community.

Patronage, of course, was just one side of the coin. While the regime co-opted many Syrians to its side, it used repression and, when necessary, extreme violence to intimidate those who might be tempted to oppose it. The regime was buttressed by effective one party rule, censorship of the media and school indoctrination. Virtually by definition, police states lack transparency. Verifiable information about the repression they conduct is scarce. It will probably be many years before a history of the vicious activities of the security and intelligence services under the Assads can be written. However, the broad outline of their role in Syria is perfectly visible. The *mukhabarat* made open discussion of political issues impossible. This had two incidental consequences that helped to degrade the regime.

The first was a tendency to believe its own propaganda. This afflicted Hafez al-Assad's sons (although probably not the canny old peasant, himself). Perhaps they could not help but be influenced by the personality cult which Ba'thist spin doctors wove around their father, and was a sign of a general intellectual dumbing down as it seemed to be aimed primarily at the less educated (and less intelligent) sections of society. Basil al-Assad's American tutor was sometimes taken for a spin by his pupil in one of his many sports cars. When gently challenged about the fact that he was very privileged to have such fine vehicles at his disposal, he retorted without any sense of irony that they belonged to the Syrian people. Similarly, Bashar al-Assad has made statements about how he was sent to study in London as an army doctor, as if the fact that he was a son of the president of the republic were irrelevant.

State repression led the regime to expect the people to believe what they were told. This meant that sometimes absurd lies were spun. The unfortunate Ibrahim Khlas, who wrote the infamous "mummies in the museums of history" article in April 1967 which contained a full-frontal attack on religion, was put on trial for acting as an American and Israeli agent and attempting to sow dissension between the Syrian people and its leadership. The charge was obviously ridiculous, but people were expected to believe it so as to save the regime from embarrassment. We might also recall Robert Fisk's conversation with the Syrian minister of information about his report on the crushing of Hama in 1982. The minister adopted an air of sweet innocence when Fisk objected to the radio broadcast that called him a liar. This was awkward for the minister, but he could deny having heard the broadcast and therefore he could disregard it. That was the end of the matter. It thus comes as no surprise that when Hamza al-Khatib's mutilated body was returned to his family, the regime expected Syrians to accept the results of the autopsy which purported to show that his injuries were not consistent with torture. Yet nothing could have been more calculated to stir up anger. Syrians knew all too well how brutal the *mukhabarat* could be.

The Syrian education system spread literacy but was poor at developing critical thinking in its students. But it was a great mistake for Syria's leaders to expect the people automatically to accept whatever it wanted them to accept. It paid the price for this, too, when it tried to demonise all its opponents as religious militants, since it was insulting the intelligence of ordinary Syrians. And all this happened against a background in which the rich seemed to grow richer and the poor grew poorer, while those in the middle were squeezed. Small wonder that Bashar al-Assad failed to rally Syria behind him when he addressed the nation on 30 March 2011, or that he blamed the demonstrations erupting across the country on agents acting on behalf of foreign conspiracies.

III

Ba'thists would not find congenial the suggestion that, consciously or not, they modelled themselves in certain respects on the oligarchic notables. They would find comparisons between themselves and the French even worse. Yet some such comparisons can be validly drawn. The first is the demonisation of their opponents as religious fanatics.

Indeed, the appearance of militant forms of political Islam, which has increasingly taken on a sectarian basis since the 1980s, has enabled the Syrian regime to don clothes once worn by the French while adjusting the tailoring to reflect the concerns of today's world. Ba'thism is not intrinsically hostile to Islam, and both Bashar al-Assad and his father tried to be pragmatic and accommodate the wishes of devout Muslims so long as Islam was not used as a banner for political opposition. But the Assads would not allow any banner of any sort to be used by opponents. It was thus scarcely surprising that political Islam, which had its own roots in Syria, should have provided a convenient rallying point against each of the Assads in turn. The attempts today by the regime to stir the sectarian pot by posing as the protector of religious minorities are thus very reminiscent of what the French did during their Mandate.

Another comparison to the French concerns the use of violence, especially the intensity of the violence which both the French under the Mandate and the Ba'thists have been willing to employ against a recalcitrant civilian population. This violence has been exercised through the bombarding of urban areas and recruiting militias like the *Shabiha* to terrorise rural ones in order to put down uprisings.

In addition, the weakness of the economy and the ineffectiveness of government efforts to help the population were among the causes of both the 1925 rebellion and the uprising which began in Syria in 2011–2. Young men, whom the countryside was unable to support, had flocked to the cities to search for work, joining an already existing urban underclass of unemployed and underemployed. On both occasions matters were made worse by drought, which had also led to a rural exodus. In 1925, the Syrian economy was suffering because of economic policies designed to suit France rather than Syria. In 2011, the economy was still only partially reformed, and the primary beneficiaries of the reforms were the elite. The children of the elite and of groups favoured through government patronage (including many Alawis) would get good jobs because of their connections, while those who lacked the right links in Syrian society (or whose families were blacklisted for various reasons) would not do so. Too little wealth was trickling down to assist the growing numbers of people who were sinking into destitution.

Coincidentally, the two Syrian revolts started in places quite close to each other. In 1925, it was on the Hawran plateau, where for a while a provisional government would even try to set itself up. In 2011, the uprising might be said to have begun in Der'a, which is now just a short drive down the road from Hawran. Both touch the border with Jordan. While one should be wary of pushing the analogy too far, proximity to Jordan enabled rebels on both occasions to gain supplies and recruits from Jordanian territory. The governorate of Suwayda in the Hawran with its large Druze population remained quiet in 2011 as the slide to civil war began. However, once the revolt began to fan out across the countryside, the area of the Ghouta around Damascus rose up on both occasions. The same occurred in some areas in and around the Orontes valley. In these and many other places, there was a strong feeling that the French (in 1925) and Bashar al-Assad (in 2011–12) lacked legitimacy. In both cases, too, expectations had been raised. Before the French arrived, Syrians had expected their country would become independent; in the case of Bashar, it had been hoped he would reform the system and bring Syrians freedom.

Some of the military tactics employed show similarities, too. In each case, once it became clear that the rebellion was widespread, the government lacked the necessary manpower to crush it. The solution was ruthless bombardment of urban areas where the rebels operated (in 1925, Damascus and Hama; in 2012 onwards Homs, Aleppo and the suburbs of Damascus in particular). Another was the recruitment of thuggish militias disproportionately from minority communities (in 1925, from Armenians, Circassians, Shi'is, Kurds and Bedouin; in 2011–12, from Alawis). Both uprisings saw a disintegration of law and order, as criminal elements and armed bands took advantage of the disorder to rob, pillage and extort. If the French had not eventually been able to transfer large numbers of Algerian, Senegalese and Madagascan troops to Syria, they might have found it impossible to regain control. Save for support from Hizbullah, across the border in Lebanon, and to a lesser extent from Iran and Shi'i volunteers from Iraq and elsewhere, manpower from outside Syria's frontiers has not been forthcoming for Bashar al-Assad's regime. Syria has a large army, but most of it has had to be confined to barracks since 2011 for fear the soldiers may defect. This explains why, as of December 2014, Assad has been unable to regain control despite the ferociousness of his crackdown.

Historical comparisons can also be drawn between the harshness of the response by Bashar al-Assad's regime against the demonstrations which grew into civil war and that of Hafez al-Assad in Hama in 1982. The position of Hafez al-Assad's brother Rif'at as commander of the defence companies has parallels with that of Maher al-Assad, Bashar's younger brother who commands the Republican Guard and the Fourth Armoured Division. Like his uncle, Maher al-Assad is the regime's enforcer. He is famed for his brutal reputation, as well as the devotion many of his troops show for him. If the regime were fully to recover its balance, a second "war between the brothers" one generation on would seem perfectly possible. This demonstrates how much the dynamics of the regime under Bashar al-Assad still follow the pattern of family rule established by his father.

But perhaps the major historical thread running through the Ba'thist era is the feud which the Assad clan and Ba'thists generally have fought with militant Islam – something that exists separately from the ongoing sectarian conflict. This goes back to the days when the teenage Hafez al-Assad fought in street brawls with young Islamists in Lattakia. It extends via the strikes and disturbances of 1964 and the unrest of the late 1970s to the pulverisation of Hama in 1982. The lesson Hafez al-Assad learned and never forgot was that the indiscriminate, overwhelming use of force had worked. Bashar and Maher al-Assad would try to implement it again thirty years later. This time they were not facing a militant Islamist uprising but people campaigning for their freedom. Yet their tendency to demonise opponents – something which comes equally naturally to militant Islamists – increasingly helped them to turn the discontent into an Islamist uprising. This was terrain with which they were familiar. In a perverse way, they felt at home. At a very basic level, it was much easier to fight with tanks and bomber aircraft against a demonised opponent in battles that destroyed half the urban landscape of Syria, than to deal with crowds agitating for their human rights and free elections.

IV

In the autumn of 2010, I heard Faisal Qasim, the deliberately provocative host on Al Jazeera (who happens to be a Syrian Druze), talk about the religious satellite channels which now beam divisive and sectarian sermons into the living rooms of many Arab homes. He drew attention to the fact that these had first appeared around the time of the 2003 US-led invasion of Iraq. In the manner of a true conspiracy theorist, he floated the idea that they were introduced by America as a wicked plot to split the Arab world. "The new Sykes-Picot," he called it. This was an allusion to the Anglo-French agreement of 1916 to partition the region. The statement was intended to wind up his guests in the studio, and was a bitter use of irony.

Throughout the many centuries of Islamic history before the modern period, religion has generally been the primary marker of identity in Muslim-majority lands. Muslims, Christians and Jews interacted, sometimes with great courtesy, but they tended to live separate lives and relations were often far from happy. Muslim minority groups and dissidents (in Syria, Alawis, Druze, Ismailis and mainstream Shi'is) also tended to keep themselves apart. This separateness, this drawing away from each other, posed dangers to the cohesion of society, particularly as it tended to be characterised by mutual disdain. Sectarianism was not brought to the Arab world by the West. Yet the Western obsession with sectarianism in Arab countries – best exemplified for our purposes by the policies of France during its Mandate – deserves a few words before we turn to the dangerous sectarianism in the conflict taking place in today's Syria.

Historically, sectarianism has been a much more destructive force in Europe than the Middle East. The Thirty Years' War and the other religious conflicts that followed the Reformation have no parallel in the world of Islam in terms of their destructiveness. Even in recent decades sectarianism has returned to haunt Europe in the dissolution of Yugoslavia and the troubles that blighted Northern Ireland. Tensions between Catholics and Orthodox are an element in the crisis threatening Ukraine today. In Britain, Catholic emancipation only took place in 1829 while it was not until the end of the 1850s that an openly professed Jew could become a Member of Parliament. Considered against this backdrop, the Ottoman decrees of 1839 and 1856 that ended the age-old disabilities on the *dhimmis*, the Christians and Jews of the empire, were hardly behind the times.

The very particular pair of spectacles through which the Western powers saw Greater Syria at the end of the Great War led to policies which exacerbated sectarianism. When negotiating the peace settlement, the powers seem to have paid great attention to religious differences in Greater Syria, but everywhere else – Central Europe, the Balkans and even Anatolia – they tended to concentrate on ethnic nationalism. This arguably tells us more about the European view of this area than about the area itself. At that time, the Sunni-Shi'i split was mentioned comparatively rarely, but attention was focused on the Christian-Muslim divide (partly because of the Maronites, but also because of France's self-assumed role of *protectrice des Chrétiens d'Orient*) and the project to create a national home "for the Jewish people" in the newly created territory of Palestine: an endeavour that was by its nature sectarian. Europeans may have conceived the Jews as sharing an ethnicity (or being members of a distinct race), but Arab Muslims and Christians always saw them as members of a religion.

Today, the policies of the French during their Syrian Mandate are only a very minor contributing factor to the sectarianism in Syria which is tearing the country apart and which the regime has undoubtedly stoked. In fact, it is a tribute to Syrian society that, on the whole, the French had such limited success in their self-serving attempts to divide Syrians along sectarian lines. The coming to power of the Syrian Ba'thists by the coup of 8 March 1963 led to a paradox. While Ba'thism is an aggressively secularist ideology, the insecurity of the position of the officers who had taken power forced them to rely on family, friends, people from their own town and province, and members of the same sect. Anti-Alawi sectarianism proved a valuable propaganda tool for the regime's opponents. These included other Arab regimes which traded venom over the airwaves with Hafez al-Assad.

On 1 May 1979, President Anwar Sadat of Egypt delivered an anti-Alawi polemic on Cairo Radio. In it, he denigrated Alawism as intrinsically evil and blended it with Ba'thism, which he viewed as not much better. He claimed the support of the late King Faisal of Saudi Arabia for the distasteful sentiments he expressed. The king was a popular figure revered by many Sunni Muslims across the world as well as by other Arabs. Sadat was trying to reach out not just to his domestic audience in Egypt but to the people of Syria and the wider Arab world. The speech was a bitter reaction to Hafez al-Assad's accusations that Sadat, by making Egypt's separate peace with Israel, had sold out the Palestinians, the rest of the Arab world and, of course, Syria. That is probably the reason for Sadat's bitterness, as well as his opening reference to the Golan Heights:

I was prepared to speak on behalf of the Golan. But no. Let these dirty Alawis speak for it. These are people who have lost all of life's meaning. By God, let them face their people in Syria and let them solve it. We shall see what they will achieve. I could have brought them the Golan,[7] but I am not responsible for it while the Alawis are in power ... We all know what the Alawis are in the eyes of the Syrian people. The Syrian people will deal with them. Afterwards things will be different ... The attitude of Syria – it is not right to say Syria, because the Syrian people are powerless in this – the attitude of the Alawis is known ... [King] Faysal of Saudi Arabia told me that Hafiz al-Asad is Alawi and Ba'thist, and the one is more evil than the other ... Faysal also told me: How can you hold hands with the Syrian Ba'thists? Al-Asad is an Alawi and a Ba'thist; one is more evil than the other.[8]

The Egyptian president is remembered today for his peace treaty with Israel (which he had signed just two months earlier). Perhaps he ought also to be remembered for this speech. Just over two weeks after he had broadcast it, the sectarian massacre of cadets at the artillery school in Aleppo took place.

The toxic sectarianism which began to afflict Syria in reaction to an authoritarian government in the steel hands of an Alawi general is closely related to another issue that has plagued the country throughout the period covered by this book: foreign interference. The revolution in Iran in early 1979 saw the overthrow of a nationalist, secular and authoritarian regime by a revolutionary form of Shi'ism. It took a few years for the sectarian implications of this to become apparent for Muslims. The Iranian Shi'i revolution provided an inspiration for the Fighting Vanguard's rebellion in Hama in 1982, although the ideology behind the Vanguard was that of the Egyptian Sunni Islamist Sayyid Qutb. How is it, then, that today Iran is the ally of the secularist Bashar al-Assad in the civil war? How is it that since the overthrow of Saddam Hussain in Iraq there has been talk of a "Shi'i crescent" stretching from Iran, through Shi'i-majority Iraq and Alawi-dominated Syria, to Lebanon, where Hizbullah is the most powerful force in the land?

The answer lies in the ideological conflict between the Iranian revolution and the ultra-conservative Sunni monarchy of Saudi Arabia with its literalist, rigid and puritanical brand of Wahhabi Islam. Syria has now become the theatre for their proxy war. Before Khomeini overthrew the Shah, the old Iranian regime was already perceived as a threat by its Arab neighbours. Iran aimed to be the strongest power in the Gulf and to dominate it. It also tore up a boundary treaty with Iraq concerning the Shatt al-Arab waterway which runs between the two countries, and used its might to extract a more favourable one. This would be a major cause of the Iran-Iraq war which broke out after the Iranian revolution.

If the threat of an aggressively nationalist Iran was gone, the revolutionary Shi'ism which replaced it was more menacing to the Sunni rulers of Arab countries. In Iraq, Saddam Hussein feared that it might undermine the loyalties of the Shi'i majority, and there was a similar nervousness about Shi'i minorities in Saudi Arabia and Kuwait and, of course, the Shi'i majority in Bahrain. Then there were the Shi'is of southern and eastern Lebanon, who became increasingly prominent during the 1980s and 1990s through Hizbullah, whose militia received training from Iranian revolutionary guards.

The Sunni monarchs and autocrats of Arab countries detested revolutionary movements of whatever hue. Anti-Shi'i sectarianism was endemic in the well-financed Wahhabism emanating from Saudi Arabia. Why not subtly encourage it, and tolerate preachers when they demonised Shi'is as idol worshippers who had forsaken the path of true Islam? To do so would placate many Sunni Islamists. It also opened the door to the use of Sayyid Qutb's revolutionary ideology against Shi'is. A new word was coined somewhere along the way: *takfiri*, "a person who denounces others as traitors to Islam and views them as worthy of death".[9] It was a very potent ideological tool for militant and easily manipulated Islamist groups to use against both heretical Alawis and the secular Ba'th, as well as just about anyone else whose conduct they disapproved of.

Sunni militants from other lands have flocked to Syria to fight for the establishment of an Islamist state, often with arms and money supplied by sympathetic individuals across the Sunni world, but perhaps especially in Saudi Arabia and Qatar. Some other Sunnis have followed them, and a proportion will have absorbed their ideology. There have been reports of money being distributed in parts of northern Syria to persuade local people to join the uprising. In April 2012, the governments of Saudi Arabia, Qatar and the UAE announced that they were earmarking $100 million to pay salaries to rebel fighters.[10] This was before ISIS appeared. Such support is partly counterbalanced by assistance for the regime from Iran as well as Shi'is in the Arab world, notably from Hizbullah and the majority Shi'i community which now dominates Iraqi parliamentary politics. Syria is once again the play thing of foreign interests. Regional actors have lined up behind sectarian ideologies, caring little for the suffering on the ground.

Across the hills of southern Lebanon pictures of Hizbullah fighters who have died in battle are to be seen by the roadside, often next to those of the movement's leader, Hassan Nasrallah. Some of his portraits have a strap-line: *haith yajib an nakun, sanakun*: "We will be wherever we have to be." This is an oblique reference to Hizbullah's entry into the conflict in Syria on the regime's side, and the fact that many of those whose deaths are commemorated have died fighting alongside the forces of Bashar al-Assad. The words blend support for the Syrian Ba'th with the struggles Hizbullah has fought against Israel: a subtle hint that the two struggles are linked, or even one and the same in the minds of Hizbullah's constituency. For these fighters, Shi'i militancy has blended with pan-Arab nationalism. But many Sunnis just across the border in Syria would now angrily reject the Shi'i troops who have come to the aid of Bashar al-Assad.

Sectarianism certainly is one of the greatest challenges currently facing Arab countries. The Syrian conflict has developed ever more bitter sectarian overtones, and has become the cockpit for the struggle between Sunnis and Shi'is, sucking in outside elements in the process. But at the same time it provides a cloak for something else. The old aspirations of pan-Arab nationalism are not dead. The sectarian conflict is also a struggle for leadership and control of the Arab world.

V

It is easy for Westerners who study the history of Syria to wonder if the solution is to redraw the map of the region. Few commentators want to sound as if they are advocating it, yet just raising the possibility can almost make it sound like something inevitable.[11] The idea that Iraq's dilemmas might be solved by splitting it into Shi'i Arab, Sunni Arab and Kurd states was occasionally floated around the time of the invasion of Iraq in 2003. Now it is sometimes hinted that Syria will be partitioned in the same way: the Kurds of the east will unite with their brethren across the border in Iraq, while the Alawis will form their own state centred on Lattakia and the Alawi heartland behind it, and there will be a Sunni Muslim state in between – possibly part of a new Sunni Arab entity which includes north-west Iraq.

This is an outbreak of the old Western disease of drawing pretty

lines on maps and then expecting the peoples of Greater Syria to step
neatly into the zones marked with the particular colour chosen for
them. Things do not work like that. It was ultimately only possible
to establish a predominantly Jewish state in Palestine by widespread
ethnic cleansing. Around 700,000 Arab Muslims and Christians lost
their homes as a result. At that time, the newly independent state of
Syria had a population of around 3.5 million.

Pretend for a moment that the events surrounding the creation of
Israel were happening at the present time. Extrapolate these figures to
what they might be today, when the population of Syria has grown to
over 22 million, and the number of Palestinian refugees permanently
displaced would be 3.5 million or more. In actual fact, since 2011 more
than 9 million Syrians have been displaced either internally or externally,
out of a population of over 22 million. If a substantial number of them
are unable to return to their homes because their country has been
partitioned, they could find themselves homeless, long-term exiles like
so many Palestinians. The effect on the neighbouring states, particularly
Lebanon and Jordan, would be crushing and might be even more
destabilising than the Palestinian tragedy of 1947–9.

The fear is sometimes voiced that the regime might retreat to a portion
of Syria based on the Alawi heartland if all else was lost. If an Alawi state
were established on the basis of the Mandate's *Région Alaouite*, this
would cut the rest of Syria off from the sea. Furthermore, it could only
be created by ethnic cleansing on the Palestine model or by following
the alternative model the French adopted in Lebanon and expanding its
borders by incorporating sufficient territory predominantly inhabited
by non-Alawis. The French were far from consistent when they set up
their *Région Alaouite* – something that underlines their motives, and
shows they were not acting out of principle. They added some Sunni
areas to the region to make it more viable (just as they did in Lebanon)
while at the same time excluding Alawi areas near Hama and Homs
because this would have antagonised powerful Sunni landlords whose
support they were cultivating.[12] Similarly, one of the more extreme
suggestions for an Alawi state since the civil war began would destroy its
purported *raison d'être* by including Damascus and Homs (both with an

overwhelmingly Sunni majority) and the Druze of the Hawran plateau. The not very Arabic name of "Alawitestan" has been suggested for this Arabic-speaking entity.[13] The name has a neo-Conservative, "made in Washington" ring to it.

But there is a much bigger objection to an Alawi state. There seems to be absolutely no sign of a movement among Alawis to set one up. At the time the Mandate began, there was a strong sense of national identity among the Maronites. This reflected their very particular history: their links with France, their Catholicism, the events of 1860, the steadily growing impact of European nationalist ideas on Maronite intellectuals, the romantic sense of an ancient Phoenician identity felt by some, and the encouragement of the French colonial lobby. Many French administrators would have loved to find a similar sense of identity among Alawis. We can be morally certain that, if it had existed, they would have found it and we would know about it. But the very different history of the Alawis meant that it did not exist. The French had to subdue the Alawi tribes in the mountains, but that was purely because of the traditional resistance to all outsiders, whether European or fellow Arab, of a largely illiterate mountain people with a strong *asabiyya* (quasi-tribal sense of identity and solidarity). Alawi resistance against the French was essentially no different from Alawi resistance to Ottoman tax collectors and press gangs.

Of course, if asked, the Alawis would always have said that they wanted to run their own affairs – what tribal and rural population would not do so? But to suggest that tribal sheikhs who were jealous of their own and their followers' ancestral rights were thinking in terms of an Alawi national identity and political independence as a modern sovereign state is completely fanciful. Very often, the Alawis joined forces as a distinct group for economic, not political, reasons. They have been described as being a "sect-class" when they united against absentee Sunni landlords in Damascus.[14] Much Alawi discontent under the Mandate merely reflected the now-familiar history of modern Syria: the struggles between country and town, and between poor and rich.

The most prominent Alawi leader to emerge during the Mandate was Sheikh Sulayman al-Murshid. The name al-Murshid means "the

Guide", and Sheikh Sulayman was given that title because he was a spiritual leader and visionary. He started life as a humble shepherd boy in Jobet Burghal, one of the poorest parts of the mountains. He claimed that, while unconscious during an illness, Khidr, the mysterious figure of Muslim legend who is often identified with St George, took him to Heaven where he received the gift of prophecy. This sounds like a near-death experience. Sulayman al-Murshid foretold the end of the world and the appearance of the Mahdi, the Muslim eschatological figure who will appear in the last days to usher in an era of justice and righteousness. He worked miracles, attracted converts among the poor, and married wives from different tribes to seal alliances. Indeed, at one point he had thirteen wives simultaneously. He then went on to become a wealthy man who was reported to have 40,000 followers and had himself elected to parliament. This colourful character collaborated with the French and went a certain way towards their separatist ideas for the Alawis, but this was with the intention of expanding his own power base. He was eventually executed for "crimes against the nation" within a year after the French departed in 1946. Sulayman al-Murshid was not an embryonic leader of a newly imagined nation but a traditional figure of a sort that by the 1930s and 1940s could only flourish in the most backward regions. The loyalty his followers felt to him was not the morning star of an Alawi national identity. Indeed, he sowed discord among the wider Alawi community rather than uniting it.[15]

After independence, most politically active Alawis joined militantly secular nationalist parties such as Antun Sa'ada's Syrian National Party and, above all, the Ba'th. Their attraction to such political parties and the Alawi overrepresentation in the army suggest the very opposite of a separatist agenda, as do the careers of both Hafez and Bashar al-Assad. This brings us to the present day. We have seen how the Assads relied on Alawis and co-opted them into their project to remain in power. That, of course, is one of the reasons why so many of them are now tied to the regime. However, there are also Alawi individuals who criticise the regime and support the opposition, such as the award-winning writer Samar Yazbek.

It has also been suggested that the Syrian Kurds might secede. They predominate locally in parts of the east and north of the country, but not in a fashion which would lend itself to a neat partition. Many of them moved south into what is now Syria when the parts of Anatolia with a large Kurdish population remained in Turkey after the Great War, and ideas of a separate Kurdish state were crushed by Kemal Atatürk. Sizeable numbers of Armenians and Syriac-speaking Christians also came from Anatolia to Syria at the same time. The newcomers began a new life in the plains east of the Euphrates, where they had to compete with Arabic-speaking Bedouin. There are thus no large, contiguous areas in Syria which could be described as exclusively Kurdish, while many Kurds are dispersed in other parts of the country, especially in the large urban centres.

Arab nationalists have, on the whole, treated the Kurds very badly. The Kurds fell foul of Adib Shishakli's cultural crackdown on self-expression by non-Arab communities. Things would get worse. A census carried out in 1962 arbitrarily deprived many Kurds of Syrian citizenship. Some were registered as foreigners, while others who were not at home on the day the census officers called were listed as "unregistered"[16] which amounted in practice to much the same thing. Large numbers of Arabs were deliberately settled in areas with large Kurdish populations through land reclamation projects. The Ba'thists tried to erase signs of Kurdish identity – such as restricting the use of the Kurdish language, replacing Kurdish place-names with Arabic ones, and even discouraging parents from giving their children Kurdish names.

The Syrian Kurds also have their own political divisions, which are bound up with the politics of the Kurdish struggle in Turkey (where they predominate in the south-east of the country to the north of the Syrian border) and Iraq, where they now have their own, oil-rich autonomous region and there is talk of pushing for complete independence. As the Syrian civil war progresses, Kurdish militias have been fighting ISIS, notably in the long drawn out battle for Kobane. However, any attempt at secession would be bound to incur the opposition of the Turkish and Iraqi governments as well as of whoever happens to be ruling in

Damascus when the civil war finally ends.[17] An independent Kurdish state which is wholly or partly on former Syrian territory remains unlikely in the medium term. The call by Kurdish leaders in Syria is therefore for the adoption of a pluralistic framework for the country which would allow minority rights for their people.

Finally, let us consider a state for Sunni Muslims created in a Syria shorn of its predominantly Alawi and Kurdish areas. There are certainly Sunni Islamists who wish to set up their own state in Syria. Yet drawing its boundaries would run into exactly the same problems that bedevilled the partition of Greater Syria after the Great War and the French attempt to divide Syria during their Mandate. In the absence of widespread reciprocal ethnic-cleansing the new state would have its own minorities. This would call into question the purpose of the partition. The erection of new barriers would hinder reconciliation, the restoration of proper government and economic development.

In its final decades, the Ottoman Empire argued that it had a right to represent Sunni Muslims as the caliphate. Before that, it claimed essentially the same legitimacy in its capacity as a sultanate: a state whose ruler is the authority[18] that enforces the Sharia, the law of God, on this earth. This was a form of legitimacy that flowed from religion and did not require the consent of the governed. This is the model that ISIS purported to adopt when it declared itself a caliphate in June 2014 and demanded allegiance from all Muslims everywhere. Its psychopathic brutality, coupled with the fact that the conditions required by Sharia for the appointment of a caliph did not exist, mean that such a pretension can have no legitimate foundation.

The claims of ISIS have encountered resistance on the ground and led to other opposition groups turning against it, despite it being one of the best organised and most effective of the factions struggling for control of Syria. Many, if not most, of its fighters are not Syrian. Despite the violent Islamist uprising which culminated in the seizure of Hama in 1982, Islamism in Syria has not always been militant. Sunni Muslim piety is strong in Syria, and we have seen how the regime has tried to co-opt it. There has been a long tradition of moderation that can be traced back to the modernists of the late nineteenth century, the pious organisations and benevolent societies that were established under the Mandate, and the Syrian branch of the Muslim Brotherhood that was established shortly after independence. The early Syrian Muslim Brotherhood accepted the democratic political process and was prepared to compromise over the position of Islam in the constitution. It emphasised that this was its position during the Damascus Spring. Today, moderate Islamist groups within the opposition call for a democratic Syria which would remain a single state: they want neither partition nor rule by ISIS.

However desperate the situation on the ground is in Syria at the moment, partition along ethnic or sectarian lines is not the answer. There is nothing to suggest that it is what Syrians want, and the original demonstrators in 2011 who called for freedom were certainly not asking for their country to be split up. The conflict has yet to run its full course. If the regime prevails, rebel groups will gradually be forced into the position in which their forebears found themselves during early 1927. As reinforcements from overseas enabled the French army to spread its control across the country, many localities made their peace with the victors. Fawzi al-Qawuqji and his dwindling band of followers no longer received the heroes' welcome to which they had become accustomed. Instead, local people pleaded with them to leave, since their presence would invite French reprisals. State terror had worked. It may yet do so again in Syria today, although the regime's shortage of troops makes this less likely.

Barring a change of heart at the top of the regime (possibly brought about by an internal coup, if the situation becomes desperate), the most likely alternative to a regime victory is that Syria descends into warlordism. The infighting on the opposition side and lack of discipline on that of the regime suggest this could already be happening. Militias from small towns and villages, as well as locally based tribal, Islamist, Kurdish and even Christian groups fight each other, agree truces and negotiate control of territory and resources. The other possibility is that the international community finally manages to take some coordinated action to put the country onto a path of transition. At the moment this looks unlikely, not least because of the superpowers' ability to veto UN Security Council resolutions and the failure of successive UN and Arab League missions. The international community was Syria's midwife; it could easily become Syria's undertaker.

Standing in the background are Russia and the USA. Russia's links with the regime survived the collapse of the Soviet Union, and it has remained Syria's main armaments supplier to this day. Ever since the 1950s, when young Syrian pilots like the then unknown Hafez al-Assad trained in the USSR, there have been strong links between the Russian and Syrian military establishments. There are also trade, cultural links (many Syrians have studied in Russia) and no doubt many personal friendships. Russia has a strong vested interest in the survival of the Syrian regime and has indefatigably supported it for this reason. It could be said that it is now doing so to the last drop of Syrian blood.

And what of America (because Europe, sadly, only punches below its weight)? America supports attempts to build a democratic Syrian opposition, but is that its main concern? Which comes first: the welfare of the Syrian people or America's geo-strategic interests? For Syria, the Cold War has never ended. It has now replaced Lebanon as a theatre for proxy wars. America cannot escape the charge of disinterest, of failure to rein in its proxies and of letting them, too, use the conflict for their own purposes while Syrian blood is shed and Syrian children starve.

Acknowledgements

Lynn Gaspard suggested I write this book in July last year. I am very grateful to her both for the confidence she has showed in me and for her patience in accompanying me through a writing process which, as is so often the case, went through a number of stages which had not been foreseen at the outset. My deep thanks are also due to her wonderful colleagues at Saqi Books. I owe a particular debt of gratitude to my editor, Lawrence Joffe, whose extraordinary erudition and ability to play the devil's advocate to my arguments have greatly enriched this book. I also wish to thank friends who read and commented on earlier drafts: Chris Doyle, whose knowledge and experience of Syria also provided me with many valuable insights, Russell McGuirk and Mike Whittingham. I am grateful, too, to Martin Lubikowski of ML Design who produced the maps. The opinions contained in this book and whatever errors may lurk inside it are, of course, entirely my fault and responsibility.

But my greatest debt is to Diana, who took me back to Damascus in 2007 and has enabled me to get to know Syria in a way that I hope is reflected in this book.

Notes

Preface

1. The UN human rights chief, Navi Pillay, estimated in August 2014 that over 190,000 had died as of April that year: www.bbc.co.uk/news/world-middle east-28892552
2. http//data.unhcr.org/syrianrefugees/regional.php
3. http://syria.unocha.org
4. www.bbc.co.uk/news/world-middle-east-26204379
5. Article 22, Covenant of the League of Nations.
6. Syria and Egypt were united as a single state called the United Arab Republic during the period 1958–61.

Chapter One

1. Acts: 9.3.
2. Masters, *Christians and Jews in the Ottoman Arab World*, p. 158
3. See Lefèvre, *The Ashes of Hama*, pp. 8–12.
4. Also sometimes called Midan.
5. Tibawi, *A History of Modern Syria*, p. 130.
6. Ibid, pp. 135 ff.
7. Cole, *Colonialism and Revolution in the Middle East*, p. 114.
8. For an introduction to the Nahda, see Hourani, *Arabic Thought in the Liberal Age, passim* but especially at pp. 245–59.
9. Allawi, *Faisal I of Iraq*, p. 33–4.
10. This was almost certainly not the position of the sultan-caliph himself or of the rank and file of the army, who saw themselves as fighting for the caliphate.
11. Longrigg, *Syria and Lebanon under French Mandate*, p. 49.
12. Hansard, *Parliamentary Debates*, Commons, 25 July 1921, Col. 36.
13. The text of the Sykes-Picot agreement may be found at http://avalon.law.yale.edu/20th_century/sykes.asp
14. Rogan, *The Arabs*, p. 197.

15. For an analysis of the drafting of the Balfour Declaration, see Schneer, *The Balfour Declaration*, Bloomsbury 2010. The final text is reproduced at p. 341. See also Kattan, *From Co-existence to Conquest*, Pluto, 2009, pp. 40–48.

16. See Grainger, p. 205, where the reaction of the Zionist settlers at Richon-le-Zion to the sacking of the Arab village of Surafend by disorderly New Zealand and Australian troops is discussed.

17. For this, see Antonius, *The Arab Awakening*, pp. 156–8. The sources for Antonius's account include what Faisal told him of these events.

18. Allawi, 53.

19. See Sir Henry MacMahon's Second Note to the Sharif Husain dated 24 October 1915, reproduced in Antonius, *The Arab Awakening*, pp.419–20.

20. Grainger, *The Battle for Syria, 1918–20*, Boydell Press, pp. 186–7.

21. Grainger, p. 187.

22. Tibawi, *A History of Modern Syria*, MacMillan, 1969, p. 271.

23. The substantive portions of the speech are quoted in Allawi, pp. 167–8.

24. Al-Askari, p. 160.

25. Allawi, pp. 184–91, 213–6. In particular, see Allawi's treatment of Lawrence's role at Faisal's meetings with the Zionist leader Chaim Weizmann (pp. 184–9). Antonius, writing closer to the time in the mid-late 1930s (and it should be noted he was a contemporary of Faisal and Lawrence), raises question marks about the depths of Lawrence's Arabic. It might be observed that acting as a translator of diplomatic Arabic would have been a very different matter from using the language to communicate with an overwhelmingly illiterate tribal army.

26. For Jafar al-Askari's role in the Arab revolt and Faisal's administration of Greater Syria, see *A Soldier's Story, The Memoirs of Jafa Pasha al-Askari*, Arabian Publishing, 2003.

27. At the outbreak of the Great War, there was a broad-gauge line running southwards from Aleppo through Hama and Homs and then through the Beqaa valley to the village of Rayaq, where it linked with the narrow-gauge line from Beirut to Damascus. Both railways were French built and had French ownership. There was also a spur from Homs to Tripoli and the Ottoman-owned Hejaz Railway system which ran south from Damascus to Medina. See Longrigg, p. 33.

28. Jafar Pasha al-Askari, *A Soldier's Tale*, p. 171.

29. Allawi, p. 193.

30. Reproduced in Hurewitz, *Diplomacy in the Near and Middle East*, pp. 38-9.

31. Ibid.

32. Ibid.
33. Allawi, p. 168.
34. Hurewitz, p. 45.
35. Allawi, pp 240–1.
36. Hurewitz, p. 62–3.
37. Ibid.
38. For the establishment of the Commission, see Allawi, pp. 210–3.
39. Moubayed, *Syria and the USA*, p. 10.
40. The King Crane Commission Report, 28 August 1919, Section III, "Recommendations", comments following sub-heading "Zionism", paragraph E (3).
41. Allenby to War Office, 29 May 1919, quoted in Grainger, p. 229.
42. On this, see Tibawi, whose book was published in 1969, at pp. 287 ff. For a very recent assessment of this topic, see Allawi, pp. 184 ff.
43. Hansard, *Parliamentary Debates*, 27 March, 1923, Cols. 655–6.
44. Moubayed, p. 26.
45. There are discrepancies in the details of the accounts of the battle, except for the fact that the general outcome was clear. See Longrigg, p. 103, Khoury, p. 97, note 1 and Allawi, pp. 290–1. Allawi states that the battle was over by 10.00 am, which does not seem consistent with the suggestion that it lasted for six hours on a hot day.

Chapter Two

1.   For an introduction to French interests in Syria in the years leading up to the Great War, see Khoury, pp. 27 ff.
2.   The text of the Mandate was published in the League of Nations Official Journal, August 1922, pp. 1013–7. It is reproduced in e.g. Longrigg, pp. 376–8.
3.   Covenant of the League of Nations, Art. 22.
4.   Khoury, *Syria and the French Mandate*, Princeton 1987, pp. 104–5.
5.   Khoury, p. 622.
6.   Khoury, p. 80.
7.   Khoury, p. 93.
8.   The word *Jazirah* means "island" (or "peninsula") and strictly speaking the name refers to the entire area between the Euphrates and the Tigris. The region to which the name of the province of *Jazirah* applies began some way to the east of the Euphrates. It was initially known as *Badiyyat al-Shaam*, "literally "the desert of Shaam", or Greater Syria.
9.   For the bare facts setting out the stages by which the Sanjak was

transferred to Turkey during the period 1936–9, see Longrigg, pp. 237–243. For a more detailed treatment, see Khoury, pp. 494–514.

10. Khoury, p.105.

11. Ibid, p. 109.

12. Ibid, p. 110.

13. Khoury, pp. 140–1.

14. Smart, Damascus, to Foreign Office, London, 25 March 1925, FO 371/10850, quoted in Seale, *The Struggle for Arab Independence*, pp.198–9.

15. Longrigg, pp. 151–2.

16. This was stated in a report to the British High Commissioner in Iraq. Despite being a British document classified as "secret", a copy of the report appears in the French archives. See Provence, p. 79 and note 41.

17. Quoted in Provence, pp. 82–3.

18. Quoted in Provence, pp. 82–3.

19. Khoury, p. 164.

20. Khoury, p. 174.

21. Smart to Chamberlain, 25 October 1925, FO 371/4310. 13028/303, quoted in Provence, p. 103.

22. Provence, p. 128.

23. Khoury, pp. 196–7.

24. Provence, p. 119.

25. Not to be confused with the modern Shi'i movement in Lebanon which has the same name.

26. White, *The Emergence of Minorities in the Middle East*, p. 52. The word translated as "communities", *tawa'if* can also mean "sects".

27. Khoury, p. 237.

28. My reflections in this paragraph are based on the analysis by Provence on the causes and consequences of the revolt. See Provence, pp. 20–2, 151–3.

29. Khoury, pp. 249–50.

30. Khoury, p. 539.

31. Khoury, p. 341.

32. Khoury, p. 374.

33. Koury, p. 265.

34. *Treaty of Alliance between Great Britain and Irak,* 10 October 1922, Article 4.

35. Longrigg, pp. 196–7.

36. Khoury, pp. 239–60.

37. Khoury, p. 545.

38. Khoury, pp. 587–9; Longrigg, p. 300.

39. Khoury, p. 465.

40. Khoury, p. 490.

41. Khoury, pp. 585–6.

42. Khoury, pp. 311, 408.

43. Sedgwick, *Muhammad Abduh*, p.64.

44. See Pierret, pp. 26–28.

45. Lefèvre, pp. 11–17. Lefèvre states that the originator of the expression is Elizabeth Thomson.

46. Khoury, p. 398.

47. Khoury, p. 275.

48. Pierret, p. 174.

49. For the strategies developed by Lyautey and his colleagues in Morocco and their attempted application in Syria, see Khoury, pp. 56–70.

50. Khoury, p. 53.

51. See Khoury, p. 466, note 38.

52. White, *The Emergence of Minorities in the Middle East*, p. 73.

53. Khoury, p. 452.

54. Khoury, p. 452.

55. Quoted in Neep, *Occupying Syria under the French Mandate*, Cambridge, 2012, pp. 199–200.

56. Longrigg, pp. 310–1.

57. Longrigg, pp. 322–3.

58. Longrigg, p. 340.

59. Moubayed, pp. 54–5. Moubayed's account is based on Arabic minutes taken at the meeting.

60. Longrigg, p. 349.

61. Moubayed, p. 61.

Chapter Three

1. Landis: "Syria and the Palestine War: Fighting King Abdullah's Greater Syria Plan", in Rogan and Shlaim, eds., *The War for Palestine*, 2nd edition, Cambridge, 2001, 2007, p. 177. The paragraphs about Syria and the Palestine War of 1948–9 in Section III of this chapter are based on Landis's scholarship in this article.

2. Owen and Pamuk, *A History of Middle East Economies in the Twentieth Century*, p.66. The information reproduced in this and the following paragraph on the Syrian economy under the Mandate is taken from pp. 64– 71 of their book.

3. For the drawing of the border between the Mandates of Syria and Palestine, see J. McTague, "Anglo-French Negotiations over the

Boundaries of Palestine, 1919–20" in *Journal of Palestine Studies*, Vol. 11, No. 2, Winter, 1982.

4.   Seale, *The Struggle for Syria, A Study of Post-War Arab Politics, 1945–58*, I. B. Tauris 1965/86, p. 45.

5.   Often known by its French acronym, PPS or "*Parti Populaire Syrien*" – *populaire* being a poor translation of the Arabic *qawmi*, "national". See Seale, 1965/86, p. 64.

6.   Tibawi, p. 363.

7.   Lefèvre, p. 27.

8.   Quotes from an interview with Siba'i in the *New York Times*, 27 February 1955, reproduced in Lefèvre, p. 25.

9.   The total number of parliamentary seats was 114 in 1947 and 82 in 1949.

10. Lefèvre, pp. 28–9.

11. One key individual who did much to develop the comparison was Ahmed Chalabi, as did other Iraqi exiles. For an evaluation of de-Ba'thification in Iraq and the flaws in both the concept and the process, see Miranda Sissons and Abdulrazzaq al-Saiedi, *A Bitter Legacy: Lessons of De-Baathification in Iraq*, International Center for Transnational Justice, March 2013. For the comparison with de-Nazification, see p. 9. It is available at www.ictj.org/sites/default/files/ICTJ-Report-Iraq-De-Baathification-2013-ENG.pdf

12. Sylvia Haim, *Arab Nationalism: an Anthology*, pp. 71–2, quoted in Seale, *The Struggle for Syria*, p.155.

13. "People to watch – Arab Ideals and Reality", in *The Times*, 8 July 1959. See Seale, *The Struggle for Syria*, p. 158.

14. Masters, *The Arabs of the Ottoman Empire, 1516–1918*, p. 190.

15. Quoted in Seale, *The Struggle for Syria*, p. 149.

16. Quoted in Seale, ibid, p. 157.

17. The summary of Ba'thist ideology that follows is largely based on its treatment by Seale in *The Struggle for Syria*, pp. 148–159.

18. Seale, *The Struggle for Syria*, p. 154.

19. Quoted in her introduction to *Arab Nationalism: An Anthology* by Sylvia Haim, at pp. 71–2 and reproduced in Seale, *The Struggle for Syria*, at p. 155.

20. Haim p. 243, quoted in Seale, *The Struggle for Syria*, p. 156.

21. He died in 1989 and was buried in Baghdad. The regime of Saddam Hussein gave him a state funeral according to Muslim rites. He is reported to have converted to Islam in secret. See Van Dam, p. 185, note 8. However, his family bitterly dispute this and maintain that his funeral was a regime propaganda exercise.

22. Ba'th Party Constitution of 1947, Article 1. This is my own translation taken from the photograph of the opening page of the Constitution which may be found at www.syrianhistory.com/en/photos1903

23. Seale, *The Struggle for Syria*, pp. 154–5.

24. Thompson, *Justice Interrupted*, p. 213.

25. Ibid.

26. I deal with this in *A Concise History of the Arabs* at pp. 176–9.

27. See Rashid Khalidi, "The Palestinians and 1948: The Underlying Causes of Failure", in *The War for Palestine*, ed. Rogan and Shlaim, Cambridge 2001/7, pp.12 ff.

28. Landis, "Syria and the Palestine War", in *The War for Palestine*, ed. Rogan and Shlaim, p. 180.

29. Ibid, p. 197.

30. See M. Fischbach, *Jewish Property Claims against Arab Countries*, pp.29 ff.

31. Seale, *The Struggle for Syria*, p. 42.

32. Quoted in Moubayed, p. 77.

33. Moubayed, pp. 77–80; Rabinovich, p. 205.

34. Rabinovich, p. 210.

35. Seale, *The Struggle for Syria*, p. 61.

36. Ibid, p. 63.

37. Rabinovich, p. 212.

38. On this, see Landis, *Shishakli and the Druzes: Integration and Intransigence.*

39. On this, see Landis, *Shishakli and the Druzes: Integration and Intransigence.*

40. Moubayed, p. 103.

41. Moubayed, p. 92.

42. Moubayed, p. 122.

43. See Moubayed, pp. 150–3.

44. The expression is Patrick Seale's. *The Struggle for Syria*, p. 255.

45. See Ben Fenton, "Macmillan backed Syria Assassination Plot", *Guardian*, 27 September, 2003.

46. Quoted in Seale, *Asad: The Struggle for the Middle East*, p. 65.

47. W. Khalidi, *Political Trends in the Fertile Crescent* in Lacqueur, The Middle East in Transition, London, 1958, pp. 121–8, quoted in Hourani, *Arabic Thought in the Liberal Age*, p. 358.

48. Quoted in Van Dam, *The Struggle for Power in Syria*, p. 76.

49. Seale, *Asad: The Struggle for the Middle East*, p. 83.

50. Ibid, p. 102.

51. Batatu, pp. 156–7.

52. Batatu, p. 24.
53. Quoted in Lefèvre, *Ashes of Hama: The Muslim Brotherhood in Syria*, Hurst & Company, London 2013.
54. Batatu, p. 157.
55. Shlaim, *The Iron Wall: Israel and the Arab World*, Penguin, 2000, p. 236.
56. Ibid, p. 236.
57. Dunstan, *The Six Day War of 1967: Jordan and Syria*, p.88.
58. Seale, *Asad: The Struggle for the Middle East*, p. 152.
59. Seale, *Asad: The Struggle for the Middle East*, p. 164.

Chapter Four

1. See Michael Young, "Patrick Seale: An Appreciation", *The Daily Star*, Beirut, 3 April 2014.
2. For a succinct account of the war, see Dunstan, *The Yom Kippur War 1973 (1): The Golan Heights*.
3. Ibid, p. 83. The same number of Israeli deaths is given by Herzog in his *The War of Atonement* at p. 145, but he records 2,453 wounded. I have given this latter figure as it appears more plausible.
4. Shlaim, *The Iron Wall*, p. 342.
5. Quoted in Seale, *Asad*, p. 256.
6. The principle that Israel would recognise the PLO as the representatives of the Palestinian People was accepted by Israel in the Oslo Accords of 1993. To this day, Israel tries to argue on a number of spurious grounds that it may annex parts of the territories occupied in 1967. However, this was unanimously rejected by the bench of the International Court of Justice in its advisory opinion on *The Legal Consequences of the Construction of a Wall in the Occupied Palestinian Territory* of July 2004.
7. Owen and Pamuk, p. 172, note 6.
8. Seale, *Asad*, p. 270.
9. Rogan, *The Arabs: A History*, p. 382.
10. Seale, *Asad*, p.284. According to Batatu, the dislike preceded the 1973 war (see Batatu, pp. 292–3) and may go back to the events of September 1970.
11. See the chapter entitled "Dirty Tricks" in Seale, *Asad: The Struggle for the Middle East*, pp. 461–491. Seale makes the point that the Arab states, Israel and Iran all indulged in dirty tricks. He states that Hafez al-Assad "gave as good or as ill as he got" and makes the well-

judged observation that none of these other state actors or their proxies could claim the moral high ground.

12. Jimmy Carter's diary, quoted in his autobiographical *Keeping Faith: The Memoirs of a President,* pp. 285–6.

13. Ibid.

14. Ibid.

15. Karim Pakradouni, quoted in Rabinovich, p. 290, p.286.

16. Lawrence Freedman, *A Choice of Enemies: America confronts the Middle East*, Weidenfeld & Nicholson, London, 2008, p.328.

Chapter Five

1. Hokayem, p. 31.

2. Batatu, p. 217.

3. Quoted in Seale, *Asad*, p. 24.

4. Van Dam, p. 32.

5. Van Dam, p. 118. Van Dam also mentions a purge of fifteen officers in 1972 who were Jadid supporters. He does not seem to mention any purge as a result of the Islamist insurgency of the late 1970s which culminated in the Hama uprising and its suppression.

6. Batatu, p. 69.

7. Batatu, pp. 71-4.

8. Batatu, pp. 63-6.

9. Batatu, pp. 53-5.

10. Batatu, p. 160.

11. Law 110 of 1991.

12. Lefèvre, p. 69.

13. On this generally, see Batatu, pp. 217–225.

14. Batatu, p. 227.

15. Batatu, p. 226.

16. Lefèvre, p. 71.

17. Batatu, p. 327.

18. Batatu, p. 229.

19. Quoted in Pierret, *Religion and State in Syria: the Sunni Ulama from Coup to Revolution*, Cambridge 2013, p. 184.

20. Batatu, p. 21.

21. Lefèvre, p. 53.

22. It is frequently asserted that the Muslim Brotherhood was behind the incident, but this is hotly disputed by Raphael Lefèvre. See Lefèvre, p.112 and note 7. For the casualty figures, see Van Dam, pp. 91–2.

Batatu (pp. 266–8), a historian as well placed as anyone to uncover the truth, also states that thirty-two cadets were killed although the figure of eighty-three is frequently repeated without qualification. As so often, objectivity has been buried somewhere between the propaganda of the regime and that of its enemies.

23. Van Dam, p. 92.
24. Seale, *Asad*, pp, 328–9.
25. Lefèvre, p. 114.
26. Van Dam, p. 108.
27. Lefèvre, p. 105.
28. This is according to the statement of the Islamist militant Abu Mus'ab al-Suri printed in Lefèvre, pp. 221–2.
29. Fisk, *Pity the Nation*, pp. 181–7
30. Ibid, p. 183.
31. Ibid, p. 184.
32. Ibid, p. 185.
33. Ibid, p.186.
34. Ibid, p. 187.
35. Hokayem, p. 33.
36. Quoted in Lefèvre, p. 77.
37. Scheller, p. 17. Scheller's source is the US envoy Dennis Ross.
38. Quoted in Lefèvre, p. 155. This conception has a long pedigree in Muslim thought. Consider the words of Laoust, speaking about Ibn Taymiyyah in his article on the great medieval polemicist in the *Encyclopedia of Islam*: "Ibn Taymiyyah considered religion and the State to be indissolubly linked. Without the coercive power of the State, religion is in danger. Without the discipline of the revealed Law, the State becomes a tyrannical organisation." However, there is little doubt that if Ibn Taymiyyah had been alive he would most certainly have considered the Syrian State of Hafez al-Assad to be a tyrannical organisation.
39. See Lefèvre, pp. 155–6.
40. Quoted in Pierret, pp. 80–1.
41. Seale, *Asad*, p. 421.
42. Ibid, p. 423
43. Batatu, p. 233
44. Van Dam, p. 119.
45. Seale, *Asad*, p. 435.
46. Owen, *The Rise and Fall of Arab Presidents for Life*, Harvard 2012, p.83.
47. Batatu, p. 193.
48. Batatu, p. 176.

49. Batatu, p. 202.

50. Batatu, pp. 212–3.

51. Batatu, p. 237.

Chapter Six

1. This is taken from the translation of the entire text of the speech at www.al-bab.com/arab/countries/syria/basharooa.htm.

2. Ibid.

3. Ziadeh, pp. 69–71.

4. For the Damascus Spring and its end, see Ziadeh, pp. 61–72.

5. Lesch, *Syria: The Fall of the House of Assad*, p. 19.

6. Owen, *Arab Presidents for Life*, p. 142.

7. Ziadeh, p. 83.

8. Leaving aside the Palestinian perspective, it was a cynical exercise in demagoguery by Ariel Sharon and was aimed at rallying broad sections of the Israeli electorate behind him.

9. Ziadeh, p. 89.

10. Scheller, pp. 182–5.

11. Ziadeh, p. 80.

12. Ziadeh, p. 116.

13. Ziadeh, pp. 37–9.

14. Ziadeh, p. 43.

15. Seifan, p. 6.

16. Lesch, *Syria: The Fall of the House of Assad*, p. 18.

17. Seifan, p. 8.

18. Hinnebusch, "Syria: From 'Authoritarian Upgrading' to Revolution?", *International Affairs* Vol. 88 No. 1, p. 103

19. See graph, GDP Growth, 1970–2005 in S. Seifan, *Syria on the Path to Economic Reform*, p. 22.

20. Ziadeh, p. 49–52. See also Seifan, pp. 8–12.

21. Seifan, p. 8.

22. "Assad cousin accused of favouring family", Lina Saigol, *Financial Times*, 24 April 2011.

23. Ziadeh, p. 59.

24. Seifan, p. 24.

25. Hinnebusch, *Syria: From 'Authoritarian Upgrading' to revolution?* p. 99.

26. Hokayem, pp. 24–5.

27. Hokayem, pp. 14, 19.

28. Hokayem, pp. 28–9.

29.   Hokayem, p. 42.

30.   Ziadeh, p. 155.

31.   This is taken from the translation of the text of the entire speech at www.
      al-bab.com/arab/countries/syria/bashar_assad_speech_110330.htm

32.   Lesch, *Syria: The Fall of the House of Assad*, p. 86.

33.   See UN Human Rights Council debate on situation of human rights in
      Syrian Arab Republic in Special Session S http://www.ohchr.org/en/
      NewsEvents/Pages/DisplayNews.aspx?NewsID=11324&LangID=E

34.   *Asharq Al-Awsat*, 1 August 2011

35.   See UN doc. S/PV.6711

36.   See Lefèvre, p. 182 and note 4.

37.   See Lefèvre, p. 187.

38.   See Liz Sly, *Washington Post*, 24 March 2013.

39.   "Profile: Syrian Opposition's Ahmed Moaz al-Khatib", BBC News, 24
      March 2013, http://www.bbc.co.uk/news/world-middle-east-20300356

40.   See e.g. "Syria chemical attack: What we know", BBC News, 24 Septem-
      ber 2013, http://www.bbc.co.uk/news/world-middle-east-23927399

41.   The statistics for Syrian refugees have been taken from the website
      of the UN High Commissioner for Refugees, www.unhcr.org/
      syrianrefugees/regional.php on 30 October 2014.

Chapter Seven

1.   For a similar view, see Grainger, p. 236.

2.   In the view of Khoury, the most accurate statistics suggest the
      ethnically Turkish element was 39 per cent. For a breakdown of the
      population, see Khoury, p. 495. Although the population consisted
      of a number of ethnic, religious and linguistic groups, the Arabic-
      speaking communities when added together were more numerous. In
      any event, Article 4 of the Mandate was clear: "The Mandatory shall
      be responsible for seeing that no part of the territory of Syria and the
      Lebanon is ceded or leased or in any way placed under the control of
      a foreign power." See Longrigg, p. 377.

3.   Covenant of the League of Nations, Article 22.

4.   Fildis quoting Klieman, *Foundations of British Policy in the Arab
      World: The Cairo Conference of 1921*, John Hopkins, 1970, p. 51.

5.   Shlaim, *The Iron Wall*, p. 235.

6.   See The Board of Deputies of British Jews, *The 2014 European Elec-
      tions: A Jewish Manifesto*, London 2014, p. 12.

7.   This was wishful thinking on the part of President Sadat and the sin-
      cerity of this assertion must be questioned.

8. Quoted in Van Dam, p. 93.

9. My own definition.

10. Hokayem, *Syria's Uprising and the Fracturing of the Levant*, p. 167.

11. See e.g. Michael Williams: "Back to the Future: Is a new Alawi Statelet a Solution to Syria's Agony" and "Martin Chulov: Lines in the Sand are blown away" in Chatham House's *The World Today*, Vol. 69, No. 3, June-July 2013; Robin Wright: "Imagining a Remapped Middle East", *New York Times*, 28 September, 2013.

12. Balanche, p. 34.

13. See the map attached to Robin Wright's article.

14. See Khoury, p. 520 referring to an article by Hananu: "Some Observations on the Social Roots of Syria's Ruling, Military Group and the Causes for its Dominance", in *Middle East Journal*, 35 (Summer 1981), pp. 331–44.

15. For Sheikh Sulayman al-Murshid, see Balanche, pp. 155–9; Khoury, pp. 523–5; Batatu, p. 154. His sect survived him, at least into the 1990s.

16. Arabic, *maktum*, literally "concealed".

17. See the report by the International Crisis Group, *Syria's Kurds: A Struggle within a Struggle*, 22 January 2013.

18. This is the literal meaning of the Arabic word *sultan*. Other translations include power, rule and dominion.

Bibliography

S. Aburish, *Nasser: The last Arab*, Duckworth, 2004

G. Achcar, *The Arabs and the Holocaust: The Arab-Israeli War of Narratives*, Saqi Books, 2010

G. Achcar, *The People Want: A Radical Exploration of the Arab Uprising*, Saqi Books, 2013

F. Ajami, *The Dream Palace of the Arabs*, Vintage Books, 1998

A. Allawi, *The Crisis of Islamic Civilization*, Yale, 2009

A. Allawi, *Faisal I of Iraq*, Yale, 2014

G. Amin, *Egypt in the Era of Hosni Mubarak*, AUC, 2011

G. Antonius, *The Arab Awakening: The Story of the Arab National Movement*, Hamish Hamilton, 1938

J. Al-Askari, *A Soldier's Story: From Ottoman Rule to Independent Iraq*, Arabian Publishing, 2003

F. Balanche, *La region alaouite et le pouvoir Syrien*, Editions Karthala, 2006

J. Barr, *A Line in the Sand: Britain, France and the Struggle that Shaped the Middle East*, Simon & Schuster, 2011

H. Batatu, *Syria's Peasants: The Descendants of its lesser rural Notables, and their Politics*, Princeton, 1999

M. Bishara, *The Invisible Arab: The Promise and Peril of the Arab Revolution*, Nation Books, 2012

J. Bowen, *Six Days: How the 1967 War Shaped the Middle East*, Simon & Schuster, 2003

R. Burns, *The Monuments of Syria: A Guide*, I. B. Tauris, 1992, 1994, 1999, 2009

J. Carter, *Keeping Faith: The Memoirs of a President*, Collins, 1982.

Z. Chehab, *Inside Hamas*, I. B. Tauris, 2007

M. Chulov, "Sectarian Pressures are tearing up the Map: A Grass-roots View of the Syrian Uprising", *The World Today*, Vol. 69, No. 3, June-July 2013

J. Cole, *Colonialism and Revolution in the Middle East*, AUC Press, 1999

M. Copeland, *Game of Nations*, Simon & Schuster, 1969

A. Crooke, *Resistance: The Essence of the Islamist Revolution*, Pluto Press, 2009

D. Darke, *The Bradt Guide to Syria*, Bradt Travel Guides Limited, 2010

D. Darke, *My House in Damascus: An Inside View of the Syrian Revolution*, Haus Publishing, 2014

N. Delong-Bas, *Wahhabi Islam: From Revival and Reform to Global Jihad*, Oxford, 2005

M. Dumper, *The Future of the Palestinian Refugee Problem*, Lynne Riemer, 2007

S. Dunstan, *The Yom Kippur War 1973 (1): The Golan Heights*, Osprey, 2003

S. Dunstan, *The Six Day War 1967: Jordan and Syria*, Osprey, 2009

B. Fenton, "Macmillan backed Syria Assassination Plot", *Guardian*, 27 September 2003

A. Fildis, "The Troubles in Syria: Spawned by French Divide and Rule", *Middle East Policy*, 2011, Vol. XVIII, No. 4

C. Finkel, *Osman's Dream: The Story of the Ottoman Empire 1300–1923*, John Murray, 2005

M. Fischbach, *Jewish Property Claims against Arab Countries*, Columbia, 2008

R. Fisk, *Pity the Nation: Lebanon at War*, Oxford, 3rd ed., 1990–2001

R. Fisk, *The Great War for Civilisation: The Conquest of the Middle East*, Fourth Estate, 2005

L. Freedman, *A Choice of Enemies: America confronts the Middle East*, Weidenfeld & Nicholson, 2008

D. Fromkin, *A Peace to end all Peace: The Fall of the Ottoman Empire and the Creation of the Modern Middle East*, Phoenix, 1989

D. Gardner, *Last Chance: The Middle East in the Balance*, I. B. Tauris, 2009

F. Gardner, *Blood & Sand*, Bantam, 2006

G. Gawrych, *The Young Ataturk: From Ottoman Soldier to Statesman of Turkey*, I. B. Tauris, 2013

J. Gelvin, *Divided Loyalties: Nationalism and Mass Politics in Syria at the Close of Empire*, University of California Press, 1998

A. George, *Syria: Neither Bread nor Freedom*, Zed Books, 2003

F. Gerges, *The Far Enemy: Why Jihad went Global*, Cambridge, 2005

M. Gilbert, *In Ishmael's House: A History of Jews in Muslim Lands*, Yale 2010

R. Ginat, *Syria and the Doctrine of Arab Neutralism: From Independence to Dependence*, Sussex Academic Press, 2005/2010

J. Goodarzi, *Syria and Iran: Diplomatic Alliance and Power Politics in the Middle East*, I. B. Tauris, 2009

J. Gordon, *Invisible War*

J. Grainger, *The Battle for Syria 1918–20*, Boydell Press, 2013

H. Haim, *Shi'ism* tr. Watson and Hill, Edinburgh, 2004

S. Haim, *Arab Nationalism: An Anthology*, University of California Press, 1976.

J. Herrin, *Byzantium: The surprising Life of a medieval Empire*, Penguin, 2007/8

C. Herzog, *The War of Atonement*, Weidenfeld & Nicholson, 1975

C. Hillenbrand, *The Crusades: Islamic Perspectives*, Edinburgh, 1999/2006

R. Hinnebusch, *Syria: Revolution from Above*, Routledge, 2002.

R. Hinnebusch, "Syria: From 'Authoritarian Upgrading' to Revolution?" *International Affairs*, Vol. 88, No. 1, 2012, pp. 95–113.

E. Hokayem, *Syria's Uprising and the Fracturing of the Levant*, Routledge, 2013

R. Hollis, *Britain and the Middle East in the 9/11 Era*, Wiley-Blackwell, 2010

A. Hourani, *Syria and Lebanon*, Oxford, 1946

A. Hourani, *Arabic Thought in the Liberal Age, 1798–1939*, Oxford Paperbacks, 1962/70

A. Hourani, *A History of the Arab Peoples*, Belknap, Harvard, 1991

S. Huntington, *The Clash of Civilizations and the Remaking of the new*

World Order, Simon and Schuster, 1997/2002

J. Hurewitz, *Diplomacy in the Near and Middle East: A Documentary Record, 1914–1956*, D. Van Nostrand Co., 1956

E. Husain, *The Islamist*, Penguin, 2007

D. Ingrams, *Palestine Papers 1917–22: Seeds of Conflict*, Eland, 1972/2009

International Crisis Group, *Syria's Kurds: A Struggle within a Struggle*, 22 January 2013

C. Kanaan, *Lebanon 1860–1960: A Century of Myth and Politics*, Saqi Books, 2005

V. Kattan, *From Co-existence to Conquest: International Law and the Origins of the Arab-Israeli Conflict, 1981–1949*, Pluto Press, 2009

M. Kedar, *Asad in Search of Legitimacy: Message and Rhetoric in the Syrian Press under Hafiz and Bashar*, Sussex Academic Press, 2005

E. Kedourie, *The Chatham House Version: and other Middle Eastern Studies*, Weidenfeld & Nicholson, 1970

B. Keenan, *An Evil Cradling*, Hutchinson, 1992

H. Kennedy, *The Prophet and the Age of the Caliphates: The Islamic Near East from the Sixth to the Eleventh Century*, Pearson Longman, 1986/2004,

G. Kepel, *Jihad: The Trail of Political Islam*, tr. Roberts, I. B. Tauris, 2002

G. Kepel, *The War for Muslim Minds: Islam and the West*, tr. Ghazaleh, Belknap, HUP, 2004

G. Kepel, tr. Ghazaleh, *Beyond Terror and Martyrdom: The Future of the Middle East*, Belknap, HUP, 2008

R. Khalidi, "The Palestinians and 1948: The underlying Causes of Failure", in *The War for Palestine*, ed. Rogan and Shlaim, Cambridge 2001/7

P. Khoury, *Syria and the French Mandate*, Princeton 1987

H. Kildani, *Modern Christianity in the Holy Land*, AuthorHouse, 2010

P. Kinross, *Ataturk: The Rebirth of a Nation*, Phoenix, 1964/2001

G. Kraemer, *Hassan al-Banna*, One World, 2010

R. Lacey, *Inside the Kingdom: Kings, Clerics, Modernists, Terrorists and the Struggle for Saudi Arabia*, Hutchinson, 2009

J. Landis, www.joshualandis.com/blog

J. Landis, "Shishakli and the Druzes: Integration and Intransigence", in T. Philipp and B. Schaebler (eds.), *The Syrian Land: Processes of Integration and Fragmentation*, Stuttgart: Franz Steiner Verlag, 1998, pp. 369–396.

J. Landis, "Syria and the Palestine War: Fighting King Abdullah's Greater Syria Plan", in Rogan and Shlaim, eds. *The War for Palestine*, 2nd ed., Cambridge, 2001, 2007.

R. Lefèvre, *Ashes of Hama: The Muslim Brotherhood in Syria*, Hurst & Company, 2013

D. Lesch, *The New Lion of Damascus: Bashar al-Asad and Modern Syria*, Yale, 2005

D. Lesch, *Syria: The Fall of the House of Assad*, Yale, 2012

F. Leverett, *Inheriting Syria: Bashar's Trial by Fire*, Brookings Institution Press, 2005

S. Longrigg, *Syria and Lebanon under French Mandate*, Oxford, 1958

Ma'oz and Yaniv ed., *Syria under Assad,* Croom Helm, 1986

B. Masters, *Christians and Jews in the Ottoman Arab World*, Cambridge, 2001

B. Masters, *The Arabs of the Ottoman Empire, 1516–1918*, Cambridge, 2013

P. Mattar, *The Mufti of Jerusalem: Al-Hajj Amin al-Husayni and the Palestinian National Movement,* Columbia, 1988

D. McDowall, *A Modern History of the Kurds*, I. B. Tauris, 1997

J. McHugo, *A Concise History of the Arabs*, Saqi Books, 2013

J. McHugo, "Borders Don't Break Easily", *The World Today*, Vol. 69, no. 4, August-September 3013

J. McTague, Anglo-French Negotiations over the Boundaries of Palestine, 1919-1920, *Journal of Palestine Studies*, Vol. II, No. 2, (Winter) 1982

B. Morris, *Israel's Border Wars, 1949–56*, Oxford, 1993

B. Morris, "Revisiting the Palestinian Exodus of 1948" in *The War for Palestine*, ed. Rogan and Shlaim, Cambridge 2001/7

B. Morris, *1948, A History of the First Arab Israeli War*, Yale, 2008

S. Moubayed, *Syria and the USA: Washington's Relations with Damascus from Wilson to Eisenhower*, I. B.Tauris, 2012, 2013

D. Neep, *Occupying Syria under the French Mandate: Insurgency, Space and State Formation*, Cambridge Middle East Series, 2012

Norton, *Hezbullah: A short History*, Princeton, 2007

Oxford Business Group, *The Report: Syria 2010,* Oxford Business Group, 2010

R. Owen, *The Middle East in the World Economy, 1800–1914*, Methuen, 1981

R. Owen and S. Pamuk, *A History of Middle East Economies in the Twentieth Century*, I. B. Tauris, 1998

R. Owen, *State, Power and Politics in the Making of the modern Middle East*, Routledge, 2000

R. Owen, *The Rise and Fall of Arab President for Life*, Harvard, 2012

I. Pappe, *The Ethnic Cleansing of Palestine*, One World, 2006

L. Parsons, "Soldiering for Arab Nationalism: Fawzi al-Qawuqji in Palestine", *Journal of Palestine Studies*, Vol. XXXVI, No. 4, (Summer) 2007

V. Perthes (ed.) *Scenarios for Syria: Socio-Economic and Political Choices*, Nomos Verlagsgesellschaft, Baden-Baden, 1998

V. Perthes, *Syria under Bashar al-Asad: Modernisation and the Limits of Change*, OUP, 2004

T. Pierret, *Religion and State in Syria: The Sunni Ulama from Coup to Revolution*, Cambridge, 2013

M. Provence, *The Great Syrian Revolt and the Rise of Arab Nationalism*, Austin, 2005

D. Pryce-Jones: *The Closed Circle: An Interpretation of the Arabs*, Paladin, 1990

N. Quilliam, *Syria and the new World Order*, Ithaca Press, 1999

S. Qutb, *Milestones*, tr. Anon., Islamic Book Service, 2001/2008–9

I. Rabinovich, *The View from Damascus*, Vallentine Mitchell, 2008

A. Raz, *The Bride and the Dowry: Israel, Jordan and the Palestinians in the Aftermath of the June 1967 War*, Yale, 2012

E. Rogan, *The Arabs: A History*, Allen Lane, 2009

E. Rogan and A. Shlaim (ed.), *The War for Palestine*, 2nd ed. Cambridge, 2007

E. Said, *Orientalism*, Routledge & Kegan Paul, 1978

J. Salt, *The Unmaking of the Middle East: A History of Western Disorder in Arab Lands*, University of California Press, 2008

B. Scheller, *The Wisdom of Syria's Waiting Game*, 2013

J. Schneer, *The Balfour Declaration: The Origins of the Arab-Israeli Conflict*, Bloomsbury, 2010

P. Seale, *The Struggle for Syria: A Study of Post-War Arab Politics*, I. B. Tauris, 1965/86

P. Seale, *Asad: The Struggle for the Middle East*, I. B. Tauris, 1988

P. Seale, *The Struggle for Arab Independence: Riad El-Solh and the Makers of the Modern Middle East*, Cambridge, 2010

M. Sedgewick, *Muhammad Abduh: A Biography*, AUC, 2009

T. Segev, tr. Watzman, *One Palestine Complete*, Abacus, 2001

T. Segev, tr. Cohen, *1967: Israel, the War and the Year that transformed the Middle East*, Little, Brown, 2007

S. Seifan, *Syria on the Path to Economic Reform*, University of St Andrews Centre for Syrian Studies, 2010

J. Shaheen, *Reel Bad Arabs: How Hollywood vilifies a People*, Arris Books, 2003

A. Shlaim, *The Iron Wall: Israel and the Arab World*, Penguin, 2000

A. Shlaim, *Lion of Jordan: The Life of King Hussein in War and Peace*, Allen Lane, 2007

A. Shlaim, "Israel and the Arab Coalition in 1948" in *The War for Palestine, Cambridge*, ed. Rogan and Shlaim, 2001/7

M. Sissons and A. al-Saiedi, A Bitter Legacy: Lessons of De-Baathification in Iraq, International Center for Transnational Justice, March 2013

E. Sivan, *Radical Islam: Medieval Theology and Modern Politics*, Yale, 1985/90

Starr, *Revolt in Syria: an Eye-witness to the Uprising*, Hurst, 2012

R. Stephens, *Nasser: A Political Biography*, Penguin Press, 1971

A. Tamimi, *Hamas: Unwritten Chapters*, Hurst, 2007

S. Tatham, *Losing Arab Hearts and Minds*, C. Hurst & Co, 2006

J. Tejel, *Syria's Kurds: History, Politics and Society*, Routledge 2009

E. Thompson, *Justice Interrupted: The Struggle for Constitutional Government in the Middle East*, Harvard, 2013

A. Tibawi, *A History of Modern Syria including Lebanon and Palestine*, Macmillan St Martin's Press, 1969

C. Tripp, *A History of Iraq*, Cambridge, 3rd edition, 2007

C. Tripp, *The Power and the People: Paths of Resistance in the Middle East*, Cambridge, 2013

N. van Dam, *The Struggle for Power in Syria: Politics and Society under Asad and the Ba'th Party*, I. B. Tauris, 1979, 1981, 1996, 2011

D. Warriner, *Land Reform and Development in the Middle East: A Study of Egypt, Syria and Iraq*, Royal Institute for International Affairs, 1957

B. White, *The Emergence of Minorities in the Middle East, The Politics of Community in French Mandate Syria*, Edinburgh, 2011/12

M. Williams, "Blurring the Borders: Back to the Future for Syria", *The World Today*, Vol. 69, No. 3, June-July 2013

R. Wright, "Imagining a Remapped Middle East", *New York Times*, 28 September, 2013

S. Yazbek, *A Woman in the Crossfire: Diaries of the Syrian Revolution*, Haus Publishing, 2012

K. Yildiz, *The Kurds in Syria: The Forgotten People*, Pluto Press, 2005

R. Ziadeh, *Power and Policy in Syria*, I. B. Tauris, 2013

E. Zisser, *Asad's Legacy: Syria in Transition*, Hurst, 2001

Index